Against
Relativism

Against Relativism

A Philosophical Defense of Method

James F. *ranklin* Harris

OPEN ❀ COURT

La Salle, Illinois

OPEN COURT and the above logo are registered in the U.S.
Patent and Trademark Office.

© 1992 by Open Court Publishing Company

First printing 1992

Printed and bound in the United States of America.

Library of Congress Cataloging-in-Publication Data

Harris, James F. (James Franklin), 1941–
    Against relativism : a philosophical defense of method /
James F. Harris.
      p.   cm.
    Includes bibliographical references and index.
    ISBN 0-8126-9201-2.—ISBN 0-8126-9202-0 (pbk.)
    1. Relativity. 2. Knowledge, Theory of. 3. Methodology.
I. Title.
BD221.H37   1992
149—dc20
                                        92-21019
                                            CIP

For My Father

To ridicule philosophy is really to philosophize.
Blaise Pascal (1623–1662)

Do not block the way of inquiry.
Charles Sanders Peirce (1839–1914)

BRIEF TABLE OF CONTENTS

DETAILED TABLE OF CONTENTS

PREFACE

This book is a critical and philosophical response to the various forms of radical relativism which have developed over the last few decades. Radical relativism is to be contrasted with simple relativism or cultural relativism. According to the different forms of radical relativism, basic epistemological notions such as truth, evidence, reason, rationality, and perhaps most importantly, the *method* of inquiry are relative to a context, frame of reference, paradigm, or cognitive scheme. The sources for such radical relativism are many, and they are located within both Anglo-American, analytic philosophy and within continental philosophy—as well as within the social sciences.

The structure of this book is the result of identifying and then responding to the most prominent, influential, and compelling sources of the different forms of radical relativism. Thus, entire chapters or sections of chapters have been devoted to the works of W.V.O. Quine, Nelson Goodman, Thomas Kuhn, Peter Winch, Hans-Georg Gadamer, Larry Laudan, and several feminist figures. Much of the recent discussion concerning the epistemological issues generated by radical relativism seems to be non-critical and glib, and to occur on a level of abstraction far removed from the detailed and considered arguments and theories which have given rise to these issues. For this reason, I have attempted to provide, in each case, enough of an initial exposition to allow the reader who is primarily interested in the methodological and epistemological issues involved in the disputes to follow the arguments, even though some readers may not have a great deal of familiarity with the original positions and theories. Thus, one advantage that the reader should find is that this book is a fairly self-contained study of those various philosophical developments which have given rise to the different forms of radical relativism.

It is very much in vogue to be a relativist of some sort or other. To that extent, if 'relativism' is understood to mean 'radical relativism', then I am swimming against the philosophical tide in this book. Consequently, I identify with what has become characterized as the conservative "old guard" in intellectual thought—holding on to essentials that are regarded by the relativists as completely outmoded. In this vein, I have, at various times, heard brash and irreverent graduate and undergraduate students dismiss Plato and Aristotle as well as Descartes, Locke, Hume, and Kant as "stupid and silly". Now there is much which might be said in response to such arrogant and presumptuous assessments; however, minimally, we might suggest that people at least *read* the writings of these figures before coming to such dismissive judgments. And we all know that no matter how high the tide rises, it always eventually turns.

One now frequently hears the adage, "Everything is relative", used either as a mantra which is recited ritualistically, much as part of a new age creed, or as an *ad hoc* premiss which is added to every philosophical argument. In this book, I have tried to show just how untrue such a claim is. While many things might be relative, not everything is; nor can everything be.

ACKNOWLEDGMENTS

There are many people to whom I owe much appreciation and gratitude. I would like to thank The College of William and Mary and the family of Francis S. Haserot for their support which gave me the time and means to complete this book. I would like to acknowledge the stimulation which I have received from my students—both past and present—and the very competent work of my research assistants, Tracey Lenox and Jon Shepard. I have benefitted significantly from the professional and friendly editorial guidance of David Ramsay Steele of Open Court Publishing Company. I am also deeply grateful to those friends and colleagues who read earlier versions of different chapters of the book and made helpful suggestions, including Larry Becker, Bowman Clarke, Ann Garry, Kevin Hoover, and especially, George Harris. Finally, I deeply appreciate the affection and encouragement of those friends without whose support completing this book would not have been possible then or nearly so satisfying now.

INTRODUCTION: FROM THE AGE OF ENLIGHTENMENT TO THE AGE OF RELATIVISM

Different periods in the history of Western thought are identified by special emphases which dominated or especially characterized those periods, such as The Age of Reason or The Age of Enlightenment. It might well be that the second half of the twentieth century will be known to future scholars as The Age of Relativism or the Age of Post-Modernism. The attacks upon "classical", or "modernistic" thinking have come from so many sources and from so many different traditions that just keeping up with all of the multifarious forms of relativism has become an almost impossible burden.

It would have been much easier perhaps to write a book on "How I Learned to Stop Worrying and Love Relativism". However, the relativism bandwagon has gotten so crowded that I am not sure that there is much room left; nor am I sure that I wish to keep intellectual company with some of the other occupants of the bandwagon. Consequently, I have chosen to throw in my lot with the remnants of Modernism, and this book represents something of a "rear-guard action" for modernists who will hopefully gather their forces and mount some kind of counterattack in defense of reason and rationality and against the onrushing tide of pernicious relativists. These are probably sufficient reasons to oppose relativism, but they are hardly sufficient reasons for writing a book. Luckily, there are also compelling philosophical arguments against radical relativism, and this volume is devoted to those arguments. At the moment, however, there are few voices being heard in defense of the cause of human reason and rationality, largely because few voices are being raised.

One factor which explains why there are so few people rushing in to pick up the fallen banner of reason and method is that the relativists have succeeded in attaching a very negative connotation to any form of non-relativism. To defend Modernism or traditional Western understandings of science and epistemology is now viewed by many to be, at best, "narrow" or "overly structured" and, at worst, "bigoted", "racist", "sexist", and "ethnocentric". Modernism has been represented in such a manner that to be a modernist is to be insensitive to and intolerant of other cultures with new and different ideas. For example, Paul Feyerabend describes the belief that there is some universal notion of human understanding which might be used to provide some theoretical approach to solving human conflicts as "conceited, ignorant, superficial, incomplete, and dishonest."[1] And we can add "sexist" to the list of pejorative adjectives since many contemporary feminist philosophers view the objectivity of modern science as uniquely masculine and the methodology of traditional Western science and epistemology as male-biased.[2] So powerful have these negative connotations become that most modernists who are left have, for the most part, become "closet modernists" and appear to come out only on rare occasions and with numerous qualifications and great trepidation.

It must count as one of the great ironies in the history of ideas that the movement which provided the mechanism to free the human race from the chains of ignorance and superstition and elevated human reason to the level where people could control not only their own affairs but their relationship with their environment should itself be accused of enslaving people. Following the spectacular successes in the sixteenth and seventeenth centuries of the pioneering efforts of Copernicus, Galileo, Newton, and Kepler, amongst others, the Enlightenment of the eighteenth century in Great Britain and France was responsible for the Gestalt shift wherein human reason came to replace religious (specifically Christian) faith as the means for understanding the universe. As a result of the Enlightenment, human beings came to be understood as naturally good and, perhaps more importantly, rational, and capable, on their own, of running their affairs—politically, socially, and scientifically—by the use of reason. According to the French *Encyclopédie,* which embodied the thinking of the members of the French Enlightenment on everything from art and literature to politics, philosophy and theology, the reason of philosophy was to replace the faith of religion.[3]

The Enlightenment was the watershed which separated modern culture from everything which had gone before, and the eighteenth century marked the "coming of age" of modern human beings. As

Peter Gay describes the processes taking place in the eighteenth century,

> Pseudo-science was giving way to science, credence in the miraculous intervention of divine forces was being corroded by the acid of skepticism and overpowered by scientific cosmology. The sacred was being hollowed out from within by the drying up of religious fervor, the call for good sense, the retreat from Augustinian theology, the campaign against 'enthusiasm', and the advance of rationalism . . .[4]

Although we cannot pursue the matter here, certainly the political consequences of the Enlightenment must not be ignored. Through the work of John Locke and Voltaire, and given Rousseau's views of the natural goodness and perfectibility of human beings, political subjects come to be regarded, for the first time, as possessing *rights* against political authority. Individuals and their interests come to be regarded as intrinsically important, and governments become limited and obligated to respect those individuals and their interests.[5]

Although there had been periods in Western civilization which would be characterized as heavily dominated by reason and knowledge (notably, ancient Greek and Roman cultures), many features of the Enlightenment were unprecedented in human history. The eighteenth century represented what Gay describes as ". . . a genuine and far-reaching novelty in human affairs; it amounted to far more than a mere recapture of old positions, and it surpassed anything the most confident of antique rationalists could have imagined."[6]

Gilbert Murray described the influence of Christianity on the human condition during the Roman Empire as a "failure of nerve", characterized by "a rise of asceticism, of mysticism . . . a sense of pessimism; a loss of self-confidence, of hope in this life and of faith in normal human effort; a despair of patient inquiry, a cry for infallible revelation; an indifference to the welfare of the state, a conversion of the soul to God."[7] Human beings were at the mercy of a hostile environment, original sin, and a future life of suffering. Part, at least, of what accounts for the uniqueness of the period of the Enlightenment is the recovery on the part of human beings of this previously lost nerve. The optimism of the Enlightenment developed out "of growing hope for life and trust in effort, of commitment to inquiry and criticism, of interest in social reform, of increasing secularism, and a growing willingness to take risks."[8]

Pessimistic theology about human nature gave way to optimistic belief in the possibility of environment and education to determine both a person's moral character and his or her intellectual character.

John Locke emphasized this point very nicely. He says, "I think, I may say, that, of all the Men we meet with Nine Parts of Ten are what they are, Good or Evil, useful or not, by their Education."[9] Human beings no longer viewed themselves as victims of their fate. Effort, inquiry, and education can not only determine the future of an individual, but they can also determine the future of the human race.

Much of the optimism concerning the educability of individuals came about because of a strongly held belief in the fundamental and universal nature of human reason. Individual differences amongst people are accounted for by their experiences, but the universally-shared ability of human beings to reason and learn is accounted for on the basis of human nature. Thus, David Hume was to say:

> It is universally acknowledged there is a great uniformity among the actions of men, in all nations and ages, and that human nature remains still the same, in its principles and operations. The same motives always produce the same actions. . . . Mankind are so much the same, in all times and places, that history informs us of nothing new or strange in this particular. Its chief use is only to discover the constant and universal principles of human nature.[10]

Given all of the talk about revolutions which is currently taking place, the Enlightenment must be one of the most important (if not the single most important) revolution to have ever taken place. The freedom and tolerance which came out of the Enlightenment creates the atmosphere within which genuine intellectual inquiry becomes possible, and ironically, the critiques of the post-modernists could never have been generated in the myopic, repressive, and intolerant intellectual climate which dominated Western culture before the Enlightenment. Thus, modernism created the possibility of its own critique.

For the last several decades, the many faces of relativism have been responsible for slowly eroding the content of modernism and the legacy of the Enlightenment until reason, rationality, and science seem to represent the last bastion for the non-relativists. The legacy of the Enlightenment with its elevation of reason—which represents for many historians of intellectual thought the pinnacle of intellectual development since the dawn of the human race and which was achieved at great risk and cost over a long period of time—is under attack and is being devoured bit by bit until there seems to be little of it left.

The rapidity of the fall from dominance of modernistic thought and all of its accompanying intellectual and methodological commitments must be surprising and paradoxical to serious students of the history of intellectual development. At the beginning of this century, scientific thought was just beginning to hit full stride, and the unprecedented successes of science in the twentieth century, in everything from medicine to space, would seemingly lead us to believe that we are all on our way to the scientific millennium. As we approach the end of the century, however, we have reached the place where science, and the scientific method and its understanding of human reason, are under attack for being ethnocentric and culturally and sexually biased. Many critics now claim that reason itself is culturally relative or "context dependent". For example, Paul Feyerabend claims

> Argument, like language, or art, or ritual, is universal; but, again like language or art or ritual, it has many forms. A simple gesture, or a grunt can decide a debate to the satisfaction or some participants while others need long and colourful arias to be convinced. Thus argument was well established long before the Greek philosophers started thinking about the matter. What the Greeks did invent was not just argument, but a special and standardised way of arguing which, they believed, was independent of the situation in which it occurred and whose results had universal authority. . . . And being rational or using reason now meant using these ways and accepting their results.[11]

Although there are a number of different ways of interpreting the course which has brought us to the "post-modern" era, I think that there are at least two significant developments in twentieth-century thought which are especially important, and there is one particularly significant political and social development.

In philosophy, much of the current reaction against empiricism and scientific philosophy can be traced to the failure of the program of logical positivism in the first part of the twentieth century. The anti-empiricist reaction which inspires many forms of relativism was a backlash against the disillusionment, frustrated expectations, and dashed hopes of those who had relied upon what proved to be the empty, failed promises and bankrupt program of the logical positivists. In its expressed aim of curing philosophy of all of its ills and eliminating all of the pseudo-problems which infested it, never had so much been promised to so many by so few, and seldom had the work of philosophers received so much attention and been so widely heralded in the intellectual world.

Since the inception of the Vienna Circle at the University of Vienna in 1922, its members were mainly unified because of a single common thesis and methodology. The shared thesis was the rejection of speculative metaphysics and the shared methodology was logical analysis and the method of the empirical sciences. These logical positivists (or logical empiricists, as some of them preferred to be known) promised a criterion for distinguishing between empirical meaningfulness and meaninglessness and a program, based upon such a criterion, which would purify philosophy and science of all of the corruption of pseudo-concerns. However, the various attempts at formulation of the verification principle for assessing cognitive meaningfulness each proved to be fraught with difficulties—to such an extent that the pursuit of an acceptable formulation of the principle occupied practically all of the writings of the early positivists.[12] The formulation which would successfully separate science from speculative metaphysics proved to be notoriously elusive.

Consequently, the general program which was to have been based upon the principle of verification also proved elusive. Perhaps there is no better example of an attempt at such a general program than that of Rudolf Carnap. Carnap's first systematic work, *Der logische Aufbau der Welt,* represents an attempt to develop a "rational reconstruction of the concepts of all fields of knowledge" while maintaining a rigorous commitment to empiricism.[13] In his *Aufbau,* through the use of "constitution theory" (a precursor to Nelson Goodman's *The Structure of Appearances* and his process of worldmaking, discussed in detail in Chapter 3 below), Carnap seeks to build a rational explanation of the world taking a single primitive relation, *similarity.* In this "rational reconstruction", observation sentences (protocol sentences) are regarded as ranging over private, phenomenalistic experiences, but Carnap was eventually convinced that such a program would lead to solipsism; so he converted to "physicalism".[14] Metaphysical issues are "external" to Carnap's constitution theory and represent the choice of one particular language over another, and he came to prefer physicalism because of its intersubjective nature through which he could attempt the unification of the sciences.[15] However, abandoning a phenomenalistic language and its epistemological certainty represented abandoning the program of the logical positivists of reducing science to immediate sense experience.

Similarly, Carnap's *Logical Syntax of Language* represented the noble attempt to construct a logical language for philosophy within which all philosophy would be conducted and which could be used to eliminate all pseudo-problems. The "logic of science" was identified with the "syntax of the language of science",[16] and consequently all problems of philosophy and science were viewed as problems of syntax. However, Carnap became convinced, mainly through the work of Alfred Tarski, that syntax alone could not accomplish the task of providing a language for logical analysis for philosophy, and Carnap began his work on semantics.[17] Only through the introduction of semantics (and intensions), Carnap came to believe, would it be possible to talk about the relations between language and facts and about truth, and he consequently moved further from the extreme empiricism of the original positivists' program. The monumental life's work of Carnap thus chronicles the gradual erosion of the logical positivists' radical program and provides some explanation of the growing skepticism of those who doubt the possibility of ever developing any single or universal theory or language for philosophy or science. Those who are sympathetic to the current wave of relativism thus point to the attempt of the positivists to successfully provide a universal and empirical 'grounding' for philosophy as an ill-advised attempt, destined to fail.

A second intellectual development of the twentieth century which has contributed significantly to the shift from the Age of Science to the Age of Relativism has taken place in the social sciences— particularly in cultural anthropology. Anthropology owes its very existence as a discipline to the Enlightenment since as a result of the Enlightenment people began to seek answers to questions which earlier had either been disallowed or answered solely on the basis of religious dogma. Thomas Hobbes and John Locke in England and Rousseau and Voltaire in France had posed questions about the origin of human beings as a species and the place of that species in the natural world. It is hard to imagine anything like a serious, scientific, anthropological study and comparison of human races, cultures, anatomies, and languages in a pre-modernist world before such questions about the origin and nature of the human species and human culture had been posed in a philosophical and scientific manner.

A single model shaped and dominated anthropological research, from its inception at the beginning of the nineteenth century, almost to the beginning of the twentieth. Nineteenth-century anthropology was practically exclusively *evolutionary* anthropology. According to the accepted evolutionary model, human cultural change is a unilinear progression, and the differences amongst cultures and races are accounted for by the positions which they occupy on an abstract, theoretical, evolutionary scale. Hence, anthropologists thought in terms of "advanced" and "primitive" societies, and anthropological research consisted mainly in locating different societies in their "proper" places and in giving some account of the causal factors for those locations and differences. Fundamental to evolutionary anthropology was an underlying belief in a universal human nature which conveniently allowed members of the dominant culture to regard themselves as more fully developed (and hence, "advanced") and to dismiss the differences with other cultures. So long as evolutionary anthropology kept the notion of a dominant culture intact, cultural differences which might suggest some kind of relativism were not taken seriously.

There had been obvious difficulties with evolutionary anthropology all along, but by the beginning of this century, evolution had collapsed as a universal model for doing anthropology. Franz Boaz's "culture history school", which has dominated much of twentieth-century American cultural anthropology, encouraged detailed, empirical "field studies" and disavowed any grand, abstract universal theory of human development. The focus came to be on differences amongst cultures rather than seeing cultures as different stages of a single line of development. The "functionalists", following Bronislaw Malinowski, focused upon understanding various features characterizing different cultures in terms of the functions of those features within the culture in question. In other words, a particular culture came to be understood not in relation to other cultures but solely in terms of itself. The notion of a grand evolutionary scale and comparison of different cultures "progressing" along that scale has now generally come to be dismissed, and even treated with scorn. Individual cultures are now regarded as simply different from one another. Each culture is autonomous, and cross-cultural judgments or comparisons are suspect if not meaningless. Hume's claims about a universal human nature and the uniformity in the principles and operations of human action[18] seem to have been completely abandoned.

Although twentieth-century anthropology is still in a state of development in the sense that there are currently several different influential schools of thought, the idea of a single, dominant, most advanced society has been generally abandoned. With the ease of travel and the astounding developments in communication brought about in this century, differences amongst peoples are now a matter of general public knowledge in much of the world, and the work of anthropologists like Ruth Benedict, Margaret Mead, Edward Sapir, and Benjamin Whorf is widely known. The development of modern anthropological theory and practice from its beginnings in the nineteenth century is thus another important factor in the current shift from reason to relativism.

One of the most important social and political developments to contribute to the rise of relativism was the end of colonialism and the emergence of nationalism in various areas of the world following World War II. The period of colonialization which accompanied the industrial revolution beginning in the second half of the eighteenth century had resulted in huge colonial empires for several Western European countries. The major difference between this period of colonialization and earlier periods was that the domination of the colonizing countries was not based simply upon military superiority but upon industrial and technological superiority, a direct result of the Enlightenment and the rise of science. Scientific and industrial developments in Western European countries during the latter part of the eighteenth century certainly had military consequences, but perhaps at least as important were the consequences for transportation (of both people and goods) and communication. In earlier periods of colonization, the dominant culture of the colonizing nation had been imposed upon the colonized culture by dint of sheer military power; however, in the wave of industrial colonization which continued during the nineteenth century, the superiority of the colonizing nations was believed by many to be cultural—based upon superior scientific development and industrial technology resulting from superior intelligence. The savagery and barbarism which accompanied this period certainly rival that of any period in human history. "The divine right of kings" had been replaced by "manifest destiny".

Although colonial expansion had largely ceased by the beginning of the twentieth century, the most significant move toward actual decolonization followed the end of World War II when, in both Africa and Asia, scores of independent nations came to replace former European colonies. The several decades since the end of World War II have seen the continual decolonialization, country by country, of both Africa and Asia. Along with decolonialization and the rise of independent countries and nationalism there has been an accompanying resurgence of cultural identity and pride in the new, independent countries. The cultural identities of the previously colonized native populations, which had long been suppressed during colonialization, were re-established and began to flourish once again. Consequently, the various cultural differences with which many relativists are concerned became much more pronounced than they had been at any other time since the Enlightenment itself.

As a result of all of these changes in the intellectual, social, and political worlds in the first half of this century, the stage becomes set for the advent of the current wave of relativism. The failure of the program of the positivists, the cultural variety revealed by anthropology, and the rise of different cultures to the level of international respectability meant that a variety of fundamentally different conceptions of the nature of reality, associated with different cultures, were suddenly loosed upon the contemporary scientific and intellectual world, and the notion of a single objective truth concerning the nature of a single reality was relegated to the intellectual dustbin. As Feyerabend describes the result: "cultural variety cannot be tamed by a formal notion of objective truth because it contains a variety of such notions."[19]

The method of science itself has also been rejected by many. Appeal to general principles or laws or methods of reasoning such as induction, which themselves could not be "justified" or defended within the framework of cognitive epistemology, has eventually led to a rejection on the part of many of those principles, rules, and methods. As Feyerabend puts it, "the idea of a science that proceeds by logically rigorous argumentation is nothing but a dream."[20] Consequently, modern thought resulting from the Enlightenment, which scholars have heretofore regarded as a unique intellectually and politically liberating force in the history of Western culture, has come to be viewed as enslaving, ethnocentric and suppressive of culturally varied views of the world.[21]

Many people casually attribute the current controversies concerning relativism to the division between analytic philosophy and continental philosophy, since analytic philosophy generally developed from the Anglo-American tradition, with its strong emphasis on formal logic and linguistic analysis, and contemporary European, continental philosophy developed from the less formal traditions of existentialism, phenomenology, and hermeneutics. Accounting for the present attacks upon traditional epistemology and science in this way is far too crude. As we shall see in Chapters 2 and 3, Willard Van Orman Quine and Nelson Goodman, both godfathers of analytic philosophy, have raised objections to traditional epistemology which have shaken it to its roots. Similarly, although Thomas Kuhn and his talk of paradigms have been adopted by many continental philosophers, the orientation of *The Structure of Scientific Revolutions* is analytic. So, amongst the many current varieties of relativism, some of them originate from within analytic philosophy while others originate from within continental philosophy, and to fully understand the kind of critique of traditional science and philosophy towards which these different attacks converge, we must turn our attention to an examination of the criticisms aimed against the methods of traditional science and epistemology which arise from within both the analytic and continental traditions in philosophy. We will find similar logical and theoretical deficiencies in the different, radical arguments against method—deficiencies which render these arguments impotent and self-refuting—and we shall stake out the high ground for reason and method upon which to take our stand against relativism.

— 1 —

A REPRIEVE FOR GALILEO

TRADITIONAL SCIENCE

The onslaughts of the different forms of present-day epistemological and scientific relativism both arise from and are directed against what I shall call the *traditional* epistemological and scientific thought which stretches from the eighteenth-century Enlightenment to the twentieth century. The fundamental epistemological understandings which have been thoroughly embedded in natural philosophy since the time of the Pre-Socratics have shaped the development of science over the last 200 years. Natural philosophy was so identified with these meta-philosophical epistemological theories that it is now difficult to distinguish sharply between the meta-scientific, epistemological concerns of the philosophy of science and the concerns of science itself. Epistemology explicitly focusses upon developing theories concerning such notions as "truth", "knowledge", "reasons", "belief", "evidence", and "fact"; however, surely science itself would be paralyzed without presupposing some understanding of these basic epistemological notions. The traditional understanding of the nature of science, the predominantly 'received' view, embodies certain definite theories and understandings of these essential, fundamental epistemological notions and distinctions.

As every schoolchild learns, the two primary purposes of science are explanation and prediction. These two crucial features of traditional scientific thought feature prominently in practically every major work on the nature of scientific investigation until recently. The few exceptions are notable. Explanation and prediction are activities which naturally arouse interest in and questions about numerous related issues and notions which quickly lead to *meta-scientific,* epistemological inquiry. "Explanation of what?" we might ask. And, "Prediction of what?" "Explanation as opposed to what, and prediction as opposed to what?" Are some explanations preferred to others? Why? Does this not mean that there are "good" explanations and "bad" ones? Why? And are some explanations "scientific" while others are not? Again, why? And similarly with predictions, why is it that some predictions command our assent or belief in preference to others? On what evidence? How do we gather the evidence? How do we come to accept and believe certain evidence? Answering such questions presupposes a fundamental, meta-scientific, epistemological inquiry into the nature of "reality", facts, truth, reasons, evidence, belief, and knowledge. Such an inquiry creates the domain of the philosophy of science.

THE EMPIRICAL BASIS OF SCIENCE

Perhaps a good way to begin unraveling some of these knotty issues is by investigating in what ways the traditional view of the nature of science has understood science to be *empirical*. After all, "empirical science", on this classical view, is a redundant expression (except to distinguish empirical science from *mathematical* science), and the controversy over the status of *social* science as scientific has centered upon whether social science is really an empirical science. Minimally, the understanding of science as empirical involves the claim that at least some of the terms and statements of scientific theory, on some level, are "about" objects, events, facts, or phenomena, and that the data concerning these objects, events, facts or phenomena are gathered by empirical observation. Such an understanding leads to a distinction between the "theoretical" and the "observable" terms and statements of a scientific theory and to all of the accompanying epistemological problems which come with this distinction. There is room for a great diversity of different ways of understanding both the nature of these phenomena and the method by which we gain any knowledge of them. Much of traditional, empirical epistemology is devoted to the various ways of exploring these problems.

SCIENTIFIC LAWS

However the distinction is drawn and wherever it is drawn, traditional scientific theory has maintained the need to distinguish between theoretical and observable parts of a scientific theory. For example, scientific *laws* must occur at some level of abstraction since, in order to provide any explanatory or predictable efficacy for events, laws must contain some information about recurring regularities amongst many events; however, as is commonly known, not all universal statements about recurring phenomena of a certain type provide a basis for prediction or explanation. To explain why some universal statements may constitute laws while others do not, it is necessary to invoke a distinction which makes scientific laws more removed from immediate observations and hence more "abstract". Since universal statements which are simply contingently or "accidentally" universal cannot be properly regarded as expressing scientific laws, it is necessary to explain the difference between those universal statements which become regarded as laws and those which do not. Within the traditional view of science, however this is done, one must eventually include some special, qualifying claim concerning "causality", or "physical necessity" (in contrast to logical necessity) and hypothetical or future events by using contrary-to-fact hypotheticals. Such law-like universals are said to have a "nomic" quality or to be "nomological universals".[1] For example, consider Archimedes's Law which says something like "the buoyancy of any object is equal to the weight of the liquid displaced by that object".[2] We can use this law to explain or predict what will happen to different objects when they are placed in a liquid only if we understand the law to be a claim which is somehow based upon some kind of physical necessity concerning the nature of physical bodies and liquids on earth and only if we understand the law to make a hypothetical claim about all bodies. We normally express such a claim by saying, "*If* a body *were to be placed* in a liquid, *then* its buoyancy *would be* equal to the weight of the liquid displaced by the object." The nomic quality of the law allows us to provide some explanation of particular events by simply subsuming the particular events under the general law.

THE EMPIRICAL AND THEORETICAL ELEMENTS OF SCIENCE

Such an understanding of the nature of scientific explanation clearly presupposes a distinction between the events, objects or phenomena which are to be explained and the scientific laws or theories which are supposed to explain them. Supposedly, the observable terms of a scientific theory provide an empirical grounding to somehow keep the theory "connected" to "reality". Otherwise, it would be difficult to distinguish science from non-science—although, as we shall see, this particular consequence might not be of great concern to some of the various, individual relativists whose criticisms of this traditional view will be examined in the following chapters. However, some philosophers who have been severely critical of a strict empiricist program are reluctant to completely abandon some form of empirical grounding for science and philosophy. For example, Alfred North Whitehead dramatically attacks the limitations of rigid empiricism, but even his "imaginative rationalization" has an empirical grounding. He says:

> The true method of discovery is like the flight of an aeroplane. It starts from the ground of particular observation; it makes a flight in the thin air of imaginative generalization; and it again lands for renewed observation rendered acute by rational interpretation.[3]

Even Whitehead sees discovery and theory construction as an interplay between the observable and the theoretical.

Empirical science and empirical epistemology are characterized by the crucial role played by the distinction between experience and interpretation of experience—between content and form or content and structure. This distinction has been drawn in many different ways by different people, and I do not intend to explore here the myriad of different interpretations of and permutations upon this general theme. However, since the various forms of epistemological relativism which we shall examine in the succeeding chapters focus their attacks primarily upon this distinction, it is necessary to identify and explore the fundamental epistemological and meta-scientific presuppositions of this traditional view of science.

GALILEO AND THE CATHOLIC CHURCH

Perhaps we can best understand the most significant and fundamental characteristics of this traditional understanding of scientific theory through an examination of the dispute between Galileo Galilei and the Roman Catholic Church in the early seventeenth century concerning the Copernican, heliocentric theory of astronomy. The general nature of this dispute is now a familiar subject to every student of the history of science. At stake in the case of Galileo, there was, of course, the matter of the *content* of the Copernican theory—its claim that the earth moves around the sun—verses the *content* of the Ptolemaic theory—its claim that the sun moves around the earth. However, far more important and more fundamental issues were also at stake—issues which lie at the very heart of the traditional understanding of the nature of scientific inquiry and of the current forms of epistemological relativism.

The most important issues in the dispute between Galileo and the Roman Catholic Church did not concern the content of the Copernican theory championed by Galileo but rather *the nature and status of the Copernican theory and the method by which Galileo determined that this theory was preferable to the Ptolemaic one.* In other words, the main disputes were not scientific ones but meta-scientific ones or philosophical ones—disputes within the philosophy of science about the nature and method of science.

Let us first consider the issue of the epistemological status of a particular theory. The Catholic Church was willing to allow Galileo to teach the Copernican theory of astronomy as a *useful* hypothesis or supposition, that is, as an *instrumental aid to mathematical calculations for making predictions in astronomy.*[4] The sticking point came over whether the new theory would be called "true". Galileo himself believed not only that the Copernican system provided a simpler and easier way of doing the calculations to account for the astronomical phenomena; he also believed that the Copernican theory provided an *accurate, factual account of reality,* and he refused to deny or vitiate this latter claim by reducing the theory to a "supposition" or "hypothesis". For Galileo, *the status* of the theory as a true, descriptive account of the heavenly bodies meant that Copernicus was right and Ptolemy was wrong.[5]

GALILEO AND CONTEMPORARY PHILOSOPHY OF SCIENCE

Ironically, though historians of science still properly regard Galileo's stand as marking a major development in the development of science as an autonomous discipline of "free" inquiry, leading figures today in both the philosophy of science and epistemology would be more likely to take the side of the Catholic Church in the dispute over these particular meta-scientific issues. In this regard, Galileo could easily find himself as out of step with many contemporary philosophers of science as he was with the Catholic Church in the sixteenth and seventeenth centuries, and Galileo's attribution of truth to his scientific theories would be as alien to much of contemporary philosophy of science as it was to The Catholic Church at the time.

For example, we shall see in the very next chapter that Willard Van Orman Quine's holistic view of theories and systems of belief is fundamentally characterized by a thoroughgoing, functional evaluation of the whole system. In order to appreciate how far twentieth-century cosmology has come since Galileo, compare Quine's description of his theory with Galileo's. Quine says:

> Physical objects are conceptually imported into the situation [scientific explanation] as convenient intermediaries—not by definition in terms of experience, but simply as irreducible posits comparable, epistemologically, to the gods of Homer. . . . Both sorts of entities enter our conception only as cultural posits. The myth of physical objects is epistemologically superior to most in that it has proved more efficacious than other myths as a device for working a manageable structure into the flux of experience.[6]

Obviously, if the gods of Homer will do as well epistemologically as physical objects (depending simply upon one's theoretical preferences), then surely other gods might also do as well—relative to different epistemological contexts. The quarrel between Galileo and the Catholic Church begins to sound very current if, as Quine claims, the *myth* of physical objects is viewed as simply a "cultural posit". Even Quine's claim that the myth of physical objects is more "efficacious" seems to mirror the Church's response to Galileo that it would be permissible to *use* Copernican theory so long as it was not claimed to be *true*.

Similarly, Nelson Goodman also insists that we construct our worlds. For Goodman, "worldmaking" is an instrumentalist activity through which we construct our world by constructing our theories according to which our world comes into existence. Theoretical and not factual concerns guide this process, and, as with Quine's holism, particular claims take on meaning and truth-value only relative to what Goodman calls a "frame of reference". Goodman explicitly discusses the exact point of dispute between Galileo and the Inquisition. The two different claims—'the sun moves' and 'the sun does not move'—are *both* true, Goodman insists, relative to different frames of reference. According to Goodman's theory of worldmaking, such claims are elliptical and always carry an assumption that they should be paraphrased as "Under Galileo's frame of reference, the sun does not move", and "Under the Catholic Church's frame of reference, the sun does move".[7] For Goodman, no one frame of reference is ontologically fundamental or privileged. Though there may be good reasons for preferring one frame of reference to another, these reasons do not include Galileo's reason for preferring the Copernican system to the Ptolemaic since, for Goodman, no one frame of reference is more factually accurate than another. Again,

Goodman's contemporary theory of worldmaking captures very closely the position which the Church attempted to force Galileo to accept and which he refused—it is all right to *use* a particular theory (with a particular frame of reference) so long as we realize that truth and ontological claims are relative to a frame of reference.

THE QUESTION OF METHOD

Secondly, and closely related to the issue of the status of the theory, is the question of *the method by which Galileo came to prefer Copernicus's theory of astronomy to that of Aristotle, Ptolemy, and the Catholic Church.* On the one hand, there were the appeals to papal authority, church history, and Biblical accounts of cosmology, the authority of the history of philosophy and the evidence from 'common sense'. On the other hand, there were his own "scientific" observations and his use of scientific "reasoning". Galileo had announced his support of Copernicanism in *Sidereus Nunicus (Starry Messenger)*[8] which was published in 1610 after he had completed his experiments with motion and had become committed to science based upon experimentation.[9] It is Galileo's commitment to the scientific method which ultimately draws the line of demarcation between the Catholic Church and Galileo—a commitment which Galileo continued to demonstrate after the publication of *Sidereus Nunicus* with his treatments of bodies in water, sunspots, and comets.[10] Galileo's observations with the telescope had shown that the surface of the moon was rough and uneven, like the surface of earth,[11] and had revealed the presence of hitherto unknown "stars" orbiting Jupiter.[12] Galileo correctly reasoned that the moon was not a perfect sphere as Aristotle had claimed but that it had mountains much like those on the surface of the earth. Based upon his observations of the changing positions of the stars, he also correctly identified these "stars" as moons orbiting Jupiter. Galileo thus provided the first empirical evidence of orbiting satellites in the heavens, and his observations of the phases of Venus, predicted by Copernicus, provided direct evidence that the planets orbit the sun.[13] However, the Copernican theory conflicted with common sense, or the experiences of the common person in the street, and the Aristotelians, while admitting that different, conflicting theories might all *work,* insisted that only their theory was *true.*[14] As the criticisms of Galileo mounted, the battle became joined over the *method* of preferring one theory to another. Religious authority and common sense were pitted against scientific experimentation and mathematical reasoning. In this regard, Galileo explicitly endorses the method of empirical science over the pronouncements of religious authority:

> It is necessary for the Bible, in order to be accommodated to the understanding of every man, to speak many things which appear to differ from the absolute truth so far as the bare meaning of the words is concerned. But Nature, on the other hand, is inexorable and immutable; she never transgresses the laws imposed upon her, or cares a whit whether her abstruse reasons and methods of operation are understandable to men. For that reason it appears that nothing physical which sense-experience sets before our eyes, or which necessary demonstrations prove to us, ought to be called in question (much less condemned) upon the testimony of biblical passages which have some different meaning beneath their words. For the Bible is not chained in every expression to conditions as strict as those which govern all physical effects.[15]

In an attempt to respond to criticisms and to provide additional scientific evidence for the Copernican theory, Galileo published his *Dialogue on the Two World Systems* in 1632. He includes what he understood as the strongest scientific "reasons" for preferring Copernican to Ptolemaic astronomy—evidence based upon sunspots and the tides. As is now well known, the arguments based upon this "evidence" fell woefully short of providing the desired scientific proof of Copernican theory which Galileo sought. Much has been made of the mistakes which Galileo made—particularly his erroneous claims regarding the tides.[16] Since, as it turns out, Galileo was mistaken about what he considered to the strongest and most primary reason for preferring Copernican to Ptolemaic astronomy, how can we regard his choice as "scientific" or "rational"?[17] What I will try to demonstrate throughout this volume is that it is the *method* of inquiry which is most important. In the present case, let us simply admit, for the sake of argument, that Galileo's scientific case for preferring Copernican theory and regarding it to be actually *true* was very weak and that much of the evidence upon which he relied (particularly that regarding the tides) was simply false. What does this prove? Well, for one thing, we should focus on the fact that it is possible to disprove Galileo's claims regarding the tides, for it is an essential part of the nature of the scientific method that one's results, data, and methods are available for public scrutiny and critical, scientific examination by others. The experiments must be public and repeatable, and it is only because of this that we can show bad science to be bad. But bad science is still science and, as we shall see in Chapters 7 and 8, bad science, in the long run, is still preferable to any other method of "fixing belief" since the scientific method is the only method which provides us with a built-in mechanism for identifying and hence correcting our mistakes.

GALILEO AND SCIENCE

Galileo should be viewed not as a champion of Copernican theory but rather as a champion of the scientific method, and in this regard, it is difficult to overestimate the significance of Galileo's stand. We can see in Galileo's stand against authority the fundamental basis for understanding the essential nature of traditional scientific theory. It is certainly difficult to imagine how the Enlightenment would have developed in the eighteenth century without the precursory changes in scientific thought which took place in the sixteenth and seventeenth centuries. Thomas Kuhn chronicles these changes in the following manner:

> During the century and a half following Galileo's death in 1642, a belief in the earth-centered universe was gradually transformed from an essential sign of sanity to an index, first, of inflexible conservatism, then of excessive parochialism, and finally of complete fanaticism. By the middle of the seventeenth century it is difficult to find an important astronomer who is not Copernican; by the end of the century it is impossible.[18]

These changes marked not only a victory for Copernican theory; they also marked a victory for human reason and the scientific method of inquiry—a victory which was to launch the Enlightenment.

Also joining the chorus of the nay-sayers to Galileo is Thomas Kuhn, who maintains that facts are relative to theory—to "paradigm-based" science according to which facts are selected and within which they exist. Like Quine and Goodman, Kuhn insists that the basis for preferring one paradigm to another is never factual, and, as we shall examine in great detail in Chapter 4, he even argues that the basis for a person's preference of one paradigm over another is not *rational*.[19] Under Kuhn's program, it is difficult to imagine how Galileo and the members of the Inquisition could ever resolve their dispute by the use of reason or argument or evidence since their paradigms—their "frames of reference" were different, which means that their facts were different and their reasons were different.

Given what Kuhn describes as the "incommensurability" of different paradigms, the switch from one paradigm to another is a

Gestalt, all-or-nothing, switch according to which one just suddenly sees the world differently.[20] Such a claim aims squarely at the second point of dispute between Galileo and the Catholic Church—the question of the method for choosing or preferring one "frame of reference" or "paradigm" to another. The Church thought that reason supported its view, and Galileo thought that reason supported his. Many of the current detractors from modernism have aligned themselves with instrumentalism so completely that some of the leading members of the current relativistic wave of criticism explicitly treat science as just one amongst many different "ideologies"—comparable to religion or magic[21]—with reason giving no more preference to one than to another.

Thus, we see that this second major meta-scientific, epistemological point of difference between Galileo and the Inquisition is also today in hot dispute, and again, leading figures in current philosophy of science would be more closely aligned with Galileo's detractors than with Galileo. This current dispute centers around the nature of human rationality and its connection with scientific method. As we shall see in Chapter 5, Peter Winch and those who follow his lead see nothing intrinsically rational about the method of science, but rather, they see rationality as essentially sociologically based and biased. Winch insists that there are different, culturally-relative standards of rationality, and any particular person's claim to rationality is only rational relative to his or her own standards of rationality.[22] According to Winch, not only is the method of science not intrinsically and universally rational as Galileo had claimed, but neither are the laws of logic.

THE LEGACY OF GALILEO

The combined forces of Galileo in Italy and his contemporary, Francis Bacon, in England provided a two-pronged development of the Renaissance which was to supplant the scholasticism of the medieval period in Western Europe. In his *Novum Organum,* Bacon provided the rules and principles for inductive reasoning as Aristotle had done for syllogistic reasoning. This canonization of the scientific method set forth the logical mechanisms for understanding the revolutionary scientific discoveries of the sixteenth and seventeenth centuries[23] since these "discoveries" were the results of the scientific method. Bacon's explanations of ways to ensure objective and unbiased observation and judgment remain as the identifying characteristics of what I am calling the traditional understanding of the nature of scientific inquiry; consequently, Bacon joins Galileo as a primary target of the current attacks of the relativists whose claims we will examine here.

The understanding of the nature of science and scientific theories has "come a long way" if a major, perhaps even dominant, contemporary school of thought in epistemology or philosophy of science is more closely aligned with the position of the sixteenth- and seventeenth-century Catholic Church than it is with Galileo. To really appreciate the significance and the irony of this development, think of the anomaly of a treatise on the history of science which championed the stance of the Inquisition in persecuting Galileo for his narrow, intolerant, realist views because the members of the Inquisition paved the way for the development of contemporary (not "modern") science! We will examine this ironic turn of events and attempt to provide a response to it—a reprieve for Galileo.

The inheritance received from Galileo and those who followed his lead in the remainder of the seventeenth century is a form of *realism* according to which the world or reality is understood to be a certain way, and the task of the scientist is to discover the most accurate theory for describing it.[24] According to this realist understanding of the nature of scientific inquiry, reality is metaphorically "out there"—"beyond" or "beneath" scientific theory; real objects, facts or events are what scientific theory is *about,* and this real world is revealed to human beings through observation. Observation thus forms the starting point for all scientific theory and provides the sounding board for checking all scientific theory. Scientific theory must "keep in touch" with reality, which is why the flight of Whitehead's aeroplane of theory construction, cited above, must begin and end its flight on *terra firma*—keeping the imaginative and sometimes highly abstract theory in touch with the actual world. It is this fundamental commitment to realism which originally gave empirical science its empirical base.

Whitehead's metaphor of the aeroplane is illustrative for capturing the empirical grounding of the "empirically minded" metaphysician; however, it probably allows too much high-soaring freedom for the realist view of the empirical scientist. Perhaps more appropriate would be the image of a hot-air balloon rising over the landscape while being firmly tethered to the ground. The *empirical grounding* of scientific theory and empiricist epistemology functions like a long cord which continually keeps theories tethered to "reality" and continually fed and nourished by empirical facts. To complete the metaphor, theories "cut off" from this continuous grounding in reality float away into speculative metaphysics. As I have indicated earlier, much of empirical epistemology has historically been given to exploring ways of trying to explain and understand the nature of this empirical grounding of human thought.

THEORY AND REALITY

The nature of the relationship between theory (or language) and reality is a theme which has dominated much of twentieth-century philosophy. The main issues which arise in the philosophy of science have rather strict parallels in the philosophy of language, and questions and problems about the theory of meaning or the theory of reference cannot be separated from the epistemological questions surrounding the realist interpretation of scientific theory and its empirical grounding. The fundamental question about the nature of the relationship between language and reality has dominated the writings of the leading figures of "analytic" philosophy—including Ludwig Wittgenstein, Bertrand Russell, and John L. Austin. For example, the Augustinian view of language which Wittgenstein uses as a stalking horse at the beginning of his *Philosophical Investigations* is simply a representative sample of this traditional view of the nature of language and its relationship to "reality".[25]

This dominant view of the relationship between language or theory on the one hand and "reality" on the other has given rise to the dominant themes of empirical epistemology: the correspondence theory of truth, the referential theory of meaning, and the verification criterion of meaning. According to this traditional view, the relationship between language or theory and the reality which theory and language are about is ontologically dichotomistic.[26] Objects, facts, and events—the objects of our observations—are all on the same ontological level—the level of the objective, physical world—while language and theories are on another distinct level. The objects, facts, or events are "out there" waiting to be experienced by an observer and discovered by the scientist, and theory formation is the process of constructing the "right" theory to describe these objective facts. Observation and experimentation are the important processes of providing evidence for theories by focussing our attention upon the crucial facts or events. Objective facts thus serve as the beginning and ending point of theory formation. The consequence of this traditional way of viewing the relationship between theory and reality is a gap or chasm between (on the one hand) facts, objects, and events "in reality" and (on the other) language and theory, which supposedly describe those facts, objects, and events.[27] Attempts to bridge this gap between theory and fact (and all of the attending difficulties of these attempts) have occupied much of empirical epistemology since the eighteenth century.

Consider, for example, the correspondence theory of truth. For this empiricist view, from a commonsense standpoint, it seems very reasonable to treat a true statement as one which properly describes or accurately labels an actual state-of-affairs. Think of what happens in a courtroom when a witness swears to tell the "truth, the whole truth, and nothing but the truth". To what does such a promise commit the witness? Well, suppose that the witness says something such as, "The red car was proceeding north on Main Street, and it went straight through the stop sign without stopping and then hit the white car." The promise to tell the truth must mean, in this circumstance, that when the witness describes the accident, she is, to the best of her knowledge, accurately describing *what actually happened*. Whether the testimony is actually true or not is determined by the judge or jury who decides whether the statement does, in fact, accurately describe the actual state-of-affairs. Truth is thus anchored in experience, and facts, or a person's judgment of the facts, become the final arbiter.

"Getting at the facts" in all of their stark, unbridled nakedness has, of course, proven to be the Achilles's heel of empiricist epistemology. The difficulties and disputes are now legendary, and I do not intend to describe those here.[28] In particular, questions concerning negative facts ("The fish are not biting today"), general facts ("The Heron is a migratory bird"), and subjective facts ("Were you to be a realist, you would be attracted to the correspondence theory of truth.") still plague attempts to "match up" true statements with facts 'in the world'.

Descartes's methodological skepticism prompted his rationalistic foundationalism. We shall examine in some detail, in Chapter 7, Charles Peirce's attack upon Cartesian foundationalism; however, traditional empiricist realism has also been very attracted to a foundationalist epistemology—though for different, or at least additional, reasons to those of Descartes. In addition to seeking safe refuge from the onslaught of the skeptic, empiricist epistemology also seeks the best place to attach the tether between language or theory and reality. Such an attempt to connect language to reality greatly encourages a foundationalist approach since an attractive and perhaps workable model would involve making the connection at some fundamental, primitive point and then building the superstructure upon this empirical foundation.[29] The primary connection has been made by different empiricists in different ways—from Locke's simple ideas and Hume's sense impressions to Russell's logically proper names and knowledge by acquaintance. Sense data, ostensive definition, and protocol sentences have all been called upon to do the job of bridging the gap between theory and reality. Thus, empiricists —from the "traditional" British empiricists of the eighteenth century to the logical positivists of the twentieth century—have sought a way of re-connecting theory and facts. However, all of these attempts have been notoriously fraught with problems, none has won universal acclaim, and even those which have won some general acceptance have proven to be short-lived.

The fundamental battle between Galileo and the Church—the battle between reason and method on the one hand and other ways of fixing beliefs on the other—has been joined once more. Galileo and Bacon served as leading figures of the Renaissance and as precursors to the Enlightenment and modernism. Now, their epistemological antagonists—Quine, Goodman, Kuhn, Winch, Gadamer, Habermas, and Laudan serve as leading figures of a form of post-modernism which seeks to completely overturn this traditional view of the nature of science and scientific inquiry. Radical feminists argue that the traditional theories of epistemology and scientific method are male-biased and simply the received view of a bunch of 'dead, white European males'. In the succeeding chapters, I will examine these attacks and criticisms in detail, and I will argue for a return to Reason and Method.

— 2 —

QUINE ON LOGICAL AND ONTOLOGICAL RELATIVISM

Logical Relativism

Willard Van Orman Quine is certainly one of the most important early figures in the current wave of relativism, and the corpus of his work represents one of the most continuous and serious challenges to traditional empirical epistemology. His claims that "No statement is immune to revision" and "ontology recapitulates philology"[1] are amongst the most notable and poignant of all aphorisms of twentieth-century philosophy. Quine conflates statements of logic and statements of fact, and he reduces all questions about ontology— questions about what exists "in reality"—to questions about language. By conflating the distinction between logic and fact, Quine abandons the distinction between structure and content and thereby undermines the epistemological view according to which there is a universal way of structuring human experience or an universal method of pursuing epistemological inquiry. At the time when he initially argued for such theories, he was one of very few people within the analytic tradition in philosophy (including, as we shall see in the next chapter, Nelson Goodman) to be found in the camp of relativism. In this chapter, I shall examine Quine's arguments concerning both logical truth and ontology in order to assess their impact upon the traditional epistemological notions of rationality and method.

Two Dogmas of Empiricism

Quine's justly celebrated "Two Dogmas of Empiricism"[2] ranks as one of the most significant pieces of work in contemporary analytic philosophy, and more generally, it must be regarded as pivotal in the development of current relativistic thought in epistemology and the philosophy of science. 'Two Dogmas' consists of a series of arguments against what he regards as the dogmas (or sacred idols) of empiricist epistemology—the analytic-synthetic distinction and reductionism. Quine's notorious attack on the analytic-synthetic distinction has received a plethora of responses; consequently, I do not intend to repeat those responses here.[3] Instead, I will examine Quine's own theory of relativistic "pragmatic holism" to see if it avoids the kinds of objections which he raises against traditional empiricist epistemology.

As is well known, Quine concludes that the traditional distinction between analytic and synthetic statements should be abandoned. On the traditional treatment of the analytic-synthetic distinction, an analytic statement like

(1) No unmarried man is married.

is regarded as logically true because of the "essential occurrence" of the logical components of the statement—quite independently of the *content*. In other words, it is the *structure* of such a statement which makes it true regardless of the particular substitutions for the non-logical elements.

An analytic statement such as

(2) No bachelor is married.

can supposedly easily be turned into a logically true statement such as (1) by analyzing the meaning of the word 'bachelor' and then putting synonyms for synonyms. Synthetic statements, on the other hand, cannot be turned into logically true statements. Statements such as (1) are usually called logical truths since their necessary truth does not depend upon semantics but completely upon the essential occurrence of the logical particles so that they remain true for all re-interpretations of the non-logical components of the statement. Quine initially raises his objections to the analytic-synthetic distinction because of the fact that analytic statements such as (2) depend upon essential predication or synonymity for their "reduction" to logical truths. His notorious attacks on the usual ways of trying to explain or defend synonymity are too well known to repeat here.[4]

QUINE'S HOLISM

Quine replaces the old, empiricist epistemology, empiricism with the dogmas, with his "thoroughgoing" pragmatism, which has at times been called Quine's *field theory, network theory, or holism.* The central idea in Quine's epistemological holism is that our epistemic beliefs form a field or network with epistemologically important relationships amongst the different beliefs. Although essentially amorphous, it is helpful to think of such a network as being structured in such manner that certain beliefs occur more toward the outside periphery of the network while others occur more toward the central core of the network. However, all positioning within the field of beliefs is simply relative to other beliefs in the field. Beliefs which occur toward the periphery are the most "loosely connected" to other beliefs in the network and correspond most closely to *observation statements,* reports of sense experience. Beliefs which occur more toward the center of the network correspond most closely to what have traditionally been called theoretical or logical statements. They are more "removed" from immediate experience and more closely and more thoroughly "connected" with other beliefs in the network.

This network of beliefs is constantly changing, with new beliefs being acquired and old ones being revised or given up. According to Quine, a person approaches each new experience with a network, or field, of beliefs, and a new, recalcitrant experience[5] occasions a belief which then enters the network at the periphery. With the process of accepting a recalcitrant experience E and some statement S1 which is a description of E, the subject has to "adjust" the rest of the statements in his or her network of beliefs. Hence, accepting S1 might force one to "give up" or revise some other statement S2 or some group of statements S2–Sn. The choice of which other statement to revise and which ones to allow to remain unchanged is one internal to the network, made on the basis, according to Quine, of deciding which statements or beliefs are the most pragmatically important to the network as a whole. Quine describes this process in the following manner:

> A conflict with experience at the periphery occasions re-adjustments in the interior of the field. Truth values have to be redistributed over some of our statements. Re-evaluation of some statements entails re-evaluation of others, because of their logical interconnections—the logical laws being in turn simply certain further statements of the system, certain further elements of the field. Having re-evaluated one statement we must re-evaluate some others, which may be statements logically connected with the first or may be the statements of the logical connections themselves.[6]

In this passage, Quine indicates that his thoroughgoing pragmatism and his rejection of the analytic-synthetic distinction lead to an epistemology where every belief in the network is epistemologically valued because of its relative pragmatic value to the network. The claim is that there is no qualitative difference—no difference "in kind"—between what have been called analytic statements and synthetic ones. Whatever differences there may be are simply differences of pragmatic degree, differences measured by the comparative value of utility which each statement has to the rest of the system. This difference amongst beliefs based solely upon pragmatic differences of degree of importance consequently explains Quine's well-known dictum that "[a]ny statement can be held true come what may" or conversely, that "no statement is immune to revision."[7]

Though statements at the periphery are described by Quine as those most closely linked with experience, he means nothing more by this than that, given a knowing subject's natural propensity to disturb the whole network of beliefs as little as possible, the ones "at the periphery" are those chosen for revision first. For this reason, the beliefs toward the periphery are said to have more "empirical reference" (relatively speaking, of course) while those toward the center are more highly theoretical.

LOGICAL TRUTH AND HOLISM

Although there is some difficulty in interpreting what Quine has to say about logical truth, evidently logical truth is to be handled in the same manner as analytic truth. In other words, statements of the form of (1) wind up in the same pragmatic boat as those of the form of (2). We have seen in the passage included above that Quine says explicitly that logical laws are "simply further elements in the system" and that we might choose to re-evaluate (and presumably revise) the statements of the logical connections amongst different statements in the system as well as we might any other statement in the system. Following the dictum that "no statement is immune to revision", Quine adds, for emphasis, that "revision even of the logical law of the excluded middle has been proposed as a means of simplifying quantum mechanics."[8]

An illustration of what Quine means here can be drawn from experiments used in quantum theory to illustrate Niels Bohr's "principle of complementarity", the claim that a complete description of light must include descriptions of different aspects of light which are both wave and particle in nature. However, the wave-like behavior of electrons and the particle-like behavior of electrons on the sub-atomic level cannot be determined by the same experiment. So, whether one describes a beam of light as a wave or a particle depends upon which experiment is conducted, and the description used depends upon the experiment. For example, in an experiment involving electron interference, if a beam of electrons is directed at screen B through screen A which contains a double slit, we find that the slits in screen A set up a pattern of electron interference which can be measured on screen B. This is evidence that the electrons should be described as a wave. However, if, in the same experiment, the slits in screen A are provided with a device for detecting electrons, we get evidence that the electrons are particles since we can now show which of the two slits in screen A an electron passes through and determine a "trajectory" for "it". At the same time, any data of interference of the slits in A (which provide evidence of the wave-like nature of electrons) completely disappear. Given the other options available when faced with such a "recalcitrant" experience and the necessity of having to revise or "give up" some claims in one's network of beliefs, one might decide, Quine suggests, to revise the Law of Excluded Middle. So, it seems, within quantum theory, it may be that electrons can be described as both waves and particles depending upon different experimental data and that the Law of Excluded Middle which would require that a claim such as "Electrons are particles" to be either true or false does not hold for quantum phenomena.

QUINE AND PRAGMATISM

The fundamental value of utility and pragmatic value for determining adjustments within Quine's field theory is reminiscent of William James's pragmatic conception of truth. James also claims that a person should be understood as having a set of beliefs and that the truth of any new belief ought to be measured by a relationship between the already accepted beliefs and the new one. Specifically, James advocates what he calls the "marriage function", meaning that we are to understand a belief as true if it unites or "marries" easily with the accepted beliefs. However, James is reluctant to ever completely abandon the notion that true ideas somehow stand in some sort of "agreement" with reality,[9] and furthermore, James never stops talking about the notion of an independent, objective reality. Thus, the ultimate purpose of a true idea for James is its pragmatic value in the sense of its serving as a *guide* for the subject in dealing with *reality*. "The essential thing is the process of being guided," says James.[10]

Many of the important measures of modern relativism can be found in James's theory of truth. Truth becomes relative to a particular system of beliefs (or, as some have suggested, to a particular individual); so there is no absolute truth, and what is true relative to a particular system may also change with time. James says:

> '*The true*', *to put it very briefly, is only the expedient in the way of our thinking, just as 'the right' is only the expedient in the way of our behaving.* Expedient in almost any fashion; and expedient in the long run and on the whole course; for what meets expediently all the experience in sight won't necessarily meet all further experiences equally satisfactorily.[11]

According to James, a pragmatic conception of truth consists in the theory that a knowing subject makes a claim true by "assimilating, validating, corroborating, and verifying" it and this process is relative to different belief systems and to different times. However, James was never able to completely lose the influence of the realism of Charles Peirce, and consequently, James's pragmatism still has some external considerations. Quine's pragmatism, on the other hand, is completely internal since pragmatic determinations concerning beliefs and the acceptance or rejection of beliefs are made internally by the consideration of the consequences for other beliefs in the system. In contrast, however, even when James temporarily drops talking about the agreement of a true idea with reality, he never abandons a notion of pragmatism according to which pragmatic value is measured by the success (or lack of success) of the organism in its environment.

James explicitly denies Peirce's belief that scientific investigation will eventually evolve toward a single determinate truth. Although he was talking about Hegel's theory of being, he might well have been talking of Peirce's theory of the scientific method when he said, "when all things have been unified to the supreme degree, the notion of a possible other than the actual may still haunt our imagination and prey upon our system."[12] And, in an obvious reference to Peirce, James says,

> There is nothing improbable in the supposition that an analysis of the world may yield a number of formulae, all consistent with the facts. . . . Why may there not be different points of view for surveying it, within each of which all data harmonize, and which the observer may therefore either choose between, or simply cumulate one upon another?[13]

But Peirce seems to have anticipated just such an objection. At any given moment, if any two theories are equally compatible with all of the data, then given Peirce's pragmatic theory of meaning, the two theories are identical: they mean exactly the same thing. One must not forget that Peirce's pragmatic theory of meaning is an essential part of his theory of scientific methodology.

Although James does suggest, in an almost off-hand way, that these different formulas, theories or views of the world would have to meet "our purely logical needs",[14] he fails to appreciate just how much is built into this phrase. The central issue of our current investigation of Quine revolves around whether "our purely logical needs" are external to any one of the views which James has described. As we shall see repeatedly, this same, central issue recurs with each major figure who advocates a form of extreme relativism.

James, of course, went too far in abandoning realism, according to Peirce. But James never went so far as Quine. If all of the criteria for evaluating the system of beliefs are internal to the system—including the pragmatic criterion of minimizing significant changes in the set of beliefs—then certainly Quine's pragmatism is more radical than James's. Not only truth but analyticity and logical truth as well become internal questions for Quine, questions internal to some network of beliefs. James explicitly denies that the same kind of marriage function which operates to incorporate beliefs about new facts into the set of accepted beliefs works for logical laws as well. On the contrary, James maintains that "the very structure of our thinking" provides the "framework" within which his pragmatism operates. And he further cautions that these "abstract relations" which comprise this structure "coerce" us and that we cannot play "fast and loose" with them.[15] When truth "happens" to an idea—when we make an idea true—this is a process which takes place within a given framework and according to certain rules, the "abstract relations". The truth of these "definitions" or "principles" or laws is not variable or relative but has, as James describes it, "an 'eternal' character"[16] to it.

HOLISM AND RELATIVISM

Quine's brand of pragmatism has the potential to be much more pernicious than James's because if logical laws are no more immune to revision than are other statements of one's network of beliefs, then standards of rationality and *reason* itself would apparently become relative to different networks of beliefs. Consequently, any absolute notion of rationality, as well as any defense of scientific method as a preferred or unique method of epistemological inquiry, are equally threatened by Quine's "empiricism without the dogmas".

Before turning to ontological questions, let us first examine Quine's claims concerning analyticity and logical truth. I will defend the analytic-synthetic distinction and will argue that Quine cannot develop his field theory if he abandons the distinction as he claims. In other words, I will argue that Quine's pragmatic field theory depends upon and uses a form of the analytic-synthetic distinction just as empiricist epistemology does. In the end, we will see, a notion of rationality based on universal and necessary logical laws remains intact as well as the method for fixing beliefs based upon those logical laws.

Consider carefully how Quine's thoroughgoing pragmatism is supposed to differ from dogmatic empiricism. A recalcitrant experience E occurs and causes a formation or a revision of some statement S1 on the periphery of one's network of statements. But, as Quine indicates in the above passage from 'Two Dogmas of Empiricism', if one re-evaluates one statement, one must re-evaluate other statements *"because of their logical interconnections"* [my emphasis]. Quine also says that "re-evaluation of some statements *entails* re-evaluation of others" and "having re-evaluated one statement we *must* re-evaluate some others." [my emphasis]. It is through this process of logical entailment that one is led—via the process of re-evaluation or re-distribution of truth-values—to a consideration of the statements at the interior of the network by a statement like S1 at the periphery. However, as we have seen, Quine is quick to point out that these logical rules are "simply further elements in the system" and that "no statement is immune to revision". Let us examine this claim of Quine's that the logical laws or rules, on the meta-linguistic level, according to which the re-evaluation of statements takes place, are of the same epistemological value as all of the other statements in the network. Let us try and formulate this meta-linguistic rule for the re-evaluation of statements in a Quinean network theory. Consider something like the following:

(Q) If some recalcitrant experience E occurs which causes a subject to regard as true (hold on to) statement S1, and if S1 and some other statement S2 are incompatible, then S2 must be regarded as false (given up or "revised"). Furthermore, if holding on to S1 or the revision of S2 causes some other inconsistency with some other statement S3, then S3 must also be revised.

The most important consideration in conducting such an evaluation is the pragmatic concern for the preservation of the system of statements and its smooth operation; therefore, the statements toward the center of the system, since they are the most important ones to the system, are the statements which most strongly resist re-evaluation.

Now on one level, Quine certainly seems to be right. On the basis of empirical evidence, it is safe to say that people do frequently "hold on to" a particular belief "come what may"—even to the point of abandoning what, on one level, might be called "logic" or "reason". For example, a cuckolded husband, wishing to retain a belief in his wife's fidelity might refuse to accede to any belief which would tend to support her infidelity—even to such an extent that observers might describe him as "crazy" or "irrational". Similarly, a parent might stubbornly refuse to believe that a child is a drug dealer by making sweeping and extensive changes within her system of beliefs. Or a theist might do the same thing regarding a belief in the omnibenevolence of a transcendent god by insisting that descriptions of human suffering and evil are false, or by otherwise adjusting the network of beliefs in such a manner that the belief about such a god's omnibenevolence is "immune to revision". All of these people seem to be employing a principle like (Q) to "pragmatically" adjust their networks of beliefs to their own liking; however, surely these examples do not touch upon Quine's main argument. He does not mean to be describing an individual's particular psychological inability to accept or reject a particular belief, and the logical laws which are at stake are much more basic and fundamental than the notion of "logical" or "rational" in these examples. All of these people might stubbornly and "blindly" persist in their "irrational" beliefs and still use *modus ponens* or The Law of Non-Contradiction or The Law of Excluded Middle quite regularly. Quine is obviously tracking much bigger game—basic and fundamental notions of logic and rationality.

PROBLEMS WITH HOLISM

It is helpful to begin trying to determine the success of Quine's arguments by examining several very interesting and difficult issues which begin to emerge when questions are raised about the status of

(Q) within a particular system and how it is supposed to operate. First, (Q) must obviously be on the meta-linguistic level since it is what allows the person to make comparisons amongst different statements in the system. So, one of the first things we must notice explicitly about Quine's network of beliefs is that it includes statements on different logical levels which are not regarded as statements of different logical types. And, since according to Quine, (Q) itself will simply be one of "the further elements of the field", it too must be revisable within the network of beliefs.

Let us pursue some of the complications of this conflation of logical types. Several difficulties are apparent immediately: Could Quine's field theory manage without (Q)? That is, could Quine's theory survive the re-evaluation of (Q)? Presumably, if no statement is immune to revision, then neither is (Q). If (Q) is not revisable, in theory, then Quine faces the same self-referential problem which has plagued so many advocates of general theories about the nature of language, and (Q) would represent an illegitimate totality. If (Q) is revisable, then Quine faces a different set of problems. The obvious initial difficulty is that if (Q) is revisable, then Quine's whole theory becomes relative to different networks and might well have nothing to recommend it to a particular person who, on whatever grounds, refuses to accept (Q). Notice also that for Quine the possible revision of (Q)—call it (QR) for '(Q) revision'—must also be just another statement in the field and as such, it also must be revisable. (QR) must be on the meta-meta-linguistic level since it is making a claim about the possible revision of (Q) which is on the meta-linguistic level. Regardless of whether a person decided to revise (Q) or hold on to it, by revising (QR), there must be an additional logical level and a statement which says something like, 'If (Q) and (QR) are incompatible and one wishes to hold onto (Q), then one must give up (QR)'; however, this statement (QQR) must also be revisable so it seems that the process of re-evaluation would never end and that one would be faced with an infinite series of different logical levels if the meta-linguistic statements, the *rules* for the re-evaluation of statements, are lumped with all of the other statements to be re-evaluated in the field.

Obviously, there are revisions, and then there are *serious* revisions. One might tinker a bit with (Q) and modify it slightly, and presumably such tinkering would cause no great problems for Quine's field theory. But what if one "chose" to give up (Q) completely? Could Quine's field theory manage with no such rule on the meta-linguistic level for the process of the re-evaluation of statements in the field? It is clear that it cannot. For one thing, the process of re-evaluation of statements in the system given the re-evaluation of others is supposed to be a *systematic* process. By calling this process systematic, I mean that since the statements of the field are related to each other (according to what Quine calls "logical inter-connections"), then the re-evaluation of some particular statement in the field causes the re-evaluation of *some other particular statement or statements in the field.* For example, suppose that one decides to accept, because of some recalcitrant experience,

(3) Richard Nixon was a crook.

Then, one might be forced to re-evaluate other statements in one's network (for example, "Richard Nixon was not a crook" would be false); however, regarding (3) as true would certainly have no bearing whatsoever on

(4) Water boils at 100°C at sea level.

or

(5) Things that are equal to the same thing are equal to each other.

or

(6) The speed of light is 186,000 miles per second.

How is one able to determine, given the re-evaluation of certain beliefs in the network, which other *particular* beliefs are to be re-evaluated? Clearly, there must be some rules on the meta-linguistic level for revising particular statements on the basis of other particular statements. Otherwise, the process of re-evaluation, the whole process of the assessment of the field, becomes a random process, and surely this cannot be what Quine intends since then there would be no way for a person to conduct the assessment with the pragmatic intention of causing minimal disruption to the network. Furthermore, if the re-evaluation is completely random, it appears that it would also simply lack the minimal conditions for what we would normally require of a theory or system.

WHAT GOES AROUND COMES AROUND

Given that there must be some meta-linguistic rules or laws operating within the network in order for the re-evaluation of statements to take place, what would they be like? Well, presumably, there would have to be some meta-linguistic formulation such as (Q) along with such logical laws as The Law of Non-Contradiction, but there must also be some semantical rules for simply telling us which statements are related to other statements in such a manner that (Q) and the logical laws are to be evoked. There must be some definitions or semantical rules which establish the relationships of meaning amongst the different statements of the network; otherwise, there would be no basis for a person to decide *which particular* statement to re-evaluate on the basis of some other particular statement. It is these relationships of meanings, the very same ones which Quine has attempted to jettison with his rejection of the analytic-synthetic distinction, which would tell a person which particular statements must be revised given the revision of others. So, it appears that some notion of synonymy (or analyticity) must be re-introduced in order for the assessment of the network to take place and for the judgment of pragmatic maximization to be made. It is difficult to understand how such semantic relationships amongst the different beliefs in a network could be established or recognized given Quine's rejection of the analytic-synthetic distinction and the attending notions of synonymy and analyticity.

Furthermore, in order for (Q) ever to be applied by a person within an actual network of beliefs or for Quine to explain how (Q) might be applied, certain *inferences* must be made. One must reason something like the following: Recalcitrant experience E has occurred. Given the occurrence of E, S1 must be true. If S1 is true, then S2 must be false. If S2 is false, then so must be S3. Or, a somewhat different description might work: Given the recalcitrant experience E, then either S1 or S2 must be true. If S1 is true, then S3 must be false, but if S2 is true, then S5 must be false. If a person is ever to reach the place where re-evaluation leads to the actual redistribution of truth-values, if any actual changes in the truth-values of the statements in the network are ever to take place, it must be on the basis of inferences based upon what Quine has called the "logical interconnections" amongst the statements of the network.

Inferences which lead to the re-distribution of truth-values amongst the statements of the network depend upon and are determined by the logical rules and laws of the network. Lewis Carroll has demonstrated very poignantly the vital importance of the need for the acceptance of some logical law in his very enjoyable story of the Tortoise and Achilles.[17] In Carroll's story, Achilles tries to convince the Tortoise that if he accepts

(A) Things that are equal to the same thing are equal to each other.

and

(B) The two sides of this triangle are things that are equal to the same thing.

that he *must* accept

(Z) The two sides of this triangle are equal to each other.

This appears to be a simple instance of *modus ponens;* however, when the Tortoise presses Achilles for a reason or justification for why he *must* accept (Z), the only reason Achilles can give is

(C) If (A) and (B) are true, then (Z) must be true.

So, (Z) would have to be true given (A) and (B) and (C), but this becomes

(D) If (A) and (B) and (C) are true, then (Z) must be true.

Achilles and the Tortoise are then "off and running" over an infinite race course since such an attempted "justification" continues *ad infinitum.* Carroll's point is clear: Unless one is willing to accept some logical rule or law and treat it on a different logical level from the inferences it generates, no justification is possible; and no actual inference can ever take place. Similarly for Quine, unless the logical laws which generate the inferences necessary for the re-distribution of truth-values in a network are accepted and treated on a different logical level than the other statements in the network, no adjustments in the network could ever be made. A person must use such logical laws to reach the conclusion of the inference that some particular statement S3 must be true or that some other particular statement S4 must be false.

LOGICAL LAWS AND HOLISM

There is some indication that Quine now recognizes the necessity of such laws for a network. In the later *Web of Belief,* contradiction is explicitly used as a general law governing all revision of beliefs. Quine says,

> When a set of beliefs has accumulated to the point of contradiction . . . we can be sure that we are going to have to drop one of the beliefs in that subset, whatever else we do.[18]

However, even given the recognition of the necessity of such laws, can these logical laws be simply "further elements of the field" and themselves capable of revision as Quine claims? I think most decidedly not. Think of how such a revision might take place. For example, how might the revision of *modus ponens* take place within a particular network of beliefs? Well, if we follow the model provided by Quine, we would say something like, "Experience E occurs and given E, S1 must be true. If S1 is true, then S2 is false and S3 is true." Finally, we could conceivably reach the point somewhere very near the center of the network where we could "decide" that if some statement Sn is true, then statement Smp *(modus ponens)* must be false. But how could one ever reach such a position and how could the inferences that *modus ponens* must be false (revised/given up) ever take place? The answer is only because of some meta-linguistic statement of the form, "Sn is true, and if Sn is true, then Smp *(modus ponens)* must be false". Obviously, though—as illustrated in Carroll's story of Achilles and the Tortoise—this statement is itself a statement form of *modus ponens*. Consequently, an attempt to revise *modus ponens* within a network according to anything like the procedure set forth by Quine using the principle (Q) for the re-evaluation of statements must use *modus ponens*.

If any attempted revision of *modus ponens* must use the same rule of inference, then this simply means that, contrary to Quine's claim, *modus ponens* is not revisable and is not just a "further element of the field" to be treated like all other statements in the field. There must be logical laws on the meta-linguistic level which are "immune to revision" and inviolate according to which judgments concerning other statements in the network are made. Exactly the same thing is true of other logical laws such as The Law of Non-Contradiction and The Law of Excluded Middle. If one tries to imagine the process by which such laws might be "revised" within a certain field of beliefs, one encounters the same kind of logical *cul-de-sac*. Quine has claimed that even a revision of the Law of Excluded Middle might be an option for simplifying quantum mechanics.[19] However, within any particular network of beliefs, quantum theory must either force a revision or not force a revision of the Law of Excluded Middle. If a person decides to revise the Law of Excluded Middle because he or she wants to "hold on to" certain recalcitrant data which result from experiments on the sub-atomic level, it can only be because the Law of Excluded Middle is still being used on the meta-linguistic level. Obviously, relative to the same particular network of beliefs, the experiment involving electron interference cannot both force a revision of the Law of Excluded Middle and not force a revision of that same law at the same time.

Quine might well be understood as advocating a "teleological suspension of the logical"; however, unlike Kierkegaard's teleological suspension of the ethical, Quine's suspension of the logical cannot even be properly stated. One cannot suspend the logical for the good of the system and make any sense of the notion at all without the logical laws according to which inferences about the consequences for the system are made. Unless the logical laws remain in place on the meta-linguistic level, there would be no way for a person to rationally project the possible outcomes of different possible revisions within the network of beliefs. Without the logical laws and semantical rules on the meta-linguistic level, there would be no rational grounds for preferring one possible revision to another. Every decision concerning the possible change in a belief in the network is supposed to be made, according to Quine, on the grounds of producing meliorative results for the network; however, as we have seen, such results cannot be reasonably projected—much less actually carried out—without the presupposition of the inviolate logical laws of the network.

It must also be added that what we have demonstrated here is that the necessity for such logical laws on the meta-linguistic level is logical and not merely pragmatic as Quine claims. It is logically impossible to give an argument or a reason or a process using anything vaguely resembling Quine's principle (Q) which could force abandoning these logical laws without using these very same laws. It is therefore logically (or theoretically) necessary that there be logical laws, rules, or principles on the meta-linguistic level of anything which we call a theory or a system of beliefs—any system, field, network, or theory within which there is a rational, systematic explanation or other accounting of experience. The necessity for such laws means, of course, that rationality is not merely pragmatic and that Quine's case against the analytic-synthetic distinction and the structure-content distinction fails. Hence, there is no logical relativity.

ONTOLOGICAL RELATIVISM

Perhaps Quine is most noted for his views regarding ontological relativity, which has been a dominant theme of Quine's work, from *Word and Object*,[20] to the more recent, "Ontological Relativity".[21]

Since Quine first introduced the notion in *Word and Object,* "onto-logical *commitment"* has now become a routine part of the nomenclature for discussing problems of existence, reference, and ontology. Although Quine's ontological relativity does not represent a frontal attack on the classical, modern notions of reason and rationality, it does require some serious attention since, for Quine, "ontology is basic to the conceptual scheme by which [one] interprets all experiences"[22] Let us look at how Quine establishes his theory of ontological relativity and then examine its implications for classical, modern notions of reason and rationality and for scientific methodology.

ONTOLOGY AND LANGUAGE

Quine, of course, did not originate the notion of treating problems of ontology by examining language. As we have seen earlier, the logical positivists' general program for the elimination of metaphysics was formulated in terms of a theory of meaning, and it will be very helpful in understanding Quine to see his position against the backdrop of positivism. A good example of the logical positivists' way of treating ontological problems linguistically is the work of Rudolf Carnap. Although he later abandoned the technique which he first applied in the *Logical Syntax of Language,* that method is illustrative and ironically precursory to Quine's position. Carnap's general approach is to try to demonstrate that ontological statements about such things as classes, abstract entities, and material objects are really disguised statements about the syntactical rules and forms of language which are conventional. Much of philosophy consists of attempting to reduce or translate language which is ostensibly about different kinds of ontological objects into language which is about the syntax of language. And although neither Carnap nor anyone else ever successfully completed such a translation, the general approach of tying ontological issues to language was not abandoned.

Given such a program, it is clear that some form of relativism will eventually emerge, and Carnap gives explicit recognition to such a conventional relativism through what has become known as his "principle of tolerance". A person is free to develop any logical system he or she wishes according to whatever conventions he or she chooses, according to Carnap, so long as the logical system is constructed clearly and the syntactical rules and conventions are properly formulated.[23] "In logic there are no morals," he says.[24]

In the mature development of his thought, Carnap distinguished between two different kinds of questions about ontological matters —one internal to a linguistic framework, and the other external to it. The first kind of question represents the domain of the scientist, and the second, the domain of the philosopher. This distinction is a crucial one for Carnap:

> it is above all necessary to recognize a fundamental distinction between two kinds of questions concerning the existence or reality of entities. If someone wishes to speak in his language about a new kind of entities, he has to introduce a system of new ways of speaking, subject to new rules; we shall call this procedure the construction of a linguistic *framework* for the new entities in question. And now we must distinguish two kinds of questions of existence: first, questions of the existence of certain entities of the new kind *within the framework;* we call them *internal questions;* and second, questions concerning the existence or reality *of the system of entities as a whole,* called *external questions.*[25]

It is obvious that the *external* variety of questions is the more interesting—and the more troublesome—for Carnap. Internal questions become rather routine and are empirical or scientific in nature and are decided "according to the rules of the [linguistic] framework."[26]

Only philosophers raise questions of the external nature—that's to say, questions about the reality of the system of the linguistic framework *as a whole.* External questions are those about the suitability of a particular entire linguistic framework or the relative merits of different linguistic frameworks. In the case of the external world, for example, with its "room-sized material objects", ontological issues are resolved by one's decision to use the linguistic framework of room-sized objects. To accept the ontological claims about such a world amounts to accepting the linguistic framework within which such claims are expressed. External questions are interesting and legitimate for Carnap because he recognizes that there are debatable reasons for accepting or refusing to accept a particular linguistic framework. He even sounds a bit like Quine by suggesting that the question of whether or not to accept a particular linguistic framework might turn out to be "a practical question".[27]

At the same time, however, Carnap recognizes that there must be some limitation on what kind of question can arise within the framework—otherwise, one winds up with an illegitimate totality. Acceptance of a room-sized, material object language carries with it the acceptance of certain statements and the possibility of raising certain questions such as the existence of the African Violet on my desk. However, the general thesis concerning the existence of the external world of material objects cannot be raised *internally,* within such a framework, since such a totally general question could not be properly formulated within the framework.[28]

Although at first blush there is a great similarity between Carnap and Quine on the relationship of ontology and language, the likenesses turn out to be apparent only, and the differences turn out to be of major importance. Perhaps the easiest and best way of comparing Quine and Carnap is to see Quine as completely eliminating what Carnap called the *external* questions concerning ontology, and collapsing all questions concerning ontology into *internal* ones. There simply are no legitimate absolute philosophical questions about the existence of objects for Quine. As he says in 'Ontological Relativity', "there is no fact of the matter [ontology]".[29] This same skepticism is reaffirmed in the most recent *Pursuit of Truth* where Quine says that "two ontologies, if explicitly correlated to one, are empirically on a par; there is no empirical ground for choosing one rather than the other."[30]

According to Quine, any and all questions concerning the particular ontology of a theory or language are internal to the theory or language, and only through the adoption of a particular language or theory does a person manage to become *ontologically committed* to certain kinds of entities. Hence, all legitimate ontological questions are relative to some language or theory, and ontological commitment is relative since different people might adopt different theories at different times and for various reasons. Actually, the ontological commitment of a particular theory is double relative since the only way to determine the ontology of a theory is by comparison to some other theory (which is already accepted) using some method for the translation of one theory into the other. One cannot question the ontological commitments of a theory completely in isolation from all other theories since, as Quine recognizes, one would eventually become involved in an illegitimate totality and problems of self-reference. He says:

> To question the reference of all the terms of our all-inclusive theory becomes meaningless, simply for want of further terms relative to which to ask or answer the question.[31]

Consequently, for Quine, determining the ontology of a particular theory can only be done relative to some other theory. Thus, the ontology of a theory becomes relative to one's choice of the second, "background" theory with which it is compared as well as one's choice of the method for translating the theory under consideration

into the background theory.[32] Through such a translation, the ontological commitments of the original theory are supposedly revealed.

Ontological Commitment and Translation

The suggestion of such a translation initially raises one's expectations of some mechanical or linguistic procedure for translation
which will quickly and easily resolve all the thorny and unresolved
ontological problems; however, Quine dashes such optimism with
his now notorious thesis of *the indeterminacy of translation* which
leads to the *inscrutability of reference.*[33] How one is to translate a
term from one language to another in terms of reference can never be
completely determined objectively since there will always be several
choices available to the translator. The reference words of one
language may be understood as individuating or "slicing up" the
world in a variety of widely differing ways, and the translator can
choose a particular single referent for a particular word only relative
to a decision about a loosely associated group of words and constructions in the background language which Quine calls the "apparatus
of individuation".[34] In other words, there is no real fact of the matter.
Quine's point is illustrated with his famous example of the difficulty
involved in attempting to translate the word 'gavagai' from some
unfamiliar, native language into English. We might think that we
could determine the referent empirically by questioning a native
language speaker in a situation where the word is used; however,
Quine argues that such an objective determination is impossible, and
that we are left with a theoretical inscrutability of the reference of the
word 'gavagai'.

> The only difference between rabbits, undetached rabbit parts, and
> rabbit stages is in their individuation. If you take the total scattered
> portion of the spatiotemporal world that is made up of rabbits, and that
> which is made up of undetached rabbit parts, and that which is made up
> of rabbit stages, you come out with the same scattered portion of the
> world each of the three times. The only difference is in how you slice it.
> And how to slice it is what ostension or simple conditioning, however
> persistently repeated, cannot teach.[35]

We are left with no objective, empirical grounds for deciding the
reference of words and thus the ontology for any given language.
Hence, according to Quine, there is no clear difference between
translating (or clarifying) an ontology and simply *specifying* one.[36]
This is true even in our home language, for example Standard
English, where we must still have some background network of

assumed terms and constructions, some "co-ordinate system", in order to determine reference.[37] The net result of Quine's treatment of reference and ontology is that there is no absolute, matter of fact, answer to the question, 'What is there?' In fact, such general, absolute questions do not even make sense. For Quine, "What makes sense is to say not what the objects of a theory are, absolutely speaking, but how one theory of objects is interpretable or reinterpretable in another."[38] Quine's "relativistic thesis" then becomes clear: "it makes no sense to say what the objects of a theory are, beyond saying how to interpret or reinterpret that theory in another."[39] Hence, it is meaningless to regard any conceptual scheme as an objective "mirror of reality" because the standard for evaluating a conceptual scheme cannot be realistic in the sense of correspondence with reality; the best one can do is to evaluate a conceptual scheme in pragmatic terms—its terms of its "efficacy in communication and in prediction".[40]

PROBLEMS WITH ONTOLOGICAL COMMITMENT

There are several issues to be pursued concerning Quine's criterion of ontological commitment, although I do not consider the question of the relativism of ontology so radical an issue as the question of the relativism of logic. However, we shall see that at a crucial level the two issues come to a juncture, and Quine's claims concerning ontological relativity are difficult to reconcile with his rejection of the analytic-synthetic distinction.

Simply within the theory of reference, there are some difficulties in understanding both the meaning and the advantages of Quine's criterion.[41] At various times, Quine has suggested that the criterion is a criterion for languages, theories, sentences, doctrines, and forms of discourse; albeit in his most recent writings, he seems to think that it applies mainly to theories. However, even if we limit the question of the application of the criterion of ontological commitment to theories, there are still remaining difficulties in deciding the nature of the theories.[42] Also, the notion of "ontological commitment" has itself been notoriously troublesome. Quine sometimes says that the ontological commitment of a theory is what a theory "presupposes", "requires", or "assumes", and, at other times, he says that it is what a theory "implies". In one of the more recent formulations of the criterion, Quine describes it in the following way:

> To show that a theory assumes a given object, or objects of a given class, we have to show that the theory would be false if that object did not

exist, or if that class were empty; hence, that the theory requires that object, or members of that class, in order to be true.[43]

One question that might be raised about Quine's criterion can perhaps best be put by asking, "What do we gain by the criterion?" Charles Chihara makes this point very explicitly:

> The sorts of objects that would have to exist in order that the theory be true are just those sorts of objects that would have to be within the range of the bound variables of the theory in order that its assertions be true. But what progress have we made? We still have the vague notion 'would have to' and instead of the term 'exist' we have the expression 'be within the range of the bound variables'.[44]

A more serious difficulty, however, lies in understanding how we are to make sense of the manner in which Quine talks about *theories* being true or false. It is simple enough to understand how statements or assertions within theories are to be regarded as true or false, but in what sense are entire theories to be regarded as true or false? On Quine's terms, would not the truth or falsity of a theory simply mean whether or not one chooses to accept the theory or not? Tying ontological commitment to the truth or falsity of a theory initially appears to give a rather definite decision procedure for ontological commitment until one remembers that truth (along with practically every other epistemic judgment) is relative to some theory for Quine.

It is at this point where Quine's notion of a background theory and the process of translation become vitally important. The above objection to Quine's criterion might be answered by the introduction of a background theory according to which one might determine the truth of one theory in terms of its translation into another. But using the notion of such a background theory as a form of bedrock to prevent an infinite regress of languages is *ad hoc* and begs the crucial questions. According to Quine, given the background theory, one is supposed to choose amongst different possible theories or languages on pragmatic grounds, and choosing on pragmatic grounds is a *rational* decision for Quine.[45] A person must be able to go through some kind of decision procedure using practical reason to make the pragmatic choice of theories or languages. As we have seen, Carnap also made the distinction between internal and external questions about the existence of objects, but he treated the external questions (the *philosophical* questions concerning the choice of theories) as pseudo-problems—reserving the internal questions (relative to a "linguistic framework") as the genuine problems of science. Quine, on the other hand, sees all questions as internal (because they involve the translation of one theory into another) and hence collapses philosophy into science. At the same time, however, Quine wishes to treat the question about the choice of a theory or language as a rational one. This, we have seen, he cannot do.

ONTOLOGICAL COMMITMENT AND BACKGROUND THEORIES

Quine's notion of a primitive background theory which we accept uncritically is a convenient, *ad hoc* solution which gives rise to the eventual relativism of ontological commitment because the only kind of background theory which would be of such a nature to explain and support the doctrine of the indeterminancy of translation and the inscrutability of reference is one which conveniently contains the necessary epistemological distinctions. The most important epistemological distinctions are the one between analytic and synthetic statements and the one between form and content.

Consider how translation is supposed to take place. We must use meta-linguistic rules which tell us something about how the translation is to be made; so we must be able to distinguish the meta-linguistic rules for translation from the object language which is to be translated. It is only such rules which could make sense of the whole process of translation and give rise to the possible, various, conflicting translations which then, in turn, generate the "indeterminacy" of translation. How else would one ever determine that the possible, various conflicting translations would be *conflicting?* For example, how is it that we would ever be able to determine that 'gavagai' cannot mean both rabbit and rabbit part? And how would we determine that 'rabbit', 'rabbit part', and 'rabbit appearance' would be conflicting translations of 'gavagai'?

TRANSLATION AND THE EXTENSIONAL THEORY OF MEANING

Quine, of course, maintains that the extensions of the words alone and just the linguistic behavior of the speakers of the native language which is being translated would be adequate for determining the differences of meaning. However, extension alone will not do the job here. The difficulties caused for a purely extensional theory of meaning by null terms are legendary. If such words as 'centaur' and 'unicorn' have no extension then the differences in their meanings cannot be accounted for simply in terms of the extensions of these terms. Attempts to provide more elaborate accounts of meaning which are completely extensional have not been successful. For example, Nelson Goodman has suggested an extensionalist account of meaning which depends upon augmenting the primary extension of the original terms with what he calls "the secondary extensions" of those original terms, in other words, the extension of any linguistic compound formed by using the original term.[46] For example, in addition to the primary extensions of 'centaur' and 'unicorn' we must also concern ourselves with the secondary extension of such expressions as 'picture of a centaur' and 'picture of a unicorn' or 'story about a centaur' and 'story about a unicorn'. Furthermore, since, according to Goodman, pictures of centaurs and pictures of unicorns are not what they are in virtue of resemblance to some object, then we should shorten such expressions to 'centaur-pictures' and 'unicorn-pictures' and treat these shortened expressions as arbitrary ways of designating different objects. In other words, the secondary extensions of such as expressions as 'centaur-pictures' are determined quite independently of the primary extension of the word 'centaur'. Goodman concludes that "two terms have the same meaning if and only if they have the same primary and secondary extensions."[47] He thus hopes to construct a theory of meaning which is completely extensional and which avoids talking about intensions altogether. I have argued elsewhere against the adequacy of Goodman's theory of secondary extensions, and I will only briefly summarize that argument here.[48] Goodman builds his case for secondary extensions using only examples of null terms. If we consider terms which do have primary extensions such as Frege's examples of 'the Morning Star' and 'the Evening Star' or 'picture of the Washington Monument' and 'picture of the Lincoln Memorial', then there is no reason to turn such expressions into single place predicates such as 'Washington Monument-picture' or 'Lincoln Memorial-picture'. Even if Goodman is right that 'centaur-picture' is a one-place predicate whose extension is independent of the extension of 'centaur', surely the extensions of 'picture of the Washington Monument' and 'picture of the Lincoln Memorial' are not independent of the extensions of 'the Washington Monument' and 'the Lincoln Memorial'. An expression such as 'picture of' may not always be a relation, but it certainly sometimes is. We cannot keep our present meanings of 'picture of the Washington Monument' and 'picture of the Lincoln Memorial' and decide to reverse the extensions of 'the Washington Monument' and 'the Lincoln Memorial'.

So, it seems, extensions alone cannot do the job of providing the rules on the meta-linguistic level necessary for translation. Conflicts amongst different possible translations must be of a logical nature since the indeterminacy which is supposedly generated by such possible conflicts is theoretical and radical; so the logical conflict can occur *only relative to a background theory which contains the analytic-synthetic distinction and semantical rules.* Translation can be radically indeterminant only within a background theory which contains the logical laws according to which the conflicts of the different possible translations are determined. So, ironically, it seems that Quine's theory of ontological relativity can work only if his theory of logical relativity fails.

— 3 —

GOODMAN ON WAYS OF MAKING WORLDS

THE NEW RIDDLE OF INDUCTION

Nelson Goodman has joined forces with Quine in rejecting the analytic-synthetic distinction and is responsible for introducing major new considerations into the debate concerning relativism and science through his "new riddle of induction" and the metaphysical relativism of his *Ways of Worldmaking*. Goodman himself describes the result of his claim that "countless" alternative world-versions may be equally "true" or "right" as "radical relativism"[1] which he explains as implying "that truth must be otherwise conceived than as correspondence with a ready-made world."[2] In this chapter, I will examine Goodman's unique brand of relativism. I will argue that Goodman's *radical* relativism is not so radical as it first appears. In the end, properly understood, Goodman's new riddle of induction and his generosity with different ways of making worlds do not seriously threaten traditional science and epistemology. Goodman's brand of relativism turns out to be fairly innocuous.

HUME AND THE PROBLEM OF INDUCTION

The original or traditional "problem of induction" is usually traced to David Hume and the objections he raised to the process of justifying induction. The difficulty is one of supplying a rationale or justification for the claim that reports of observations concerning known or observed cases provide some logical basis for making judgments about *un*observed cases. Induction is the process of inference whereby one concludes that unobserved cases will resemble observed cases in some crucial respect. But, as Hume's question goes, why would one ever be justified in believing this to be so? The question is neither simply why one believes that it is so nor simply why one trusts in or uses induction, but rather why such beliefs are epistemologically *justified.*

According to Hume, of course, any such justification of induction is impossible since any epistemological justification would require that there be some "connection" between events in such a way that the occurrence of one event would impose some necessity upon the occurrence of another event.[3] Since Hume argued very convincingly that we cannot justify the claim that there are necessary connections between matters of fact, there would then seem to be no *grounds* for believing that what has happened or what has been observed gives any *reason* whatsoever for concluding something about what has not happened or what is yet *un*observed. Hume's own "solution" to this problem is skeptical—skeptical because he concludes that even though people do indeed believe in induction or operate using induction, there is, in the end, no logical justification for induction. The belief in induction is generated by the regular concatenation of events in experience which eventually is responsible for the formation of a habit of expectation. Because of this habit, the human understanding is led to associate two events in such a way so that whenever one event occurs, the second is expected to follow. In other words, Hume provides an explanation of why human beings use induction to form judgments about the future or other unobserved events, but he does not provide a justification for induction.

Alfred North Whitehead's characterization of Western philosophy as simply a series of footnotes to Plato is a claim which many philosophers would dispute; however, the observation that most of the history of the epistemological treatments of inductive logic is simply a footnote to Hume would perhaps be less controversial. Attempts to justify induction may end up in different places, but they all seem to begin with Hume in an effort to avoid the problems which he raised and the skeptical resolution which he proposed. Through all of the efforts to defend induction, the original stigma attached to induction—and hence to science—has remained. If induction is not logically, rationally justified, then neither is science.

HUME AND GOODMAN ON INDUCTION

In his "recasting" of the problem of induction, Goodman also begins with Hume if only to draw the contrast between Hume's original way of casting the problem and his own. Indeed, the "new" problem of induction can best be understood through a simple comparison with the traditional problem posed by Hume. For Hume, regularities amongst occurring events produce beliefs because of the mind's habitual association of those events, but, according to Goodman, the crucial point which Hume overlooked is that not all regularities amongst events produce such beliefs. Why is it that some regularities which we experience between two events result in the development of some habit of association and the accompanying expectations concerning future events and others do not? Why does the mind form habits based on the experience of some regularities but not of others? Hume's way of putting the problem was to say that observed regularities between two events, though never a good logical reason for an inference about unobserved events, still gives rise to beliefs about unobserved events. Goodman, though agreeing with Hume that experience provides us with no justification for claiming to know in advance which predictions will turn out to be accurate,[4] maintains that there are numerous regularities—perhaps even an infinite number—which the mind chooses to ignore. So the problem becomes one of not simply asking whether or how observations ever justify claims concerning unobserved events but rather one of asking whether or how *certain* claims about unobserved events are justified on the basis of *certain* observations of regularities. As Goodman puts it, "Hume overlooks the fact that some regularities do and some do not establish such habits; that predictions based on some regularities are valid while predictions based on other regularities are not".[5]

To understand Goodman's new riddle of induction, he suggests that we use the model of deduction.[6] What does it mean to justify an instance of deduction? According to Goodman, a deductive argument is justified (or valid) if it conforms to the general rules of deductive logic and unjustified (or invalid) if it does not. Thus, the process of justification leads to an investigation of the rules and proceeds on the basis of certain rules rather than certain other rules. The process of justifying induction should be thought of, Goodman says, in analogous terms. Justification of induction should lead to an investigation of the rules of inductive logic and any justification would then proceed on the basis of certain rules. Justification of an inductive argument would then consist of showing that the argument conforms to those rules.

Of course such an explanation must eventually lead to some examination of the rules themselves and the issue of the justification of those rules. In the case of deduction, the rules themselves must be valid. Certainly, a deductive argument is not considered valid or justified if it just happens to conform to just any old rule. Goodman's own position is based upon what he describes as the virtuous circularity of assessing the general rules by their conformity to the valid inferences which they justify. He puts this matter very clearly: *"A rule is amended if it yields an inference we are unwilling to accept; an inference is rejected if it violates a rule we are unwilling to amend."*[7] Now this way of justifying deduction is interesting and debatable; however, the pertinent point here is that Goodman maintains that the process of justifying induction follows a strict parallel to the one described for deduction. Induction is also justified by an appeal to general rules which, in turn, are justified by the inferences justified by those rules. He again says, "predictions are justified if they conform to valid canons of induction; and the canons are valid if they accurately codify accepted inductive practice."[8]

So, according to Goodman, rather than putting the question in terms of how a certain kind of knowledge is possible, we should ask why certain inductive inferences are valid and others are not. Hume's problem might be described as "the problem of induction" while Goodman's might be described as "the problem of inductive validity". For Goodman, the issue is not one of justifying induction but rather one of justifying valid inductive inferences over invalid ones—one of distinguishing between valid and invalid inductive inferences. This manner of justification will lead to a search for the rules or canons of inductive logic.

The Grue Paradox

As formidable as this task might seem—since the rules and canons of induction are notoriously less explicit and obvious than those of deduction—the matter is seriously complicated further by the novel twist which Goodman now adds. His point is illustrated by the now well-known "grue paradox". 'Grue' is a new predicate introduced by Goodman to apply to all things examined before a certain time t and found to be green and to all other things only if they are blue.[9] Now consider how the introduction of this new predicate complicates predictions which we might make based upon our observations of green things. For example, suppose that all of the emeralds observed before a certain time t (say, the present moment) have all been found to be green. Normally, on the basis of those observations, we might make the usual inductive generalization, "All emeralds are green." Hume would then pose the question of why and how we are justified in believing that the observed cases of green emeralds have any necessary connection at all with unobserved emeralds. However, with the introduction of the predicate 'grue', a new and different problem emerges. Exactly the same evidence which confirms 'all emeralds are green' also confirms 'all emeralds are grue'. That is, for each observation of an emerald which is described by the true observation statement 'a is green', 'b is green', and so forth, there is a corresponding true observation statement 'a is grue', 'b is grue', and so on. Consequently, the two generalizations, 'all emeralds are green' and 'all emeralds are grue' are each equally confirmed by any and all of exactly the same observations (before t).

Having two different hypotheses confirmed by exactly the same data may not be troubling in some circumstances; however, in the present case the situation becomes particularly intolerable given the mutual inconsistency of the two hypotheses. A green emerald will be green after t, but a grue emerald will be blue after t given the definition of 'grue'. Whichever of the two hypotheses we might regard as confirmed, the other is equally confirmed, and hence, we are left in the very unenviable position of being unable to give an evidential reason for choosing one hypothesis and rejecting the other since, to emphasize the point, there is absolutely no evidence which confirms one which does not also confirm the other. "Moreover," as Goodman points out, "it is clear that if we simply choose an appropriate predicate, then on the basis of these same observations we shall have equal confirmation, by our definition, for any prediction whatever about other emeralds—or indeed about anything else."[10]

Consequently, whereas Hume's way of putting the problem of induction was one of trying to justify how it is ever the case that *any* observation *ever* justifies an inference concerning unobserved events, Goodman's way of putting the new problem of induction is one of explaining why we prefer certain inferences to others since *any* observation *always* equally justifies *any* inference concerning unobserved events (even conflicting ones). This is the grue paradox, and things seem to be at least as difficult as they are with the problem as posed by Hume. If Hume is right, then, it seems, we are never justified in making an inductive inference. If Goodman is right, we are always equally justified whatever the inductive inferences might be. In both cases, the very rationality of induction and hence, of science as well is at stake. Hume's proposed solution to his problem of induction results in induction being a psychological belief or habit induced by regular association of events, and Goodman's proposed solution to the new problem of induction results in raising the ugly specter of relativism with theory-relative facts.

The key issue for Goodman is not one of just choosing one hypothesis in preference to another. It will not do merely to say, "Well, we use 'green' and not 'grue'" or "We just prefer green emeralds to grue emeralds". The point is to explain and justify why we choose one hypothesis and not the other. As Goodman says,

> Regularity in greenness confirms the prediction of further cases; regularity in grueness does not. To say that valid predictions are those based on past regularities, without being able to say *which* regularities, is thus quite pointless. Regularities are where you find them, and you can find them anywhere.[11]

Goodman's solution to this dilemma is to be found in the distinction between *lawlike* and *accidental* hypotheses. Only lawlike hypotheses are confirmed by positive instances and hence can be used to justify inferences about unobserved cases. For example, "all copper conducts electricity" is partially confirmed by the observation of a particular piece of copper which conducts electricity; however, if we discover that a particular philosopher is a middle child, that fact does not add any additional confirmation to the claim that "all philosophers are middle children".[12] The difference is accounted for in terms of describing the former as a *lawlike* hypothesis and the latter as an *accidental* hypothesis. Now the problem of distinguishing between lawlike and accidental hypotheses is a thorny one indeed, and the usual move is to attempt to remove from lawlike hypotheses any and all spatial and/or temporal references which identify any specific individual. Accidental hypotheses refer to some particular individual while lawlike hypotheses refer either to an entire class of individuals or some unspecified, ambiguous, representative individual.[13] Aside from the difficulties of ever successfully distinguishing lawlike from accidental hypotheses on these grounds, it is apparent that such a characterization would be only necessary and not sufficient for drawing the distinction. Goodman, therefore, despairs of ever adequately distinguishing between lawlike and accidental hypothesis on purely syntactical or semantical grounds.[14]

ENTRENCHMENT AND PROJECTION

It is Goodman's use of his theory of *entrenchment* to distinguish lawlike from accidental hypotheses which ultimately provides one of the routes to one form of the present relativism in science. The theory of entrenchment begins with an explanation of *projection* which, Goodman suggests, we approach within the context of "accepted statements" or at least "some stock of knowledge". The main problem then becomes one of defining *valid* projections or the notion of *projectibility*,[15] and this will be done on the basis of *actual projections*. The contrast between Goodman's approach to the new problem of induction and Hume's approach to the traditional problem of induction is now a stark one:

> Hume thought of the mind as being set in motion making predictions by, and in accordance with, regularities in what it observed. This left him with the problem of differentiating between the regularities that do and those that do not thus set the mind in motion. We, [Goodman] on the contrary, regard the mind as in motion from the start, striking out with spontaneous predictions in dozens of directions, and gradually rectifying and channeling its predictive processes. We ask not how predictions come to be made, but how—granting they are made—they come to be sorted out as valid and invalid. Literally, of course, we are not concerned with describing how the mind works but rather with describing or defining the distinction it makes between valid and invalid projections.[16]

If a hypothesis is adopted after some of its instances have been determined to be true and while other of its instances are still "outstanding", still to be determined, the hypothesis is *actually projected*. Actual projection may involve lawlike or accidental hypotheses since this is simply the explicit formulation and adoption of a hypothesis in order to make predictions about hitherto unobserved cases. A *supported* hypothesis is one with some positive instances, a *violated* hypothesis is one with some negative instances, and an *exhausted* hypothesis is one with no undetermined instances. Actual projection of a hypothesis requires that the hypothesis be supported, unviolated and unexhausted.

Hypotheses which at some earlier time were projectible but which have since become violated or exhausted are no longer projectible; however, we are still not in a position to distinguish between lawlike and accidental hypotheses. 'All emeralds are green' and 'all emeralds are grue' are both still projectible since both are supported (by exactly the same evidence) and neither is violated nor exhausted. We are still not in a position to say why we prefer 'all emeralds are green' to 'all emeralds are grue'.

The answer, according to Goodman, is finally to be found in his theory of *entrenchment*. We must consult the history of the earlier actual projections containing the two predicates 'green' and 'grue' to determine which has the more "impressive biography"—that is, to determine which has occurred more frequently in earlier actual projections. When we do this, we find out that 'green' has occurred much more frequently than has 'grue' in actual projections (even though both 'green' and 'grue' were available for projection) and is therefore the better entrenched predicate. Since 'all emeralds are green' contains the better entrenched predicate, it is the preferred hypothesis.[17]

Entrenchment derives from linguistic practice or, in terms of scientific theories, theory formation. On the one hand, predicates occurring in actually projected hypotheses which are violated will become less firmly entrenched compared to other predicates occurring in unviolated projections. In other words, the wrong predicates, the ones from violated actual projections, do not become or stay well entrenched. Conversely, Goodman says, "The reason why only the right predicates happen so luckily to have become well entrenched is just that the well entrenched predicates have thereby become the right ones."[18]

THE NEW RIDDLE OF INDUCTION AND RELATIVISM

There are many avenues still to be explored concerning Goodman's new riddle of induction and his theory of entrenchment. For example, there has been much debate concerning the status of the predicate 'grue',[19] and there has been equal attention given to the proper formulation of the rules of projection.[20] However, the most salient feature of Goodman's new riddle of induction and his resolution of the riddle is the fact that the theory of entrenchment ultimately resolves into matters of language. His conclusion is that given a great variety of ways of viewing the world—of observing regularities upon which to base projections concerning unobserved cases—the particular ones which we happen to choose to project upon the future are those which contain the best entrenched predicate. Entrenchment, as Goodman himself observes, "derives from the use of language".[21] Projection of a particular predicate depends upon the entrenchment of that predicate, and entrenchment depends upon linguistic practice. Consequently, it appears, both the factual claims we make about the world and the predictions we make based upon those factual claims are simply the result of linguistic practice. This is the source of the relativism arising from Goodman's new riddle of induction, and, as we shall see in the next chapter, it is very much akin to the relativism arising from the work of Thomas Kuhn (as well as the "post-Kuhnians") for whom facts become theory-relative. In the case of Goodman, facts become language-relative and language-dependent. Whether a particular emerald is green or grue depends upon whether the observer speaks a green language or a grue language—upon whether 'green' or 'grue' is better entrenched in the language of the observer. Similarly, whether one projects 'all emer-alds are green' or 'all emeralds are grue' again depends upon the language of the person making the projection.

Using the theory of entrenchment to account for the projection of certain predicates begins to lead us toward a view of knowledge very different from the one which we get from Hume's treatment of the original problem of induction or the one which we get from what I have characterized as the traditional view of the nature of science. Truth is now subordinate to linguistic convention and theory forma-tion. Whether it is true that all emeralds are green or that all emeralds are grue depends upon whether we play "the green game" or "the grue game". Green and grue are relative to the language of the beholder. Any notion of a reality "out there", "behind" or "beneath" for a theory to explain, describe, or predict becomes epistemological-ly irrelevant. Epistemological bedrock is the choice of predicates and the relative entrenchment of those predicates. Relativism lurks around every corner of the zig-zag pattern of linguistic practices used to determine the entrenchment of predicates.

The initial, ostensible consequences of reducing scientific obser-vation and prediction to linguistic usage appear to undermine the two main functions of traditional science: explanation and predic-tion. If these two functions are dependent upon the use of language, as Goodman's theory of entrenchment requires, then it seems that any realistic or absolute basis for science is undermined, and science does indeed become relative. Both what we conceive as scientific fact and what we regard as scientific prediction using induction would incorporate all of the arbitrary conventions and cultural differences which we normally associate with language itself. Indeed, perhaps most seriously, if induction is dependent upon language, then the very method of science would appear to be relative.

THE NEW THEORY OF INDUCTION AND ABDUCTION

Briefly, I will suggest a way of understanding Goodman's new riddle of induction (as well as his proposed resolution of the riddle in terms of his theory of projection) such that none of the threatened relativistic consequences for science follow. In particular, I will argue that induction as part of the scientific method emerges unscathed from Goodman's grue paradox. In the end, we shall see that Goodman's "new riddle of induction" is neither new nor a riddle of induction.[22]

One answer to Goodman's "grue paradox" and one key to understanding its lasting impact upon science lies in the analysis of scientific reasoning developed by Charles Sanders Peirce. In contrast to the traditional division of inference into simply deduction and induction, Peirce insists on a tripartite division—deduction, abduction, and induction.[23] By deduction, Peirce means what is traditionally meant; its subject matter includes mathematics and logic. Peirce limits induction to the process which we would now call confirmation—the process of confirming a hypothesis through observation of the particular instances deduced from the hypothesis. However, Peirce identifies the process of *the formation of the hypothesis* as an independent form of reasoning, and this, he calls *abduction.* Peirce regards this distinction as vitally important to the proper understanding of scientific reasoning. He says,

> Nothing has so much contributed to present chaotic or erroneous ideas in the logic of science as failure to distinguish the essentially different characters of different elements of scientific reasoning; and one of the worst of these confusions, as well as one of the commonest, consists of regarding abduction and induction taken together . . . as a simple argument.[24]

Obviously, there were also many "chaotic" suggestions and "erroneous ideas" floating around concerning scientific reasoning in Peirce's day as well, and Peirce intends that his distinction between abduction and induction be used to sort out these confusions. Using this distinction between abduction and induction, I think that we can eliminate some of the confusion surrounding Goodman's new riddle of induction and the alleged relativistic consequences for induction and science.

It appears that Goodman's new riddle of induction results from, as Peirce has said above, the "failure to distinguish the essentially different characters of different elements of scientific reasoning." The new riddle of induction—whether it is a riddle at all or not—is not, in any case, a riddle of *induction.* Goodman obviously treats abduction and induction as "a single argument" and conflates abduction and induction. If we adopt Peirce's distinction, then the new riddle of induction is properly viewed as a riddle of abduction, a *meta-scientific* riddle. Goodman is certainly correct in claiming that what he calls the new riddle of induction differs from Hume's problem of induction, but Hume's problem had to do with the process of explaining how an observed case can ever impart any justification for inferences concerning an *unobserved* case if there is no necessary connection between matters of fact. This "traditional problem" seems obviously to be a problem within confirmation theory: How does probability accrue to a general hypothesis on the basis of observed particular instances of the hypothesis? For Hume's problem to arise, the hypothesis must already be in place. Goodman's new riddle of induction is clearly a problem concerning how a hypothesis gets selected for confirmation. Will we select 'all emeralds are green' or 'all emeralds are grue'? This question is an issue of abduction, not induction.

There is some evidence that Goodman himself recognizes that the grue paradox raises questions that are pre-inductive. In *Ways of Worldmaking*, for example, he seems to admit this very point:

> Induction requires taking some classes to the exclusion of others as relevant kinds. Only so, for example, do our observations of emeralds exhibit any regularity and confirm that all emeralds are green rather than that all are grue.[25]

Further evidence that the new riddle of induction really raises problems on the meta-inductive level can be seen simply by a close analysis of the new riddle itself. How is it that the grue paradox becomes a paradox? Goodman tells us that it is because 'all emeralds are green' and 'all emeralds are grue' are equally "confirmed by evidence statements describing the same observations."[26] Now how is it that the two competing hypotheses get confirmed in order to generate the paradox unless induction is being used with each hypothesis? In other words, the new riddle of induction becomes a riddle only if induction itself is used since both hypotheses must be confirmed (by induction) in order for Goodman's paradox to arise. This is clear evidence that the problem raised by Goodman's new riddle of induction is on the meta-scientific level involving the selection of hypotheses rather than on the level of confirmation of hypotheses by induction.

Peirce recognized the importance of Goodman's claim that "regularities are where you find them, and you can find them anywhere." Peirce says explicity that "any two things resemble one another just as strongly as any two others, if recondite resemblances are admitted." (2.634) Peirce, then, recognizes Goodman's claim that it is not adequate simply to say that regularities exist without specifying which are the important regularities, the ones to be projected. It is this concern which leads Peirce to the Rule of Predesignation, which explicitly recognizes and requires that an abduction always precede an induction. We must select 'all emeralds are green' or 'all emeralds are grue' before we can deduce the particular instances from the different hypotheses and begin the process of confirmation.

With more than just a hint of anticipation of the grue paradox, Peirce uses the following example to illustrate this point:

> A chemist notices a surprising phenomenon. Now if he has a high admiration of Mill's *Logic,* as many chemists have, he will remember that Mill tells him that he must work on the principle that, under precisely the same circumstances, like phenomena are produced. Why does he then not note that this phenomena was produced on such a day of the week the planets presenting a certain configuration, his daughter having on a blue dress, the milkman being late that morning and so on? (6.413)

The chemist is faced with a difficult problem in the logic of discovery—that of theory formation or hypothesis selection—but this is not a problem of induction. As we have seen, this is a problem on the meta-inductive level, on the same level as the problem raised by the grue paradox—the problem of choosing between green theory and grue theory. So far as raising serious questions of relativism for induction is concerned, the new riddle of induction is a sheep in wolf's clothing because the alleged pernicious, relativistic consequences of the grue paradox for induction do not follow.[27] The scientific method which uses induction in the process of confirmation for providing epistemological warrant for a hypothesis must be presupposed by the grue paradox since, in order for the paradox to be generated, conflicting projections must be equally confirmed. Seen in this manner, the new problem of induction is neither new nor a problem of induction. It is the old problem of theory formation, Peirce's process of abduction, and induction is not threatened by new charges of relativism. Surely, induction is relative to a particular theory, but this simply amounts to saying that confirmation is relative to a particular hypothesis.

All of which is not to say that there is not something new and valuable in Goodman's new "problem of induction". Although Peirce treated abduction as a form of inference and maintained that it is regulated and structured by rules and "leading principles" in such a manner that a theory of abduction can be treated by critical logic in a manner analogous to deduction and induction, he never made much progress toward completing such a formal treatment of abduction. Nor has anyone else. The best that Peirce can do in answering the questions which he himself raises about why the chemist attends to certain features and includes them in his hypothesis and ignores other features and does not include them is to say that "The answer will be that in early days chemists did use to attend to some such circumstances, but that they have learned better" (6.413).

Goodman's theory of projection based upon the theory of entrenchment can best be understood as an attempt to provide the rules and 'leading principles' for a theory of abduction. Whether or not, in the final analysis, Goodman's theory of entrenchment is successful as a leading principle for the process of hypothesis, he has certainly made a better attempt than anyone else. Ironically, then, if Goodman's new riddle of induction is seen as an attempt to supply grounds or reasons for hypothesis selection, Goodman's work can actually be regarded as providing additional support for the superstructure of traditional science.

PROBLEMS OF ENTRENCHMENT

However, there are several reasons for doubting that Goodman's theory of entrenchment will work for supplying some reasons or grounds for hypothesis selection. First, there is a strong psychological component in Goodman's treatment of projection. For example, actual projection of a particular hypothesis requires, Goodman says, "something like affirmation [of that particular hypothesis] as sufficiently more credible than alternative hypotheses."[28] "Credibility" raises strong, subjective psychological connotations. Peirce warns that the "likelihood" of a hypothesis under consideration in abduction is nothing more than "an indication that the hypothesis accords or discords with our preconceived ideas" (7.220). And although the experience which gives rise to our preconceived ideas will, in the long run, provide some economy in the selection of hypotheses, this same experience teaches us that likelihoods are "treacherous guides" (7.220).

As a hedge against this psychologism, Goodman does suggest that it would be theoretically possible to develop a mechanical procedure for the selection of hypotheses based upon comparative quantitative indices for different predicates.[29] However, using such a mechanical, quantitative guide for the selection of competing hypotheses creates more problems than it answers. For example, if the projection of a hypothesis means to seriously adopt it for testing, then it seems, many other considerations rather than simply the quantitative determination of the entrenchment of the predicates should be considered. Suppose that a scientist is trying to decide which of two competing hypotheses—h1 and h2—to project.[30] If she is able to determine through some quantitative, mechanical index that the predicate(s) in h1 are more thoroughly entrenched than those in h2, then h1 is the hypothesis to be chosen for actual projection according to Goodman's proposed mechanical procedure. Consider, however, the possible other relevant factors which might conceivably affect the choice. Suppose that h1 will take much longer (even *years* longer) to test and will also completely exhaust the resources of the scientist whereas the testing of h2 is relatively quick, easy and cheap. Ought not h2 to be tested first then, even if its predicates are not the better entrenched? Consider also, that in a scientific community where information is shared freely and easily amongst the members of the community, the chances are that all or nearly all of the scientists would actually project the same hypothesis based upon the same mechanical, quantitative index. The result might well be that enormous amounts of time and resources would be wasted with everyone in a particular scientific field testing the same hypothesis which might well turn out to be also the most complicated, time-consuming and expensive to test. Peirce's suggestion is that the testing of a particular hypothesis ought to be guided more by "pragmatic" concerns. Given an understanding of how complicated and involved the testing of a hypothesis might turn out to be, Peirce says, "Perhaps we might conceive the strength, or urgency, of a hypothesis as measured by the amount of wealth, in time, thought, money, etc., that we ought to have at our disposal before it would be worth while to take up that hypothesis for examination" (2.780). Using a rule of projection based upon simply the mechanical, quantitative index of entrenchment, a scientist might well find herself in the position of projecting a hypothesis which neither she nor anyone else will ever be in the position to test. Peirce's aphoristic rule for projecting hypotheses, "Don't block the path of research" (1.135), is concerned much more with the results of the actual projection—not only for the individual but for the scientific community as well.

Thus, we see that Goodman's new riddle of induction is a riddle of abduction—a riddle of hypothesis selection and theory formation. As such, Goodman's work represents, in some measure, an advance in the attempts to develop some logic of discovery and some logic of abduction; however, the new riddle of induction with the grue paradox does not pose any threat to the rationality of induction nor does it demonstrate that induction is relative.

WAYS OF WORLDMAKING

Another route which Nelson Goodman takes toward a thorough epistemological and metaphysical relativism is through his *Structure of Appearance* and his *Ways of Worldmaking.* In these works, Goodman develops what he calls a "radical relativism" resulting in a position according to which we are faced with a choice amongst many theories (or systems) which are purported to describe reality but none of which has any special epistemological, ontological, or scientific status. One system may be preferable for certain reasons and relative to a particular purpose, but other systems will be preferable on other grounds and for other purposes. The title, *Ways of Worldmaking,* is appropriately chosen because Goodman really means that we actually make different worlds by creating different theories or systems. There is no realistic ontology of physical objects to make any one of the choices metaphysically or scientifically more desirable than any other choice. The only guiding principles for system choice and "worldmaking" are pragmatic. Obviously, Goodman's position amounts to a thorough and complete rejection of the kind of scientific theory which I have called traditional or classical theory—science before the relativist revolution. I will first briefly examine how Goodman develops his position of relative ways of worldmaking. Then, I will look at the ways in which I think that Goodman has gone wrong, and finally, I will offer an assessment of the consequences of Goodman's relativism for traditional scientific theory.

In *The Structure of Appearance,* Goodman "constructs" a phenomenalistic system to explain the universe in such a manner to eliminate philosophical confusions. Given that "the real" and "the apparent" differ, there is always a rich source of philosophical confusion and error. Faced with a situation, for example, where a thing which is really blue *looks* green, and later becomes red, how are we to describe the difference between the apparent change in color which we capture by saying that the thing "looks" green and the "real" change in color which takes place when the blue thing *actually* becomes red?[31] Of course, all of this presupposes that there is an intelligible difference between the real and the apparent, and Goodman sets out to try and make sense of attempts to explain the world—both the real and the apparent—in terms of different kinds of systems. Competing systems, Goodman says, "may be founded on many different bases and constructed in different ways. And several quite different programs may be equally correct and offer equal if different advantages."[32]

WORLDMAKING AND RELATIVISM

It may be helpful to emphasize two important aspects of Goodman's title, *Ways of Worldmaking*. First, notice that we are talking about ways of world*making*. Although Goodman might occasionally talk about *descriptions* of the world, those descriptions result from the conventional actions of a *world-maker*—not some omnipotent creator of the universe from some theistic belief, but from you and me as we construct theories or systems. One builds worlds by building systems of beliefs, and Goodman explicitly rejects the notion that there is any sort of criterion or test for measuring the accuracy of a theory by its correspondence with the world in any realist sense.[33] Secondly, the use of the plural to talk about *ways* of worldmaking is also very instructive. There is no single way of describing the world or building the world through building a system. There is no way that the world is; there are many. Goodman says,

> There are very many different equally true descriptions of the world, and their truth is the only standard of their faithfulness. And when we say of them that they all involve conventionalizations, we are saying that no one of these different descriptions is *exclusively* true, since the others are also true. None of them tells us *the* way the world is, but each of them tells us *a* way the world is.[34]

Consider two competing systems for explaining the universe—one which attempts to explain things on the basis of qualia (characteristics of appearances or presentations) and the other on the basis of physical objects. Goodman examines the alleged superiority of each system in terms of epistemological priority and decides that there are no good epistemological grounds for preferring one kind of system to another. Goodman opts for a phenomenalistic system himself but for quite different reasons. Even given the choice of a phenomenalistic system, there is the further choice between a nominalistic system and a Platonistic one, and even here, Goodman claims that it is possible to go either way, depending upon one's preferences and reasons.[35] Certainly, any pretext of any underlying "reality" which is a part of traditional or classical scientific theory has been stripped away, and competing systems or theories cannot be assessed in terms of any "correspondence" with reality.

Goodman's pluralism is so highly developed by the time that he produces *Ways of Worldmaking* that he claims that "the fact that there are many different world-versions is hardly debatable."[36] Worlds are created through systems of description, and different worlds are created by different systems of description. It is important to interpret Goodman correctly here. He is not suggesting some version of possible world theory, and he takes some care to distance himself from the possible world theorists. He explicitly cautions that he is "not speaking in terms of multiple possible alternatives to a single actual world but of multiple actual worlds."[37]

Multiple worlds are actually composed through the construction of different systems of interpretation or "frames of reference". Goodman's own description of the process of worldmaking in terms of composition and decomposition is very illustrative:

> Much but by no means all worldmaking consists of taking apart and putting together, often conjointly: on the on[e] hand, of dividing wholes into parts and partitioning kinds into sub-species, analyzing complexes into component features, drawing distinctions; on the other hand, of composing wholes and kinds out of parts and members and subclasses, combining features into complexes, and making connections. Such composition or decomposition is normally effected or assisted or consolidated by the application of labels: names, predicates, gestures, pictures, etc.[38]

Differences amongst different worlds are accounted for mainly in theoretical terms. If one chooses to divide the world in such a manner that points are basic elements, then one winds up with a Newtonian world, and if one chooses to make events basic, then one winds up with a Whiteheadian world. Or again, one might choose a physical object world or a qualia world. The bases for the choices and the differences between the outcomes are not factual but theoretical.

As will become more apparent in the next chapter, Goodman's process of making multifarious worlds places him squarely in the same camp as Thomas Kuhn. Also, since individual statements have truth-values only relative to some theory of description or some frame of reference, Goodman also aligns himself very closely with Quine's holism. These similarities are readily apparent in Goodman's discussion of the comparison of 'the sun never moves' and 'the sun always moves'. These two claims, though mutually exclusive, are still both true if we interpret them as true only relative to some theory or frame of reference, and the individual statements should be understood as making an assumption about the frame of reference within which they occur. Thus, 'the sun always moves' should be interpreted as "Under frame of reference A, the sun always moves", whereas 'the sun never moves' should be interpreted as "Under frame of reference B, the sun never moves".[39] All true descriptions of the world must be relative to some frame of reference without any presumption whatsoever that there is a single "basic" frame of reference to which all of the others are reducible. We are left with a pluralistic position which embraces many worlds—none absolutely fundamental or basic—but some preferable to others for different reasons and on different grounds.

Unlike Quine, who gives ontological preference to a world composed of physical objects, Goodman does not attribute ontological priority to any particular frame of reference. Whether the world is composed of physical objects or qualia really has no answer since any answer to what the world is ultimately composed of must be given with respect to some particular frame of reference.

RIGHT AND WRONG WAYS OF MAKING WORLDS

Such an "ontological relativity" would seem to be the source of Goodman's "radical relativism"; however, Goodman is quick to add an important qualification—a qualification which, temporarily at least, staves off radical relativism and raises the difficult problem of interpreting just exactly what Goodman's brand of relativism really means. Goodman places constraints on the multiple worlds which are possible ways of worldmaking: some ways of worldmaking are ruled out. Goodman insists that some ways of worldmaking yield "true" or "right" worlds and that others yield "false" worlds. He says,

> What I have said so far plainly points to a radical relativism; but severe restraints are imposed. Willingness to accept countless alternative true or right world-versions does not mean that everything goes, that tall stories are as good as short ones, that truths are no longer distinguished from falsehoods, but only that truth must be otherwise conceived than as correspondence with a ready-made world. . . . The multiple worlds I countenance are just the actual worlds made by and answering to true or right versions. Worlds . . . answering to false versions have no place in my philosophy.[40]

The resulting pluralism and the rejection of anything resembling the correspondence theory of truth does not lead to the multiplicity of worlds; it simply leads to the multiplicity of world-versions. The question of whether two different "true" or "right" versions are two different versions of a single reality or whether they create two different realities is still debatable. Goodman just insists that such a debate does not get us anywhere and that we would then do better to simply focus on the world-versions and forget about the question of the "reality of the world". Whether there is what Goodman calls "something solid underneath" is simply not a profitable avenue to pursue.

On the one hand—by placing "severe restraints" on his radical relativism—Goodman seems to be making some concession to the realist; however, he immediately rescinds whatever appearance of compromise one might find in his gesture to the realist. The things that the descriptions contained in "right" world-versions refer to are constructed in the process of world making—whether they are mind, matter, energy, electrons, quanta, or quarks. Goodman explicitly holds that facts are "theory-laden", and "facts", he says, "are small theories" just as "true theories are big facts".[41] There appears to be no doubt then that facts and worlds are constructed along with the world-versions or as a result of the construction of the world-versions.

Although Goodman calls his brand of relativism "radical relativism", he is, at the same time, intent upon distinguishing it from the kind of relativism in which "anything goes". That is, although Goodman clearly thinks that we can give different accounts of the world (choosing, for example, either physical objects or qualia), he does not wish his generosity concerning world-views to extend to embracing spirits, gremlins, or leprechauns. If some world-versions are to be right and others wrong, there must be some standards or "rightness" according to which such an assessment is made. Goodman's standard of rightness[42] is his notion of *fit with practice.* He says that "rightness of categorization, which enters into most other varieties of rightness, is rather a matter of fit with practice; that without the organization, the selection of relevant kinds, effected by evolving tradition, there is no rightness or wrongness of categorization, no validity or invalidity of inductive inference. . . . "[43]

PROBLEMS WITH MAKING WORLDS

There have been several questions raised about the adequacy of Goodman's notion of "fit with practice".[44] At the present moment, I wish to pursue a line of reasoning which will demonstrate that there is a fundamental epistemological difficulty in using Goodman's notion of fit (or, indeed, any criterion of rightness) to assess world-versions on Goodman's account.

The "ways of worldmaking" which Goodman's theory is about are ways of constructing theories about the world on the object level—that is, the world-versions created by various ways of worldmaking take as their arguments the world itself, however it is described.

The criteria of rightness which allow one to choose right from wrong object-level world-versions must themselves be on the meta-linguistic or meta-world-version level since the criteria are supposed to be world-version neutral and since they involve the "fit" of the world-version with some practice "in the world". Goodman's criteria of rightness must be a part of his general meta-theory about worldmaking. We can imagine, indeed we shall examine, other theories about worldmaking; so if one is to accept Goodman's theory about worldmaking over some other one, one must examine Goodman's meta-worldmaking theory (including its criteria of rightness) and decide, on balance, which meta-theory is most attractive.

Goodman, of course, recognizes the status of his theory of worldmaking. He admits explicitly that his "outline of the facts concerning the fabrication of facts is of course itself a fabrication",[45] but what he fails to recognize are the consequences of his own theory. Goodman wishes to maintain that the criteria of rightness will prevent a complete laissez-faire situation in which "anything goes"; however, this attempt at restraint is doomed to fail for several reasons.

On the one hand, Goodman's criteria of rightness might be interpreted as relative to his own, unique meta-theory of worldmaking. In other words, just as facts on the object level are created by the creation of world-versions through the process of worldmaking, likewise, facts on the meta-theory level are created through the process of meta-worldmaking—constructing theories *about* worldmaking, part of which consists in formulating criteria of rightness. On this account, the criteria of rightness are world-version neutral but not meta-world-version neutral. Harvey Siegel has recognized the ill consequences for Goodman if his criteria of rightness are so understood. He says that Goodman's

> meta-version is itself only one of countless possible meta-versions. So the restraints on radical relativism which keep it from being the case that "everything goes" in [Goodman's relativism] are themselves rela-

tive to Goodman's meta-version. Relativity of versions re-arises at the level of meta-version. In short, it is the case that not "everything goes" *only in Goodman's meta-version.*[46]

Siegel argues that since Goodman recognizes that his own meta-theoretic account of worldmaking is only one amongst numerous such accounts—many of which would be mutually incompatible— that Goodman must also allow the "equal legitimacy" of competing meta-theories with criteria of rightness which are incompatible with Goodman's. On Siegel's account, Goodman's criteria of rightness become impotent for distinguishing right from wrong world-versions since "they are, on Goodman's own scheme, no more authoritative than rival, incompatible criteria . . . which offer different judgments regarding the rightness of (object-level) versions."[47] This interpretation of Goodman's criteria of rightness undermines Goodman's distinction between right and wrong world-versions and makes of his "constrained" radical relativism a "real" radical relativism where, it seems, anything goes.

I certainly agree with Siegel that if Goodman's account of the criteria of rightness are relative to and internal to his own unique meta-worldmaking version, then "all bets are off" for picking amongst rival world-versions on any epistemological grounds at all. However, although Goodman himself might not be very happy about such consequences, people like Gerald Doppelt or Paul Feyerabend might well applaud and gladly embrace the resulting unrestrained radical relativism. To turn the present argument into a complete *reductio ad absurdum,* we must also point out that *if Goodman's criteria of rightness are completely relative on the meta-theory level, then so is everything else he says in his meta-theory of worldmaking, including the central claim that worlds get constructed through the process of worldmaking.* Not only would Goodman's criteria of rightness be simply powerless to distinguish right from wrong world-versions, but Goodman's entire account of world-making would be arguably no better or worse off than the realist accounts of traditional science, science before the relativist revolution.

RIGHT AND WRONG THEORIES ABOUT MAKING WORLDS

This is the real crux of the matter with Goodman's theory of world-making. Why ought we to prefer his account of worldmaking to any other? This is a question on the meta-meta-worldmaking level. It is a question about the criteria for assessing and choosing meta-world-versions. As Goodman himself recognizes, the different world-versions which result from worldmaking do not themselves cut across many of the major, relevant disputes involved. We have seen, for example, that different ways of constructing the world might be equally compatible with realism and nominalism or with physicalism and phenomenalism; so, on the object-level the consequences of worldmaking seem to be relatively non-threatening and uninteresting so far as questions of relativism are involved.

There must be reasons on the meta-worldmaking level for preferring one account of worldmaking to another. Presumably, for Goodman, logical consistency would be one such criterion for assessing meta-worldmaking theories. Elegance might well be another such criterion. Additionally, there would probably be pragmatic criteria of a very similar nature to the notion of fit for world-versions. Certainly, there is now a well-established and long-standing practice of theorizing about the construction of theories about the world. Until the criteria for assessing meta-world-versions are supplied and analyzed, Goodman's theory of ways of worldmaking remains incomplete in a very important respect.

In any case, we have seen that Goodman's version of relativism is a relatively mild-mannered one with little or no serious consequences for the traditional scientific and epistemological notions of rationality. When compared to some of the other brands of radical relativism, Goodman's particular variety of relativism seems very tame. For example, Richard Rorty has declared the death of epistemology since, according to him, epistemology fails in its attempt at commensurability—interpreting different theories or systems in such a way that they all fall under a single set of rules or principles for comparing the different theories and for settling disagreements in a rational manner. Goodman, however, must embrace commensurability. In order to compare two different world-versions on grounds of fit, Goodman must assume that they are commensurable. The judgment that world-version A is preferable to world-version B because A's fit with practice is judged to be "better" than B's presupposes that A and B are commensurable; otherwise, the judgment could not be made. Consequently, for Goodman, traditional standards of rationality must be alive and well on the meta-theoretic level in order to compare world-versions to decide the question of fit; so, induction and the scientific method remain intact.

— 4 —

KUHN ON SCIENTIFIC REVOLUTIONS AND RELATIVISM

SCIENCE BEFORE THE REVOLUTION

Since the appearance of Thomas S. Kuhn's justly celebrated *Structure of Scientific Revolutions,* traditional epistemological and metaphysical issues have been catapulted into the forefront of the philosophy of science. Concern about such issues has "trickled down" to the level of the practicing scientist to the point where now the entire enterprise of science and the nature of science are being debated not only by philosophers of science but by practicing social and empirical scientists as well. In particular, debate concerning the rationality of the methodology of science (as well as the notion of progress in the history of the development of scientific theories) is now being hotly waged amongst philosophers and scientists alike. In addition, the ancient debate between realism and anti-realism has emerged once again but with entirely new dimensions.

Many of the issues prompted by the current discussion are traditional ones. For example, many of the basic epistemological and methodological questions were anticipated by several major figures in the history of philosophy including David Hume and Charles Peirce. However, these debates are now explicitly formulated within the philosophy of science, and the stakes certainly have been raised. On the table now are the very rationality of science itself and the viability of epistemology as a philosophical enterprise. The ugly specter of relativism is raised, skepticism is clothed in new sheep's clothing, and science is in danger of becoming, as has been suggested by some, just another ideology. The plethora of recent literature on the current debate testifies to the essential character of the issues under discussion.

As I have explored in some detail earlier, the main purposes of science, according to "science before the revolution" and as learned by every school child in general science in elementary school, is to explain and predict phenomena. Generations of school children have had this lesson thoroughly drilled into their heads—explain and predict. This rather simplistic account embodies all of the underlying, epistemological complexities which give rise to the current controversies. Explain and predict what? "Phenomena" or "reality" or "the world" (or some comparable vague description) are the answers. Any such description of the purposes of science is clearly, on the surface, realistic, and dichotomistic. Scientific theories, hypotheses, and even simple observation statements are *about* something—facts, events, reality, or the nebulous "phenomena" which are in some metaphorical sense "out there" for science to describe and predict. The implication seems obviously realistic— however elusive "reality" or "phenomena" turn out to be.

I have argued that this same view has dominated much of Western philosophy's view concerning the nature of language and the relationship between language and reality.[1] At the beginning of *Philosophical Investigations,*[2] as Wittgenstein begins his exploration of the nature and limits of reality and of how language is able to represent reality, he identifies what he calls the Augustinian view of language. He then proceeds to attempt to dismantle the elaborate epistemological and metaphysical constructions which had developed out of this view. It is this view of the nature of language, or in the case of science, scientific theory, which explains, within empiricist epistemology, the concerted efforts to provide some justification for "bridging the gap" between language or theory and the "reality" which language or theory is "about". These efforts have given rise to the special status ascribed to ostensive definition, the referential theory of meaning, the correspondence theory of truth, and the verification criterion of meaning. In each case, there is an effort to provide a tether to anchor theory or language in some objective, independent reality. If ever there were an obvious candidate for the elusive philosopher's stone, bridging the gap between language and object (theory and phenomena) is it.

Finally, the difficulty of bridging this gap between theory and reality, the attempt to develop an adequate account of *representation* in language, has frequently led to foundationalist understandings of the nature of both epistemology and ontology. Connecting theory to facts requires some sort of meta-theory which takes as its argument both theory and reality. Theories of reference, theories of meaning, theories of verification, and theories of truth all serve this purpose in different ways. Attempts to provide such accounts easily become foundationalist. Methodologically, a very simple approach is to give some account of how theory and reality are connected at some privileged, particular point and then construct an account for the entire, complicated structure based upon such a "foundation". Candidates, from within the empiricist tradition, for the elementary linguistic components which connect with reality are legion. They include sense-data reports, atomic propositions, logically proper names, and protocol sentences.

It is at this point that questions about rationality in science begin to be interwoven with problems of explanation. The process of providing an explanation for a particular phenomenon involves providing some *reasons* for entertaining certain beliefs about the phenomenon or for making certain claims about it. And presumably, *the best* explanation is the one which provides us with *the best* reasons. Obviously then, science is fundamentally and essentially concerned with the epistemological justification of beliefs and with the basic problem of adjudicating between properly held beliefs and improperly held ones.[3]

Once we begin to explore what makes some reasons good reasons and others not so good, the wide and straight path to foundationalism which has appealed to so many philosophers begins to get clearer and clearer. Traditional understandings of science, science before the revolution, as well as classical theories of rationality both require similar conditions to be met in order to arrive at rational belief. As Harold I. Brown describes the process,

> reasons are provided by the information we begin with, along with the rules that establish the connection between this information and the proposition believed. But as soon as the model is put this starkly, two questions arise—or, rather, the same question arises in two contexts: on what basis do we select the information from which to begin, and on what basis do we select our rules? If a belief is to be genuinely rational, it must be rational on both of these counts. There would not be much point in claiming that a conclusion had been arrived at in a rational manner if we arrived there on the basis of an impeccable algorithm from randomly chosen premises, or if we proceeded from appropriate premises in strict accordance with ridiculous rules. The classical model requires that we begin from an appropriate starting point and use appropriate rules.[4]

It is through the search for the beginning point of justification, for the original premisses of justification, that we have been led by foundationalists in various guises to account for self-justifying claims in terms of self-evident ones. Empiricists and rationalists

alike have sought some beginning point for the process of explanation, some ending point for the process of justification. In this
enterprise, the model of science has attracted many philosophers to
emulate it, and science and scientific theory have served as paradigm
cases of rationality. Brown again says,

> science provides a crucial test case, since science, and particularly
> physical science, currently stands as our clearest example of a rational
> enterprise. . . . Moreover, proponents of the classical model of rational-
> ity have typically considered science to be a clear instance of rationality
> in action.[5]

That is, "science before the revolution" was not only understood
as providing us with the best answers as to what constitutes a justified
belief (an explanation), but *the method of science* was also regarded
as a model of rational inquiry and justification. Given this view of
the nature of science, the history of science is seen as a continual
search for the proper starting point and the equally important search
for the rules, the method, or *the process* of justification, and *progress*
in science is determined by the way in which constant refinement on
method is able to produce more epistemically compelling results.

SCIENCE, EPISTEMOLOGY, AND PARADIGMS

The most important new direction in the course of philosophical
investigation into the nature of science and scientific method can be
traced to the appearance of Kuhn's *Structure of Scientific Revolutions.* His views concerning the nature of science and the history of
science have given rise to what is now being regarded as a new school
of thought—post-modernist or post-positivist philosophy of science.

Kuhn's investigation into the nature of science raises the same
fundamental issues about the relationship between scientific theory
and reality and the nature of rationality as concerned the positivists;
however, Kuhn approaches these issues from a completely new
direction. He argues, of course, that what I have called the traditional, Enlightenment view of science is ill-conceived and fraught with
misunderstandings and blind prejudices.

The single most important—and, at the same time, one of the
most controversial—aspect of Kuhn's analysis of science is that it is
paradigm based.[6] Kuhn's view of the nature of science and scientific
reasoning as based on paradigms can best be understood by looking
at the way in which Kuhn sees the history of science developing.
Following an initial "preparadigmatic" stage during which there is

little or no agreement amongst scientists about the methods, techniques, or questions (much less the answers) in a particular field, there comes a point when a particular model begins gradually to gain wide acceptance and emerge as dominant in the community of scientists. This "paradigm" eventually gains wide or universal acceptance within a particular field and provides the practicing scientists within that field with what become commonly accepted and recognized as the model ways of posing problems, conducting investigations, designing experiments, and considering solutions.[7] In one of his earliest characterizations of a paradigm, Kuhn says,

> I mean to suggest that some accepted examples of actual scientific practice—examples which include law, theory, application, and instrumentation together—provide models from which spring particular coherent traditions of scientific research.[8]

Such a paradigm becomes established when it is successful enough to attract a group of scientific practitioners to tackle the problems defined by the model, and when the paradigm is also "open-ended" enough to leave sufficient unresolved problems to occupy the scientific endeavors of the newly-attracted scientists.[9]

NORMAL SCIENCE

Paradigm-guided science becomes "normal science" whose chief activity is trying to solve the problems generated by the "open-ended" paradigm. This is a process of "puzzle-solving"—showing how the accepted paradigm applies to various phenomena in more detailed and precise fashion, a process of refining, extending, and articulating the existing paradigm. Scientists who are committed to the same paradigm are engaged in an enterprise which is structured in the same way by the paradigm; thus, their theories, methods, practices, and even the puzzles which they attempt to solve are very similar. Consequently, paradigms are responsible for the entire nature of normal science and its activities. Kuhn says,

> The study of paradigms . . . is what mainly prepares the student for membership in the particular scientific community with which he will later practice. Because he there joins men who learned the bases of their field from the same concrete models, his subsequent practice will seldom evoke overt disagreement over fundamentals. Men whose research is based on shared paradigms are committed to the same rules and standards for scientific practice. That commitment and the apparent consensus it produces are prerequisites for normal science, i.e., for the genesis and continuation of a particular research tradition.[10]

The rather unflattering picture of the practicing scientist within normal science which emerges from Kuhn's depiction of normal science is that of a person who mindlessly and endlessly (and almost feverishly) twists a Rubik's Cube to try and solve the puzzle without ever asking why one is trying to solve this particular puzzle and without considering the possibility of trying a different puzzle.

However, as normal science proceeds and puzzle-solving activities are carried out, anomalies inevitably begin to develop—situations in which the paradigm just does not work as it is supposed to work. Circumstances invariably arise which the currently accepted paradigm cannot explain or even make intelligible. A crack begins to develop in the accepted paradigm, and, to paraphrase Quine, no paradigm is immune to anomaly. In the course of the history of science, these discrepancies continue to mount until some practitioners begin to doubt the paradigm itself, and a crisis develops. Eventually, competing paradigms emerge, and a *scientific revolution* occurs when a new paradigm unseats the old, established one. It is this process of scientific revolution which is one of the most controversial aspects of Kuhn's theory and which raises questions about the fundamental nature of scientific reasoning and rationality itself.

INCOMMENSURABILITY OF PARADIGMS

The new paradigm which replaces the old one during a scientific revolution is, according to Kuhn, "incommensurable" with the old paradigm, that is: since the new paradigm "necessitates a redefinition" of the old[11] and since the standards and criteria for the evaluation of paradigms are *internal* to the paradigms, it follows that the change from the old paradigm to the new one cannot come about by appealing to some neutral criteria or method of paradigm selection. Perhaps most importantly, the replacement process is not the old, familiar falsification/verification process from science before the revolution where certain data might either falsify or verify one paradigm or the other. Since the new paradigm is incommensurable with the old, the process of abandoning the old in favor of the new cannot be a gradual, logical or "scientific" process based upon evidence or some form of reasoning. The anomalies cannot logically force a change in paradigm. As a matter of fact, Kuhn tells us, "paradigms are not corrigible by normal science at all".[12] The differences between different proponents of competing paradigms at a time of crisis will be so great that they are unlikely even to agree on what would constitute sufficient scientific grounds for scientifically preferring one to the other since the criteria for such preference are internal to the competing paradigms. Paradigm change is something like a Gestalt switch in perception[13] and does not simply involve a new interpretation of the data by the proponents of the new paradigm.[14] The paradigm switch is abrupt, according to Kuhn, a "sudden and unstructured event".[15] One cannot reason oneself into the new paradigm. Kuhn describes the process of adopting a new paradigm as a "conversion experience"[16] which often occurs "in defiance of the evidence"[17] and which "can only be made on faith."[18] Kuhn summarizes this process in the following manner:

> If two men disagree, for example, about the relative fruitfulness of their theories, or if they agree about that but disagree about the relative importance of fruitfulness and, say, scope in reaching a choice, neither can be convicted of a mistake. Nor is either being unscientific. There is no neutral algorithm for theory-choice, no systematic decision procedure which, properly applied, must lead each individual in the group to the same decision.[19]

Many of the current controversies involving rationality, methodology, relativism, and realism/anti-realism are spawned from this view of science which seems to make of science a matter of nonrational, intuitive flashes of insight, or political clout, or mass psychology. Minimally, however one interprets Kuhn's position, the consequence is to force a re-examination of the nature of science and rationality.

INCOMMENSURABILITY AND RELATIVISM

Some have interpreted Kuhn's position as skeptical and relativistic since Kuhn is understood as claiming that "choices between competing scientific theories . . . *must be irrational*"[20] while others have called such interpretations "gross distortions".[21] The most radical interpretations of the Kuhnian position have led to regarding science as just another ideology—like religion or magic.[22] The result, heralded by some and deplored by others, is what Robert Baum has called "intellectual anarchism",[23] the end of the reign of reason.

Exactly how Kuhn himself stands on the matter of relativism is a matter of some controversy. Initially, it certainly appears that, given the description of the epistemological force of paradigms and the incommensurability of paradigms, there can be no paradigm-neutral or paradigm-independent standards for paradigm assessment and that the selection of paradigms must therefore be "irrational". This is the interpretation of Kuhn which has become known as "the irrationality thesis", and it is based largely upon Kuhn's original formulation of his theses concerning the nature of and the incommensurability of paradigms. Israel Scheffler understands Kuhn in the following manner:

> to accept a paradigm is to accept not only theory and methods, but also governing standards or criteria which serve to justify the paradigm as against its rivals, in the eyes of its proponents. Paradigm differences are thus inevitably reflected upward, in criterial differences at the second level. It follows that each paradigm is, in effect, inevitably self-justifying, and that paradigm debates must fail of objectivity: again we appear driven back to nonrational conversions as the final characterization of paradigm shifts within the community of science.[24]

Scheffler argues very successfully that although criteria for puzzle-solving may be internal to a paradigm, it does not follow that criteria for paradigm selection, the "second level" criteria, are also internal. He thus sees Kuhn as unjustifiably collapsing external criteria into internal ones, or, more poignantly I think, collapsing meta-linguistic criteria into object-language ones. In other words, even if one grants that criteria for puzzle-solving are internal to the paradigm which gives rise to the puzzle, it does not follow that standards or criteria for choosing amongst paradigms must also be internal. The kinds of puzzles generated might differ from paradigm to paradigm, and what counts as a solution to a puzzle might differ from paradigm to paradigm as well, but one can still reasonably argue over the choice of paradigms. A solution to the Rubik's Cube is certainly different from a solution to the Monkey Puzzle, and even the criteria for what counts as a solution differs from puzzle to puzzle, but one can still give reasons for preferring one puzzle to another and argue for the preference of one puzzle to another by appealing to criteria which are external to either the Rubik's Cube or the Monkey Puzzle.

In other words, the sense in which paradigm-criteria are internal is exactly the sense which Kuhn has identified and emphasized. This is the sense according to which a "paradigm is understood as defining a range of acceptable problems and modes of solution within a particular scientific domain. . . . "[25] However, when we consider the problem of choosing from amongst different paradigms, the criteria for making the comparisons amongst paradigms which must occur as a prelude to choice, must function on a different level. Even if we admit that paradigm-criteria are internal in the first sense, there is no reason that we should think that the criteria on this second level are internal. As Scheffler again observes, if paradigms are understood as sets of rules for conducting normal science, no set of rules contains explanations of how they are to be applied nor instructions for comparing them with other sets of rules.[26]

At one time at least, Kuhn seems to have clearly dismissed the possibility of rational theory choice. Given the limitations imposed by the incommensurability of paradigms, Kuhn maintained that no person could entertain the considerations necessary to make a rational choice. Such considerations would involve a careful examination and comparison of the two competing paradigms. The limitations on what a person who holds one paradigm can understand of another, "make it difficult or, more likely, impossible," according to Kuhn, "for an individual to hold both theories in mind together and compare them point by point with each other and with nature. That sort of comparison is, however, the process on which the appropriateness of any word like 'choice' depends."[27] Supposedly, just as one cannot hold two different Gestalt perspectives of a picture simultaneously or just as one cannot slowly and carefully move from one Gestalt perspective to another, likewise, one's perspective of phenomena which is controlled by a paradigm—one's scientific point of view—is a perspective which one comes to hold suddenly and completely. One cannot slowly and carefully reason oneself from one paradigm to another since this would require or presuppose the ability to compare rationally two different paradigms. It is this radical position with its sudden, non-inferential, "all-or-nothing" switch which has provided the impetus for the attacks of many of the radical relativists upon the traditional view of science and the denunciations of the general enterprise of epistemology.

The situation seems closely akin to the issue involving Goodman's *Ways of Worldmaking* which we investigated in Chapter 3. Just as, for Goodman, metaphysicians construct worlds through the conventional force of theories, similarly scientists "construct" worlds through the fact-making force of paradigms for Kuhn. In both cases, there is no criterion for assessing the accuracy or preference of a theory or paradigm by any notion of correspondence with a "real" world, and in both cases we are faced with a multiplicity of different worlds. Goodman's notion of "frame of reference" comes across easily into Kuhnian jargon as "paradigm", and the distinction between fact and theory is also undermined by the theories of both men. Given the important similarities between the positions of Goodman and Kuhn, it is reasonable to expect Kuhn to be faced with the same kind of issues and difficulties with which Goodman is faced in his theory of worldmaking. One issue involves the status of the theory itself, and another involves the question of the bases for paradigm preference.

The Status of Kuhn's Theory

Consider whatever may be judged to be an accurate version of Kuhn's theory. The actual formulation of Kuhn's position is not important here because the issue concerns the status and fundamental coherence of the theory—not its content. Just for the sake of argument, let us take

(K) Science is based upon paradigms which are incommensurable.

as a formulation of Kuhn's position. Now clearly, K is a meta-paradigm theory. Paradigms take as their arguments facts—theory-laden though they may be—about the world. K takes as its arguments paradigms and what, for Kuhn, are facts about paradigms—for example, that they are incommensurable.

Suppose we raise the simple question of why one should prefer K to any other theory of science—say, to a realistic one which is paradigm-free. In pursuing an answer to such a question, indeed, the question which is now preoccupying much of the philosophy of science, one is faced with only two possible ways of assessing K—the same two alternatives with which we are faced when assessing Goodman's theory of worldmaking. Either the criteria for evaluating K and comparing it with other meta-scientific theories are internal to K, or they are external to K.

Are the Criteria for Evaluating Kuhn's Theory Internal to It?

Consider first the alternative wherein the criteria for assessing K are internal to K.[28] On this understanding of the nature of the criteria for assessing K, facts concerning paradigms and scientific theory—indeed, the very existence of paradigms themselves, are relative to K. Just as facts on the object language level are relative to paradigms according to K, likewise, facts on the meta-language level—on the meta-paradigm level—are also relative to K. If the adoption of a paradigm is not really a choice but a conversion experience, as Kuhn claims, then, it appears, *a fortiori,* that one's adoption of K would be similarly a conversion experience made "on the basis of faith". On this account, one would not be able to reason oneself into adopting K but would have to wait for that blinding flash of insight which results when "the scales fall from one's eyes".

This interpretation would make a farce of the entire debate currently raging concerning the nature of science and completely vitiates the significance of all of the seriously scholarly tomes on the controversy—including Kuhn's and the present one. If the criteria for preferring K to any of its competitors are internal to K, then, of course, those criteria apply only to K and cannot be a basis for comparing K to any other theory about scientific theories. Obviously, such internal criteria for K cannot be reasons for preferring K to any of its competitors. Hence, the whole issue of which understanding of the nature of science and which philosophy of science is preferable becomes non-debatable.

Similarly, it would seem that a condition of incommensurability would exist on the meta-paradigm level as Kuhn claims exists on the level of paradigms. As we have seen, Kuhn insists that the existence of "significant limits" of what one person under the influence of one paradigm can understand of another means that it is highly unlikely or impossible that any one individual could ever understand both paradigms simultaneously in order to compare them to make a rational choice.[29] But if this is true on the level of paradigms because the criteria for paradigm-assessment are internal to paradigms, then it would also be true on the meta-paradigm level if the criteria for meta-paradigm theories are internal to those theories. The result would be a radical relativism according to which there could be no *reasons* for a person to adopt K, and even Kuhn himself would not be able to compare K with any of its competitors since he could not understand two different meta-paradigm theories at the same time. If the criteria for assessing K are internal to K, then there is little else to be said philosophically about the matter. The only thing one might do is to meditate or silently repeat some mantra (such as "paradigms are incommensurable") until "the penny drops" and "the scales fall" and one suddenly becomes a convert to K.

OR ARE THEY EXTERNAL TO IT?

On the other hand, if the criteria for assessing K are external to K, then, as the saying goes, that's "a whole new ball game". Certainly, if the criteria for assessing K are external to K, we can easily compare K to other competing theories about the nature of scientific theories and use the same criteria to assess those competing theories as well. This would certainly seem to be the more reasonable alternative for pursuing an answer to the question of why one should prefer K since it allows for the comparison of meta-scientific theories and for the possibility, at least, for *reasons* for preferring K or some alternative account of the nature of scientific theories. Understanding criteria for meta-paradigm theory as external would also account for the abundance of literature produced by pro-Kuhnians and anti-Kuhnians alike.

However, as reasonable as treating criteria for assessing K as external might initially sound, there is an unavoidable problem of self-reference involved which ultimately leads to paradox. Given that the criteria for paradigm-assessment are internal to paradigms, as Kuhn insists, then it seems impossible that the criteria for meta-paradigm theory assessment could be external. Since K is a theory about the nature of and the relationships between paradigms, K requires its proponents to be able to compare and understand different paradigms—even to be able to say that two paradigms are incommensurable. But K makes an even stronger claim: K claims that science is *generally* paradigm-based and that paradigms *generally* are incommensurable. If the criteria for assessing meta-paradigm claims about the nature of paradigms are external to the particular theory making the claim (K, in this case), then it appears as if the criteria for assessing paradigms must also be external to the paradigms. Otherwise, how could the comparative advantages and disadvantages of K be discussed and considered carefully? Since a major component of K involves the claim that the criteria for paradigm choice are internal, how could one ever evaluate this part of K and compare it with other claims about the nature of paradigm evaluation unless one could examine and compare different paradigms and their different criteria for paradigm evaluation? In other words, K's claim that paradigms are incommensurable can be assessed by criteria which are external to K only if paradigms are not incommensurable.

The result is what Wittgenstein would have recognized as an illegitimate totality. To say that two paradigms are incommensurable requires one to assume an intellectual position such that one can "stand outside" the totality of any single paradigm. The point is one recognized by many philosophers from Plato to Wittgenstein. To develop any general theory about any totality which includes drawing the boundaries or limitations of that totality, one must also include as part of the argument of the general theory something which is outside of the totality. In the cases of The Third Man Argument against Plato's Theory of the Forms and Wittgenstein's famed ladder analogy in the *Tractatus,* the difficulty is caused by the complete generality of the theories. In the case of Kuhn, he imposes the limitation upon his own theory by his claim of the incommensurability of paradigms. Since rules and criteria for paradigm evaluation (including presumably even logical consistency) are clearly supposed to be internal to a paradigm, according to Kuhn,[30] then 'incommensurable' is a predicate which can only take on meaning relative to a single paradigm. Obviously, however, incommensurability is a relationship between or amongst paradigms; so it must follow as a result of criteria or rules which are not internal to any given paradigm. Hence, the self-referential paradox: paradigms are and can be incommensurable only if they are not incommensurable.

We are back once again to Rudolf Carnap's conclusion regarding possible internal and external questions about the kind of linguistic framework which we have examined in some detail earlier. Carnap recognized, long before Kuhn, that empirical questions are internal to a particular framework and that one's choice of frameworks cannot be empirical in the same manner. However, Kuhn's claim of the incommensurability of theories involves a much stronger claim, and whether the criteria for K are understood to be internal or external to K, we have seen that K becomes self-referentially refuting. It is one thing to say that empirical questions are internal to a theory and that theory choices are not empirical in the same way as that in which the choices made within a theory are; it is quite another thing to say that there are no reasons for theory choice and that one cannot understand any two theories at once in order to make a reasonable choice between the two.

DAVIDSON AND CONCEPTUAL RELATIVITY

Kuhn's general theory of science as based on incommensurability requires us to make intelligible the imagined situation where several different groups of people are (or have been) committed to different points of view from which they understand (or have understood) the nature of reality, with no group able to understand another group's point of view. The "privacy" of each group's theory and language is the result of the incommensurability amongst the theories, that is, the failure of translatability amongst theories. Since the meanings of terms within a theory follow from the principles, rules, and laws of the theory, and since these principles, rules, and laws are understood to be internal to each theory, there is no meaning invariance across theories. Kuhn says explicitly that in the imagined move from one paradigm to another "words change their meanings" and consequently no language is available for the "comparison of two successive theories."[31] The lack of such a general language leads directly to incommensurability for Kuhn. But if we abandon the notion of meanings which apply across theories or paradigms and the analytic-synthetic distinction upon which such a notion is based, then as Donald Davidson has correctly pointed out, what is left is some sort of vague distinction between scheme and content, the third dogma of empiricism.[32] According to Kuhn (and, as we have seen in Chapter 2, Quine), the scheme or paradigm organizes and shapes the content whether the content is understood as reality or experience. For Davidson the elements of such a theory include

> language as the organizing force, not to be distinguished clearly from science: what is organized, referred to variously as "experience", "the stream of sensory experience", and "physical evidence"; and finally, the failure of intertranslatability is a necessary condition for difference of conceptual schemes; the common relation to experience or the evidence is what is supposed to help us make sense of the claim that it is languages or schemes that are under consideration when translation fails. It is essential to this idea that there be something neutral and common that lies outside all schemes. This common something cannot, of course, be the *subject matter* of contrasting languages, or translation would be possible.[33]

Now, whether we understand the "failure of intertranslatability" as complete, radical failure or as simply partial failure, Davidson has argued convincingly that the notion of conceptual relativity does not make sense. Whether we regard a scheme as organizing reality (facts) or experience, organizing a content boils down to a matter of which statements one takes to be true. A different conceptual scheme becomes one which some other group of people accepts as true but which is not translatable into our own. As Davidson argues,[34] if the criterion for a conceptual scheme necessarily involves the notion of truth, then what we need to make sense of the notion of different conceptual schemes is a notion of truth which does not involve translation. Using Alfred Tarski's semantic conception of truth as a paradigm of a successful criterion of truth, Davidson concludes that "there does not seem to be much hope for a test that a conceptual scheme is radically different from ours if that test depends on the assumption that we can divorce the notion of truth from that of translation."[35]

What would it mean to say that another person holds a paradigm-based view which is incommensurate with our own? Surely, Kuhn's view requires us to be able to make sense of such a claim, but exactly how are we suppose to analyze such a claim of incommensurability where terms and definitions as well as facts are relative to the two different paradigms? Such a claim is both based upon and used to support a theory of radical meaning variance according to which the meanings of terms are essentially dependent upon, and hence variant upon, the theory within which they occur.[36] One might agree with the claim that the meanings of scientific terms are essentially dependent upon the theoretical context in which they occur, but this does not support the more radical claim that the meanings of scientific terms must change radically if the theoretical context within which they occur is changed.[37] If meanings of terms change radically when the theoretical context in which they occur is changed, then to say that another person holds a paradigm which is incommensurable with one's own is to say that the terms of the other's paradigm cannot be understood in one's own paradigm or translated into one's own paradigm. To understand how this is supposed to happen, consider the situation where L1 is our own conceptual scheme and 's' is some sentence in some conceptual scheme, L2, different from and incommensurable with our own. How are we to understand the claim, occurring within L1, "s is true in L2"? The sentence, let us call it t, "s is true in L2", must occur in L1 in order for us even to say that there is a conceptual scheme (theory or paradigm[38]) which is different from our own; so we can understand the claim that s is true in L2 only if we understand the claim that t is true in L1, our own conceptual scheme. Now it must be possible for one to *name* s in L1 in order for t to occur in L1. In other words, L1 must be rich enough to contain the names of whatever sentences we want to say are true in L2 and the names of the ones which, if we want to maintain that L1 and L2 are incommensurable, we want to say are not translatable into L1. However, although we use the name of s to *say* that s is true in L2 (t) or that s is not translatable into L1, it is not the name of s which is actually true in L2 or non-translatable into L1. It is the sentence itself about which we would want to say that it is true in L2 or non-translatable into L1; so, it seems, for either of these claims to make sense in L1, the sentence itself and not just its name must occur in L1. Thus, the kinds of prohibitions which the doctrine of incommensurability is supposed to set up regarding the occurrence of *s* in L1 can be understood by a person using L1 only if *s* is translatable from L2 to L1. The very notion of a conceptual scheme different from one's own seems to depend then upon a notion of truth which essentially involves successful translation. So, it seems, that incommensurability of L1 and L2 cannot be accounted for in terms of failure of translation or else our ability to understand the original claim is also lost. Davidson concludes that there is no way of making intelligible the claim that there are other people whose conceptual schemes are radically different from our own.[39] What I have shown is that, *a fortiori,* if the claim of incommensurability rests upon the claim of non-translatability, we cannot make sense of that claim in our own language and Kuhn's claim becomes self-referentially unintelligible.[40]

Davidson concludes that it would be equally wrong to claim that all of humankind shares a common conceptual scheme. He says: "if we cannot intelligibly say that schemes are different, neither can we intelligibly say that they are one."[41] But surely this is mistaken. It may well be the case that the claim that all people share the same conceptual scheme is *wrong,* but surely it is intelligible. I have argued that Kuhn's claim about the incommensurability of different paradigms and the resulting relativism are self-referentially inconsistent since in order to understand the claim in our present conceptual scheme we must assume translatability—which is exactly what the original claim denies. However, if I claim that all people share the same conceptual scheme (hence denying the claim of incommensurability), my claim is not self-referentially unintelligible, and appears to be a perfectly *reasonable* claim to make—even if it is not true. Indeed, the kind of argument which would make the claim of a shared, universal conceptual scheme unintelligible is simply the reassertion of the claim of incommensurability, which is to say, the reassertion that the laws, principles, and criteria of paradigm evaluation are internal to a particular paradigm. We have already seen that such a claim is unintelligible. In other words, Kuhn's claim of incommensurability, if true, must itself be paradigm relative too, that is, relative to *some* paradigm since the criteria for paradigm evaluation are supposed to be paradigm relative also. According to some theory of paradigms one might be able to understand other paradigms, but relative to Kuhn's one cannot. Furthermore, relative to *some* paradigm—if laws, principles, and criteria of paradigm evaluation are internal—other paradigms might be both commensurable and incommensurable at the same time. The situation with Kuhn's incommensurability thesis seems to parallel exactly the difficulties with Goodman's ways of worldmaking.[42]

KUHN'S SHIFT OF POSITION

We have seen in what Kuhn has said so far that competing paradigms are supposed to be incommensurable because the criteria for paradigm evaluation are claimed to be internal to a particular paradigm. Such an understanding of Kuhn's doctrine leads directly to a radical relativism with all of its attending difficulties. More recently, Kuhn has apparently attempted to recant his early extreme views about the incommensurability of paradigms and move to a more moderate position—although it is still difficult to make out clearly exactly what his present view is. In his responses to the interpretation which leads to the radical "irrationality thesis," Kuhn has denied that his notion of incommensurability leads to either irrationality or relativism. He says,

> My critics respond to my views on this subject [the incommensurability of paradigms] with charges of irrationality, relativism, and the defence of mob rule. These are all labels which I categorically reject, even when they are used in my defense . . . To say that, in matters of theory-choice, the force of logic and observation cannot in principle be compelling is neither to discard logic and observation nor to suggest that there are not good reasons for favouring one theory over another.[43]

All of this seems to be a far cry from Kuhn's earlier claims which we have examined in some detail. Kuhn now claims that he simply means that there is no "neutral algorithm for theory-choice"[44] and not that "there are no good reasons" to prefer a theory.[45] It is certainly difficult to reconcile this more modest position with Kuhn's earlier, and more radical, claims that theory-choice is a matter of conversion rather than choice and that one cannot reason oneself from one paradigm to another.

Kuhn's explanation for his shift from his earlier, radical position to his apparently more moderate, current one is to be found in his introduction of the notion of *values* into the process of paradigm selection. In the Postscript which was added to the Second Edition of *The Structure of Scientific Revolutions,* he says,

> Nothing about that relatively familiar thesis [that theory-choice is not the result of a logical or mathematical proof] implies either that there are no good reasons for being persuaded or that those reasons are not

ultimately decisive for the group. Nor does it even imply that the reasons for choice are different from those usually listed by philosophers of science: accuracy, simplicity, fruitfulness, and the like.[46]

At this point, one might wonder what all the fuss has been about because Kuhn seems to be saying nothing terribly radical or controversial at all, and the stark contrast with his earlier remarks on the incommensurability of paradigms ought to be obvious. Kuhn seems to have given up the notion of incommensurability completely, but in fact, he wants to eat his cake and have it too. He wants to maintain the notion of incommensurability but in a much weakened form. Consequently, he adds,

> What it should suggest, however, is that such reasons function as *values* [my emphasis] and that they can thus be differently applied, individually and collectively, by men who concur in honoring them.[47]

What Kuhn now suggests is that scientists share certain "values" but that differences amongst paradigms are to be accounted for by the way in which those "values" are applied by different scientists within different paradigms. He says:

> Two men deeply committed to the *same values* [my emphasis] may nevertheless, in particular situations, make different choices [of paradigms] as, in fact, they do. But that difference in outcome ought not to suggest that the values scientists share are less than critically important either to their decisions or to the development of the enterprise in which they participate. Values like accuracy, consistency, and scope may prove ambiguous in application, both individually and collectively; they may, that is, be an insufficient basis for a *shared* algorithm of choice. But they do specify a great deal: what each scientist must consider in reaching a decision, what he may and may not consider relevant, and what he can legitimately be required to report as the basis for the choice he has made.[48]

Now it is extremely difficult to know what to make of these latest claims of Kuhn's. He appears to have reached the point where the earlier, radical and controversial claim of the incommensurability of paradigms has deteriorated into the claim that theory-choice is not the result of an algorithm. But, of course no one ever seriously maintained that it was. As we have seen, Charles Peirce did maintain that theory formation, or the formation of hypotheses, was the result of a reasoning process, which he called abduction, but he never claimed mathematical, deductive certainty for abduction nor did he ever manage to identify rules or principles of abduction. Richard Rorty understands Kuhn's denial of an algorithm of theory-choice as threatening all of epistemology since, according to his interpretation, the lack of such a mathematical procedure would indicate epistemology's inability to discover "the common ground of as much of human discourse as could be thought of as 'cognitive' or 'rational'."[49] But Rorty's dire projections for epistemology can be dismissed as the expression of relativistic zeal. There is absolutely no need to impose such strenuous requirements upon epistemology unless one adopts the geometrical model of Spinoza or the foundational model of Descartes. Otherwise, epistemology would have stopped after David Hume.

Kuhn's claim that values provide a person with a "good reason" for paradigm choice is unfathomable given that he still wishes to maintain the claim of incommensurability. As we have clearly seen, according to incommensurability, rules, principles, and criteria of paradigm evaluation are internal to paradigms, and if anything is going to be meaning variant—paradigm-dependent for meaning— the notion of what constitutes a "good reason" would be.[50]

In the above passage, Kuhn also indicates that people can now deliberate meaningfully about the different applications in different paradigms of their "shared values". But, as Harvey Siegel has observed, it is exactly this kind of deliberation which is prohibited by incommensurability.[51] Suppose, for example, that two people share the value of "consistency". How might a debate about different applications of this "shared value" be conducted? Well, the debate can be carried on only if the disputants share a commitment to the same rules and logical principles, and it is exactly these rules and principles which are supposed to be paradigm-relative given the thesis of incommensurability; so, again it seems, the thesis of incommensurability is self-defeating even in the guise of "values".

Finally, there appears to be nothing to be gained by the introduction of the notion of values. If accuracy and consistency are called "values", the suggestion is that they are to be regarded in the same category as something like social "utility"[52]—as something "subjective" and "relative" from which one might pick and choose. But consistency cannot be the same kind of "value" as social utility. Consider what is necessary for the kind of debate concerning incommensurability, of which this book is a part, to be waged. Certainly, nothing about social utility is necessary; however, without some agreement upon logical laws and rules which ensure consistency, no one can reasonably agree or disagree with another person. Similarly, for two scientists to agree or disagree about what Kuhn describes as the "application of shared values", requires a commitment to those same logical laws and principles. Calling such rules, laws and principles "values" suggests a subjectivity and relativity which is simply not present and obfuscates the difference between a paradigm-choice criterion like consistency and what one might agree to call a "value" of a paradigm such as social utility. If one allows Kuhn to include consistency within the same set of "values" of a paradigm as social utility, then the head of the relativists' camel is in the tent, and the case for relativism is much easier to make. So, it is at this point that one must resist Kuhn's claim that all criteria for evaluating theories are in the same bag of "values". What we have shown is that some "values" must be necessary and universal.

Others have made similar arguments. For example, Steven Lukes has insisted that some criteria for assessing rationality are universal, not paradigm-dependent,[53] and Martin Hollis has added that the kind of criteria for rationality which Lukes is talking about is not just universal but necessary.[54] That is, we are talking about a Kantian notion of absolute universality, not simply accidental or empirical universality. Our argument above has confirmed that there must be such necessary and absolute criteria of rationality. To borrow a favorite metaphor from both Kuhn and Norwood Hanson,[55] there may be many kinds of spectacles which do different things to one's perception which one might wear at different times, but there is one pair of spectacles which one can never take off, and that is simply to say that human reason is necessary and universal.

In summary, Kuhn's attempt to avoid the relativistic and irrationality consequences of his thesis of incommensurability by the introduction of the notion of "values" comes to nought. As Siegel concludes concerning Kuhn's attempt to avoid radical relativism, "it is difficult to take that denial [of the irrationality thesis] seriously, in light of his reluctance to give up the incommensurability thesis, his hedging over the status of reasons, and his continued descriptions of theory choices as gestalt switches and conversion experiences."[56]

KUHN AND HERMENEUTICS

Another way of understanding Kuhn is to see him as involved in a hermeneutical reading of the history of science; indeed, Kuhn himself indicates an autobiographical sympathy with a hermeneutical approach by his example of a hermeneutical reading of Aristotle's theory of motion. Aristotelian scholars have long been perplexed about how one of the recognized geniuses of human thought could believe so many ridiculous and completely mistaken things about motion. Finally, Kuhn tells us, he discovered a way of reading Aristotle which explained the earlier "perplexities".

> For the first time I gave due weight to the fact that Aristotle's subject was change-of-quality in general, including both the fall of a stone and the growth of a child to adulthood. In his physics, the subject that was to become mechanics was at best a still-not-quite-isolable special case. More consequential was my recognition that the permanent ingredients of Aristotle's universe, its ontologically primary and indestructible elements, were not material bodies but rather the qualities which, when imposed on some portion of omnipresent neutral matter, constituted an individual material body or substance.[57]

Illustrated in Kuhn's reading of Aristotle is his earlier denial of the possibility of any "neutral algorithm for theory choice" or any "systematic decision procedure" which must lead different individuals to the same decision. Clearly, it seems, Kuhn abandoned reading Aristotle in such a way so that he was applying the "algorithm" of Newtonian mechanics. His "insight" into Aristotle and into how a man with such a brilliant mind could make such apparently absurd claims seems to parallel the "lightning flash" of intuitive insight which accounts for a change in paradigm view. And, in a way, Kuhn has undergone a "change in view" in his reading of Aristotle so he now, in some fashion, "sees the world" as Aristotle did.

Kuhn goes on to explicitly advocate a hermeneutical reading of scientific works. He offers the following maxim for trying to understand the history of science:

> When reading the works of an important thinker, look first for the apparent absurdities in the text and ask yourself how a sensible person could have written them. When you find an answer, . . . when those passages make sense, then you may find that more central passages, ones you previously thought you understood, have changed their meaning.[58]

The form of post-modernism arising from hermeneutics and the challenge to the traditional understanding of human reason and scientific method from hermeneutics requires attention in some detail. I now turn to an investigation into that "continental" or hermeneutic tradition.

WINCH AND GADAMER ON THE SOCIAL SCIENCES, HERMENEUTICS, AND RELATIVISM

THE NATURE OF THE SOCIAL SCIENCES

We have seen in the previous chapter how Kuhn's *Structure of Scientific Revolutions* proved to be a major catalyst for prompting the current critical re-examination of traditional epistemology and science. Two other works, which have proven to be of major importance within the tradition of hermeneutics, appeared at about the same time as Kuhn's book. These are *The Idea of a Social Science and Its Relation to Philosophy* by Peter Winch[1] and Hans-Georg Gadamer's *Truth and Method.*[2] As we shall see, these two books were as responsible for generating methodological concerns within the social sciences and hermeneutics as was Kuhn's book for generating the same kind of methodological concerns within the analytic philosophy of science. Since both Winch's work and Gadamer's hermeneutics have been responsible for a particular variety of the current relativism which now abounds in the social sciences, I will first examine Winch's views concerning the social sciences and then look at the hermeneutical accounts of understanding and interpretation of Gadamer and Jürgen Habermas.

As we have seen earlier, the social sciences, in their infancy, very explicitly adopted the methodology and techniques of the "empirical", natural sciences. The earliest model for studying and understanding the differences amongst different cultures was Darwinian evolutionary theory which anthropology borrowed from biology. Along with the general scientific approach borrowed from the natural sciences came all of the hidden epistemological assumptions of traditional science—the epistemological underpinnings of modern philosophy. These include the dichotomy between knowing subject and known object and the desirability of objective, unbiased knowledge. During their early, formative years when the social sciences were still searching for their identity as sciences, an approximation to natural science was universally considered to be the only avenue for examining the various aspects of human culture which are the subject matter of the social sciences.

Winch is responsible for offering an analysis of the nature of the social sciences which places them in sharp contrast with the natural sciences. Instead of trying to duplicate or emulate the natural sciences, Winch argues that the social sciences ought to embrace a very different kind of methodology—a methodology which abandons all pretense of objectivity and leads to a radical relativism.

One of the standard and "informal" criticisms of analytic philosophy has been that it is "dry"—artifical and "only about language". Analytic philosophers have been viewed as "nit-picking" linguists who have nothing to say about the important philosophical issues by which people live their lives. Winch must be credited with generating potentially revolutionary consequences for the social sciences by applying what is straightforward, analytic philosophy—linguistic analysis of the first order—to issues in social science.

Using as his point of departure the later Wittgenstein's development of language games and forms of life in the *Philosophical Investigations,* Winch sharply separates the social sciences from the natural sciences. He abandons the notion of a unified and formalist account of science which includes the social sciences just as Wittgenstein abandoned the essentialist notion of meaning and the notion of a formal, logical language. Winch draws the parallels between the variety of different language games and the plethora of different social practices by arguing that since both are rule governed, meaning and understanding must be relative to the context— whether it be linguistic or social. Indeed, for Winch, the notion of "social" comes to include some grounding in a particular set of social practices, a particular Wittgensteinian "form of life".

All of this means that "research" in the social sciences, and any understanding of different social practices in different cultures which might follow from it, are not the results of the "scientific method" of the natural sciences. The data available to the social scientist always require some interpretation and any understanding of different social practices must be relative to a particular language game and the underlying form of life. Winch concludes that there is an essential, "subjective" and interpretive element in sociology and anthropology which cannot be eliminated, and by thus using a straightforward analytic argument, Winch finds his way to a hermeneutic-style understanding of the social sciences.

THE SOCIAL SCIENCES AND RATIONALITY

For many, the path from Winch's analysis of social science to a radical relativism is short, straight, and wide. If understanding and interpretation of all social practices are subjective and relative, then what is not? As Richard Bernstein points out,

> Winch seems to be suggesting that forms of life may be so radically different from each other that in order to understand and interpret alien or primitive societies we not only have to bracket our prejudices and biases but have to suspend our own Western standards and criteria of rationality. We may be confronted with standards of rationality about beliefs and actions that are incompatible with or incommensurable with our standards.[3]

The stakes have suddenly been escalated to the point that from Winch's concerns about the notion of "social" and about the methodology of the social sciences, we have moved to an examination of our notions of "rationality" and "human reason". Indeed, Winch goes on to say,

> the forms in which rationality expresses itself in the culture of a human society cannot be elucidated *simply* in terms of the logical coherence of the rules according to which activities are carried out in that society. For . . . there comes a point where we are not even in a position to determine what is and what is not coherent in such a context of rules, without raising questions about the point which following those rules has in the society.[4]

In other words, an observer is not in a position to impose his or her own standards of rationality upon a different culture in order to try and understand it since there will always come a point where one must determine what counts as following the rules which set the context for rationality in that particular culture. Winch, cavalierly juxtaposing the early and later Wittgenstein, insists that since "the limits of my language mean the limits of my world" and since there are many different languages, then each of us is faced with limitations of our understanding—limitations which are rooted in our language and "form of rationality".[5] The main issue, according to Winch, becomes one concerned with differences in *criteria of ration-*

ality. Any time we talk about standards or criteria of rationality, we are to ask, "Whose?"[6] To complete Winch's analogy to Wittgenstein's notion of games and the rule-governed nature of language, we might say that the main issue becomes whether there is a single game of rationality with a single set of rules or whether there are different games of rationality with different rules. Winch's position is clear: He says that "intelligibility takes many and varied forms". There is, he continues, no "norm for intelligibility in general".[7]

THE AZANDE AND RATIONALITY

The controversy can be clearly seen in the exchange which has taken place between Winch and Alasdair MacIntyre about E. E. Evans-Pritchard's research concerning the African Azande's use of magic.[8] The Azande practice what Winch and Evans-Pritchard identify as *witchcraft,* the belief in the power to influence the course of events through "mystical" means. This practice is frequently manifested in terms of oracles which the Azande use to direct their lives. Winch says, "A Zande would be utterly lost and bewildered without his oracle. The mainstay of his life would be lacking."[9] According to Winch, oracles function for the Azande in much the same way as mathematical calculations or clocks function in modern American society.[10] How are we to *understand* and make intelligible this facet of the life of the Azande? The Azande *see* the same events that we would see, but they see them *as* events controlled by witchcraft. Their understanding of causality and why and how events occur is so different from that of modern science that it appears to be very difficult to make any sense at all of the practice.

When the question of the intelligibility of the Azande's practice of witchcraft is raised, Winch argues that the first thing that we must consider is the question of *to whom* the question is being put. If we relativize intelligibility itself, then we might answer that witchcraft is intelligible to the Azande when it is not, relative to modern American culture. Our ways of explaining why and how events occur might be just as unintelligible to them. Their ways are not our ways, and our ways are not theirs. If the non-relativist persists by arguing that even relative to Azande thought their practice of witchcraft is fraught with *contradiction,* Winch concludes that since the basic epistemological notions of evidence, confirmation, and contradiction differ from our culture to the Azande's, such comparisons and such objections to trans-cultural criteria of rationality are not possible according to Winch.[11]

LANGUAGE GAMES

It is at this point that Winch introduces his now well-known use of Wittgenstein's notion of language games. Just as Wittgenstein abandoned his beliefs in essentialism and the possibility of any universal character of language or any general form of propositions for the non-essentialism and irreducible variety of language games, so, Winch says, ought we to abandon any single essentialist notion of rationality. If we follow this line of reasoning, then we realize that every society has some form of rationality which is imposed by its language, according to Winch, since the use of language means that there must be a right way and a wrong way of saying things, but different societies might have different norms of rationality. Every society must appeal to some norm of rationality, but these norms might well differ from one society to another, and the best that we can ever do is to talk about "our standards and yours".[12] Thus, for Winch, in any discussion concerning rationality, "it is obviously of first importance to be clear about *whose* concept of rationality is being alluded to", since "something can appear rational to someone only in terms of *his* understanding of what is and is not rational".[13] For this reason, Winch concludes that trans-cultural rational criticism is precluded, and understanding and intelligible interpretation are culturally relative.

Although there are still some gaps to be filled in, this is the rough outline of one of the routes which has led through the social sciences to relativistic positions concerning rationality and human reason. There is much to be gained from paying close attention to the lesson which Wittgenstein taught us and of which Winch reminds us—not to look for essentials where essentials do not exist; however, Winch's position goes far beyond this fundamental Wittgensteinian maxim. Winch grossly distorts Wittgenstein's original notions of language game and form of life.

Let us begin an examination of Winch's claims by comparing the magic of the Azande with something in modern American Culture with which we are more familiar. Consider Christian and Jewish religious believers who believe that god is immanent in the course of human events; in other words, they believe that god acts causally to produce or alter events. Such a belief might be manifested on a grand scale such as by believing that god directed the people of Israel out of Egypt and into the promised land, or it might be manifested on a much more limited scale by a person believing in the power of prayer to save the life of a loved one who is in danger. Such a belief is still very common in modern American society as evidenced by the accounts given by survivors of such disasters as plane crashes, hurricanes and earthquakes. Now on Winch's account of rationality with different norms of rationality tied to different language games, the Azande and the Christians and Jews would obviously have different standards of rationality since they are obviously playing different language games.

RATIONALITY AND BEHAVIOR

I wish to argue that there is a basic notion of rationality common to the Azande, the Christians, and the Jews—a notion of rationality which provides the essence of human rationality and which is ignored in Winch's position. The clue to the existence of such a common, fundamental notion is provided by Winch himself when he says that "[a] Zande would be utterly lost and bewildered without his oracle. The mainstay of his life would be lacking".[14] Suppose for a moment that the Christian and the Jew are equally religious so that their religious beliefs provide the "mainstay" of their lives and that they also would be "lost and bewildered" without their religious beliefs. Now, obviously there is something different going on in each case. The Azande attribute causal efficacy to magical potions or incantations, while the Jews attribute such power to Yahweh, while the Christians do the same thing with (let us say for the sake of as much variety as possible) Christ. However, there must also be something which the three share in common. In what sense can a person's belief, whatever the content of the belief, actually influence that person's behavior or understanding of the world? A belief must always preclude other beliefs. A belief which leads to one course of action must preclude other courses of action. A belief which leads to one understanding of the world must preclude other understandings of the world.

If a Zande uses an oracle to decide any issue upon which to predicate any behavior or understanding, it can only be because the oracle is not consistent with all possible behavior and all possible understandings. A Zande cannot act on the basis of an oracle and not act on it at the same time and in the same respect. If the oracle is to

be the "mainstay" of the lives of the Azande, and if this means that the oracles are to provide some means for deciding some behavior (such as avoiding dangers) or arriving at some understanding (such as fixing blame), then this can only be because certain behaviors and understandings are consistent with or implied by the oracle while others are not.

Winch anticipates something like my argument and correctly identifies the main issue as one involving the notion of *contradiction*.[15] Winch insists that if we press the question about the consistency of the Azande's beliefs, we are simply revealing the prejudices of our own norms of rationality. Since, according to Winch, the Azande do not treat their oracles in the same manner as scientists treat scientific hypotheses[16] and since they do not press their thinking about oracles to the point where they would become involved in contradictions,[17] the issue of logical consistency is a non-issue.

Apparent contradictions are explained away or the Azande apparently refuse to consider them; they simply refuse to apply logical rules or epistemological principles to their beliefs. But might we not say the same thing about some Christian or Jewish religious believers? If we point out to the Christian, for example, that the belief that Jesus was both divine and human at the same time involves what is apparently a blatant contradiction, there is a standard response according to which some religious believers simply "bracket" the religious belief, set it aside as a special case, and just refuse to apply logic to this particular belief. The problem of the consistency of belief systems arises then not simply in the context of comparing different cultures but within a particular culture. What are we to say about this kind of situation?

Winch deals with the problem of contradiction within the Azande belief system by insisting that the oracular revelations are not the kind of beliefs about which one can reasonably raise the problem of consistency, and he claims that to insist that the issue of the consistency of beliefs be pursued to its logical conclusion is to be guilty of "misunderstanding" and "a category-mistake".[18] He explains that the Azande's beliefs about the oracles "are not a matter of intellectual interest but the main way in which Azande decide how they should act".[19] This suggestion amounts to a kind of bracketing where a person simply separates a certain sub-set of beliefs and refuses to apply the same standards or rules to that sub-set as is applied to the remainder of the system of beliefs. It may be possible to do such bracketing with beliefs upon which no behavior is predicated. However, I have shown that this cannot be done with any set of beliefs which serves as the basis for any possible action on the part of the individual, but, according to Winch, this is exactly what the beliefs about oracles are supposed to do for the Azande.

We are concerned here with beliefs upon which a person is willing to act. Any such belief which functions in a manner to direct a person's behavior or to provide an understanding of the world upon which a person is willing to act can do so only because it excludes other behavior and other understandings. A Zande might refuse to pursue a thorough epistemological examination of all of his or her beliefs, but a Zande cannot both act on an oracle and not act on it. For any person to act intentionally, for any person to plan his or her behavior, for any person to act in such a way to pursue certain ends, for any person to act to satisfy certain desires, one course of action must be inconsistent with others. For example, suppose one is warned not to journey by a certain route because of some possible danger. Now it really does not matter whether this warning comes from an oracle or from the National Weather Service; the way in which the belief functions to direct a person's behavior is the same. *If a person holds a certain belief,* then, on the meta-belief level, there must be ways in which that belief excludes other beliefs, and there must be ways in which that belief is tied to specific behavior. Winch fails to recognize that a game with an inconsistent set of rules is the same as a game with no rules. An inconsistent set of beliefs excludes no behavior—any behavior is just as likely as any other behavior to bring about a desired result. This simply means that, in such a situation, a person could not act intentionally, and, in such a situation, a person could not act rationally.

UNIVERSAL CRITERIA OF RATIONALITY

Martin Hollis and Steven Lukes have also argued for a universal, commonly shared set of beliefs and inferences.[20] For example, Hollis has claimed that all interpretation is based upon "rationality assumptions", assumptions about some set of beliefs shared by all people. This set of commonly shared beliefs which provides the basis for all rationality and, at the same time, a "bridgehead" for interpreting one culture from the standpoint of another "consists of what a rational man cannot fail to believe in simple perceptual situations, organized by rules of coherent judgment, which a rational man cannot fail to subscribe to".[21] Lukes distinguishes between two senses of "rationality"; one is universal and applicable in all contexts and for all peoples while the other is context-dependent and varies from society to society. Universal criteria of rationality are "criteria of rationality that simply *are* criteria of rationality".[22]

There are two distinct concerns here. One concern is the criteria of rationality used in interpreting another culture; the other is the criteria of rationality operative in the other culture. The question of the criteria of rationality used in interpreting another society is primarily a problem of social science; the problem of the criteria used in different societies is primarily a problem of epistemology. Although my interests here are primarily epistemological, I maintain that there must be universal criteria of rationality, in Lukes's sense, in both the epistemological and social science contexts. We have already seen, in Chapter 2, that in the case of the issues raised by Quine's theory of ontological relativity, the issues are genuine problems only if there is some presumed logical universality. Different possible interpretations or translations are recognizably different only if one interpretation excludes another or conflicts with another, and interpretations can exclude or conflict only by assuming logical relationships. I concluded there that Quine's ontological relativity can succeed only if his logical relativity does not. The same conclusion applies to any question of interpretation of another society. Interpretations of different societies are possible only given certain universal logical criteria of rationality which are not relative to those different societies.

BARNES AND BLOOR AND RATIONALITY

Ironically, then, attempts to argue for relativism by arguing for indeterminacy in translations or interpretations are arguments for the universally shared criteria of rationality for judgments. For example, to bolster their claim of radical relativism, Barry Barnes and David Bloor use the example of how the word 'yakt' is employed by the Karam in New Guinea.[23] While one might initially think that 'yakt' might be translated as 'bird', they tell us, the fact that bats are counted as yakt and cassowaries are not complicates the situation. Barnes and Bloor use this example and others like it to conclude that particulars of perceptual experience "are ordered into clusters and patterns *specific to a culture*"[24] and that hence, there is not a "bridgehead" of commonly shared perceptual experience in Hollis's sense. Yet, how is it that one would ever come to be in a position to determine that different interpretations of 'yakt' conflict? Why can 'bird' not be understood to include bats? Why can 'yakt' not be understood to include bats and not include them at the same time? Different possible interpretations are *different* only because of the assumed, underlying universal criteria of rationality.

The second issue is whether there are universal, commonly shared criteria of rationality in all societies. It is here that the epistemological issue and the conflict between epistemology and Winch's form of relativism are brought into focus most sharply. I have already argued above that there must be such universal criteria for any rational behavior on the basis of belief, but let me here respond to two points made by Barnes and Bloor. First, Barnes and Bloor object that the claim for universal criteria of rationality based in the form of inferences or "rules of coherent judgment" is spurious since deductive inferences cannot be justified. In defense of their position they use Lewis Carroll's clever dialogue, 'What the Tortoise Said to Achilles'.[25] They conclude that the tortoise demonstrates that any attempt at the justification of deduction fails since "justifications of deductions themselves presuppose deduction".[26] According to Barnes and Bloor, the defender of universal criteria of rationality is in the "predicament" of having to admit that "[w]e have reached the end-point at which justification goes in a circle".[27]

The "predicament" which Barnes and Bloor describe is only the predicament of the rational person. Justification of deduction does presuppose deduction, but so does all justification. *'Justification'* means a process which can take place only within a certain context, and it is the laws and principles of deduction which create that context. It is the tortoise and not Achilles which is in the "predicament" since, as I have shown elsewhere, absolutely nothing follows from the tortoise's position without assuming the very logical law which is at stake.[28] The same is true of Barnes and Bloor. Consider the various things which they have to say about this matter. They say, "We have reached the end-point at which justification goes in a circle" and "The attempt at justification fails" and "[J]ustifications of deductions themselves presuppose deduction" and "They [justifications] are circular".[29] Absolutely none of these conclusions follows from the tortoise's position in Carroll's dialogue without assuming the very rule of inference which the tortoise (and Barnes and Bloor) are challenging. Each claim supposedly follows from some argument such as, 'If Carroll is right that the laws of deduction cannot be proved, then all justification of deduction is circular. Carroll is right. Therefore, all justification of deduction is circular'. But any such claim about the "predicament" of deductive logic based upon

Carroll's dialogue follows only if we use the same rule of inference which is being attacked; thus, Barnes and Bloor's position is self-defeating. Any *argument* against the "bridgehead" must confirm the very rules of inference and forms of judgment upon which the claim for such a bridgehead is based. If Barnes and Bloor really think that the tortoise has demonstrated that the rules of logic cannot be proved, then they, like him, must simply say nothing.[30]

There is one final point about the issue of universally shared, common forms of judgments. Consider any person S who holds any belief B as the result of whatever method or upon whatever grounds one might choose—science, oracle, witchcraft, or voodoo. Let us call the method which produces B, M. Now suppose we ask how it is that S comes to believe that B is the result of M. If B is to be a belief upon which this person predicates any behavior whatsoever, then, as I have argued, both B and not-B cannot both follow from M (at the same time, under the same conditions, and so forth). Consequently, there must be some mechanism, some warrant, some criterion c by which S determines that B follows from M. Perhaps c is simply the recognition and implicit acknowledgment of an authority, or perhaps it is a certain ritual or procedure, or perhaps it is the application of a particular method to certain data. But whatever c is, S must be able to reason, 'If c, then B follows from M and if not-c, then B does not follow from M'. *This* is the force of Wittgenstein's famed call for the necessity of a criterion or rules. As we shall see in Chapter 7, it is the ability to provide such a criterion which sets the scientific method aside as unique. On the meta-oracle level, the Azande must be able to determine when a belief is based upon an oracle and when it is not, and to do this, there must be some criterion or set of conditions for assessing oracles, to distinguish legitimate oracles from illegitimate ones. This process of distinguishing legitimate from illegitimate oracles must be possible since, as Winch tells us, the oracles constitute the "mainstay" of the lives of the Azande and are the source of the beliefs upon which they act. But such a process is possible only because the kind of rules and form of judgment which Winch denies are operative are indeed operating on the meta-oracle level.

INFERENCE AND MEANINGS OF WORDS

Secondly, Barnes and Bloor maintain that because rules of inference depend upon the meanings of logical words (that is, semantics) any claim to universality has been "completely devastated" by A. N. Prior's demonstration that different logical connectives with different meanings would justify different inferences.[31] Consider, for example, the new logical connective 'tonk'. Prior defines 'tonk' in the following manner:

> Its meaning is completely given by the rule that (i) from any statement P we can infer any statement formed by joining P to any statement Q by 'tonk' (which compound statement we hereafter describe as 'the statement P-tonk-Q'), and that (ii) from any 'contonktive' statement P-tonk-Q we can infer the contained statement Q.[32]

Defining 'tonk' in this manner means that from any statement we can infer any other statement, and Barnes and Bloor conclude from this example that we cannot use "rules and meanings" to justify intuitions about validity since we must rely upon our intuitions to prove that 'and' is an acceptable logical connective and 'tonk' is not. However, one need not rely upon intuition to prove that 'tonk' is an unacceptable logical connective. One cannot act upon inferences using 'tonk'. No belief could direct any behavior using 'tonk'. One could not act intentionally in an attempt to bring about any intended state of affairs, to satisfy any need or to pursue any end. No society—no matter how disparate from our own—can exist in which inferences based upon 'tonk' are performed and acted upon or relied upon for an understanding of the world. There are rules and forms of judgment which are rational simply because they are, and the proposed rule using 'tonk' is not among them. We must use *these* common rules and forms of judgment even to understand the intended meaning of 'tonk'.

Prior concludes that "the forms in which rationality expresses itself in the culture of a human society cannot be elucidated *simply* in terms of the logical coherence of the rules according to which activities are carried out in that society."[33] However, this is exactly the ground upon which rationality can be elucidated in *any* society. Winch claims that "there comes a point where we are not even in a position to determine what is and what is not coherent in such a context or rules, without raising questions about the point which following those rules has in the society."[34] Well, of course, there may come a point where an observer cannot determine what is and what is not coherent, but we can rest assured that if beliefs are to direct behavior, they must be coherent, and they must be coherent in the same manner and according to the same rules as we count logical coherence. A person cannot act upon a simultaneously held set of inconsistent beliefs.

Winch accuses Evans-Pritchard of introducing the notion of a "reality" revealed by science in an *ad hoc* manner as a way of avoiding what Winch takes to be the basic relativistic aspect of rationality. Winch argues that the notion of reality cannot be used to distinguish between science and mysticism since some conception of reality must be presupposed before we can make any sense of the notion of "what science reveals to be the case".[35] However, as we shall see in Chapter 7, it is not necessary to presuppose any pre-methodological notion of reality if, following Charles Peirce, one defends the *method* of science as intrinsically rational. It is the method of science rather than any presupposed notion of reality which brings an end to relativism.

MacIntyre comes close to making the same point against Winch, but MacIntyre does not press his point hard enough. MacIntyre insists that there are cases where one can use one's own standards of rationality to "criticize" what people in a different society do since it is only through such process of criticism that we are able to determine that there are difficult cases of apparent conflict between different standards of intelligibility.[36]

DIFFERENT STANDARDS OF RATIONALITY

While I certainly agree with MacIntyre on this point, Winch can still maintain his relativism if he concedes that there may be some such cases as MacIntyre describes but still claim that the process of "criticizing" and trans-cultural interpretation must always come to an end at some point. The proper question is not whether there are cases such as the ones which MacIntyre describes, but whether there are ever any ones which Winch describes—the cases "where we are not even in a position to determine what is and what is not coherent".[37] The proper answer clearly seems to be that it simply all depends upon what one means by 'intelligibility' and 'rational'. If one means something such as 'Well, one cannot *really* understand what it is like to believe in magic unless one is a Zande', then one would have to admit that there is a sense of 'understand' or 'make intelligible' where this would be true. This is a loose and informal sense of 'making sense' which is captured in the old adage that one cannot really understand another person unless one walks a mile in that person's moccasins. There is definitely a sense in which we can all learn a great deal from a study of other cultures by putting aside our prejudices and trying to understand the different culture in a fresh manner, without imposing our own beliefs upon the beliefs of the other culture. But even on this level, Winch does not provide any direction or guidelines about how we are to do this. As Richard Bernstein points out, "Even if we concede everything that Winch wants to claim about how we can learn from the study of alien cultures and forms of life, he has not given us the slightest clue about what *critical* standards we are to employ in doing this".[38] In the absence of any guidelines for how one is supposed to manage to study different cultures with their different "norms" of rationality, it appears that one would have to rely upon the "blinding flash" of insight, the gestalt shift, described by Thomas Kuhn, which accompanies a paradigm shift. We have already examined, in the previous chapter, the bankruptcy of such a claim; however, it appears particularly difficult to make out exactly how one would ever be in a position to say anything intelligible about another culture if this is what Winch has in mind. It seems that one would always either be in one culture with one set of norms operating or in another culture with a different set of norms operating with never the twain meeting. This approach seems to eliminate social science altogether.

When the level of controversy is the basic, fundamental one of strict, logical consistency, then we must say that the process of toleration of differences comes to an end. If we press MacIntyre's objection to Winch to its "logical conclusion," we see that any set of beliefs which are used to direct behavior and any social practices which are governed by rules must be logically consistent. Indeed, this is exactly what Wittgenstein meant by insisting that language is rule-governed. The force of the rules is to establish a context within which the possibility of error and hence, the notion of correct and incorrect usage, become possible. Any such context must be logically consistent, and on this level of logical consistency, relativism comes to an end.

HERMENEUTICS AND RATIONALITY

Winch's treatment of the social sciences is an attack upon the direct opposition between epistemology and sociology which one finds in traditional epistemology. An attack upon this same sharp distinction between traditional epistemology (including the nature of knowledge and the notions of reason, arguments, evidence, and epistemological warrant) and sociology, history, and particular cultural and social characteristics lies at the very center of philosophical hermeneutics. For example, Aristotle said, "Man is a rational animal." Now if we eliminate the sexism and paraphrase this as something like "human beings are rational animals", we get a clear, essentialist claim about the nature of human beings. This is a claim which Aristotle intends to be true of human beings as a species (at least in our non-sexist translation). It is a claim which is supposed to transcend time and place. Thus, though there may be some debate about whether this characterization of human nature is accurate, the approach is to try and determine a general, essential characterization of the species, human being, in the abstract—devoid of particular location in space and time. If a person wants to know anything about human beings, the proper route is to try and gain knowledge of this abstract, general essence. Thus, we get one classical picture of human beings and human endeavor being essentially epistemological.

Heidegger, by contrast, maintained that human beings are essentially historical—that the very nature of human beings is tied to the historical processes and development through which we came to be whatever it is that we are. According to Heidegger, any attempt to derive some general, completely abstract characterization of human being—or any related notion such as knowledge, reason or truth—is completely misguided. For Heidegger, there is no essential aspect to human nature which transcends particular, historical situations; rather, human nature and all human endeavor are essentially historical. The study of history and the place of human beings in history (historicity) takes on an important ontological role for Heidegger since human nature and one's being are determined by their place in history. The basis for all human understanding thus shifts from epistemology to historicity.[39]

HISTORICITY AND METHOD

Given the shift from epistemology to historicity, the nature of historical inquiry and human understanding, the *method* of historicity, becomes a matter of primary concern, and Hans-Georg Gadamer's *Truth and Method* is more responsible for shaping the philosophical hermeneutical critique of method than any other single work. Gadamer's focus in *Truth and Method* is upon history, literature, and art; however, given the usual German division between the natural sciences and the *human sciences* (including what Americans and British call the humanities and social sciences), the application of Gadamer's critique to the other social sciences has been direct and immediate.

Gadamer's critique of method is focussed upon the kind of epistemological method generated by modern philosophy generally and by Descartes in particular. One of the most significant characteristics of this method, according to Gadamer, is the way in which it both generates and is dependent upon dichotomies which separate and divide the universe in an arbitrary and unjustified manner. For example, consider the distinctions between knowing subject and known object, self and others, and experience and reality. Consider also the kinds of epistemological issues to which these distinctions have given rise—conditions for knowledge, the problem of other minds, and theories of perception. Such distinctions are the result of our "alienation" from the natural world, according to Gadamer, and are the result of the industrial revolution and the imposition of the model of the natural sciences upon the human sciences. What should be normal parts of our experience and nature such as our connection with the past and with others get artificially objectified and are relinquished to the role of "data" to be studied or collected or researched.[40] In order to impose the distinctions which are necessary for epistemology, we must impose (or presuppose) distinctions upon our experience and nature which separate and isolate us—from nature, from art and literature, and from history. Thus, method originates from a process of alienation and fragmentation which is most evident in the way in which the natural sciences claim to produce knowledge of an aspect or process in nature "only when we are able to reproduce it artificially".[41] For Gadamer, method creates a need for itself by first artificially separating people from the parts of their existences which ought to be familiar and natural and then proffering itself as the only way of bridging the gap and overcoming the separation; however, Gadamer claims, the attempt to use epistemology to re-establish the unity of experience is doomed to failure. Joel Weinsheimer captures this aspect of Gadamer's critique nicely:

> Like nature, art and history no longer belong to us, nor we to them [after the introduction of method]. They no longer belong to the *selbstverständlich:* the things which are to us self-understandable, self-evident matters of course. Method, then, aims to redeem this loss by substituting itself for the kind of understanding that is not reflective knowledge because it understands everything in advance by belonging to it, before knowing and its methodological regulation come into play. But the paradox of the substitute is operative here as elsewhere: method famishes the very craving for homecoming that it is designed to satisfy.[42]

According to Gadamer, we must abandon what Richard Rorty calls "the desire for constraint and confrontation",[43] artificially imposed by epistemology, and give ourselves to hermeneutical *understanding*. Since the time of Plato at least, knowledge has been contrasted with opinion, and at least one of the crucial differences has been that knowledge has been understood to be objective and based upon evidence and rules which can be identified, explained, and scrutinized while opinion is subjective and based upon prejudice and biases. Since the fundamental purpose of epistemology is to establish method as a way of objectifying experience and providing some way of analyzing it and justifying it, the imposition of method upon experience results in the cancellation of its natural origin and history. According to natural science, Gadamer says,

> Experience is valid only if it is confirmed; hence its dignity depends on its fundamental repeatability. But this means that experience, by its very nature, abolishes its history. This is true even of everyday experience, and how much more for any scientific version of it.[44]

The main problem with knowledge based on the model of the natural sciences, according to Gadamer, is that it "tolerates no restriction of its claim to universality".[45] Others, as we shall see, turn Gadamer's claims for philosophical hermeneutics upon the natural sciences as well as the human sciences; however, Gadamer's main criticism of epistemology and method is its claim to universality. As Weinsheimer aptly describes it, "the fundamental hubris of method [according to Gadamer] consists in its presumption that it exhausts the sphere of truth".[46] This blanket claim of universality is what Hesse calls the "imperialism" of empiricist philosophy of science.[47] But, Gadamer insists, method and the natural sciences do not exhaust truth.

HERMENEUTICS VERSUS EPISTEMOLOGY

For Gadamer, it is through philosophical hermeneutics and the human sciences that we are able to explore the understanding of experience independent of the "idealization" imposed upon it by method and the natural sciences.[48] Hermeneutics "goes beyond the limits that the concept of method sets to modern science".[49]

> It [hermeneutics] is concerned to seek that experience of truth that transcends the sphere of the control of scientific method wherever it is to be found, and to inquire into its legitimacy. Hence the human sciences are joined with modes of experience which lie outside science: with the

experiences of philosophy, of art, and of history itself. These are all modes of experience in which a truth is communicated that cannot be verified by the methodological means proper to science.[50]

Gadamer thus attempts to circumscribe the limitations of science and the kind of truth dependent upon the method of the natural sciences. Science is seen as having no monopoly on truth, and Gadamer sets out to "legitimize an avenue to truth that lies outside and in opposition to the methodological control of the natural sciences".[51]

As it is for Heidegger, historical knowledge, for Gadamer, is fundamental to all understanding and possesses an ontological efficacy for determining the very nature of human beings. Part of what makes us what we are is our understanding of our history and our place in it. Each generation's understanding (in each culture) of itself and of all of the various cultural institutions and beliefs and values are filtered through a hermeneutical understanding of its history. As different texts from the past are interpreted differently by different generations in different cultures, they produce effects upon the present generation and culture; they develop a *tradition*. For Gadamer, these current effects are a part of the meaning of the texts. What develops is a reciprocal causal conditioning where a current reading and interpretation of a text is conditioned by the text and the meaning of the text is conditioned by the present interpretation.

Gadamer insists that it is a mistake to characterize hermeneutical understanding as attempting any kind of reconstruction of some original meaning of the author. Such an understanding of the nature of hermeneutics amounts to a re-introduction of the artificial distinctions of method—knowing subject and known object, for example. Understanding essentially involves interpretation which cannot be reduced to knowledge in a traditional sense. Gadamer emphasizes the mutual importance of the original text and current interpretation to understanding:

> [I]t is undoubtedly true that, compared with the genuine hermeneutical experience that understands the meaning of the text, the reconstruction of what the author really had in mind is a limited undertaking. It is the seduction of historicism to see in this kind of reduction a scientific virtue and regard understanding as a kind of reconstruction which in effect repeats the process of how the text came into being. Hence it [the reconstruction of original meaning] follows the ideal familiar to us from our knowledge of nature.[52]

Hermeneutical understanding is never "mere reconstruction" of some original meaning;[53] it always includes the "historical self-mediation of present and tradition".[54] Thus, according to historicity, and in contrast to Aristotle, the only essence of human beings is that there is no essence. The nature of human beings is ontologically determined by the historical situation in which we exist, and any understanding of that historical situation will always involve the interplay of "subjective" prejudices and tradition.

Most critics agree that Gadamer did not intend to undermine or replace the traditional view of science. The objectivity of traditional scientific inquiry is part of a particular kind of enquiry and is thus part of a particular tradition. The aim of Gadamer's philosophical hermeneutics is not to directly challenge such a claim to objectivity but simply to show its limitations.[55] The objectivity of traditional natural science cannot be demonstrated by its own method, according to Gadamer; so, if we attempt any justification or understanding of the objectivity in the natural sciences, we must acknowledge the necessity of our commitment to tradition (interpretation).[56]

SCIENCE AND LEGITIMATION

The move from a limited theory of hermeneutics which applies in the human sciences to a more general theory which applies in all fields of human inquiry is a quick and easy one for some philosophers. When hermeneutics is turned into a general, radical theory, it becomes the antithesis of epistemology and scientific knowledge. For example, Richard Rorty says,

> [H]ermeneutics is an expression of hope that the cultural space left by the demise of epistemology will not be filled—that our culture should become one in which the demand for constraint and confrontation is no longer felt. The notion that there is a permanent neutral framework whose "structure" philosophy can display is the notion that the objects to be confronted by the mind, or the rules which constrain inquiry, are common to all discourse, or at least to every discourse on a given topic. Thus epistemology proceeds on the assumption that all contributions to a given discourse are commensurable. Hermeneutics is largely a struggle against this assumption.[57]

Jean-François Lyotard also sees in *postmodern* philosophical hermeneutics a general and radical end to epistemology. Lyotard insists that the *modern* notion of knowledge as based upon some grand, legitimizing 'metanarrative' has been replaced; in particular, the Enlightenment's view of a metanarrative of "possible unanimity between rational minds"[58] which legitimizes knowledge is just an example of "cultural imperialism".[59] Even Jürgen Habermas's view that truth is ultimately the result of consensus through discourse is not radical enough for Lyotard because, he claims, since Habermas ignores the "heteromorphous" nature of language games, his view is "outmoded and suspect".[60] According to Lyotard, postmodern culture is characterized by the loss of credibility of the grand narrative[61] —by a complete loss of confidence in the ability of any grand narrative to legitimize science and knowledge. In Lyotard's criticism, we find implicitly the recognition of the failure of the positivists' program of distinguishing science from metaphysics, as a contributing factor in the development of his radical form of hermeneutics.

Lyotard traces the "delegitimation" of science by arguing that, according to the science-narrative, "[a] science that has not legitimated itself is not a true science"; however, "if the rules of the science game . . . are applied to science itself", science is revealed to be just another "ideology".[62] This self-referential argument is very reminiscent of the well-known problem of self reference in the various versions of the verification criterion of meaning which contributed to the failure of logical positivism. Lyotard decries any attempt to introduce any kind of type-theory to deal with this problem as just a matter of scientific knowledge reduplicating (sic) itself and thus justifying itself on a second level.[63]

HERMENEUTICS AND LEGITIMATION

The general attempt to "delegitimate", relativize, and "hermeneuticize" knowledge surely amounts to one of the grandest narratives ever told about the nature of knowledge. Lyotard surely intends his critique of epistemology and science to be a general critique applicable to all knowledge. However, if we drop the talk of legitimation for a moment, and simply ask what it is that Lyotard is doing in offering his theory for our consideration, the answer must be that he is proposing a grand narrative for the understanding of the nature of knowledge, a grand narrative in exactly the same tradition which he is "delegitimating". What could ever lead Lyotard or anyone else to prefer his version of the narrative?

Gadamer, at least, recognized this problem—though he never dealt with it satisfactorily. Does Gadamer's theory of philosophical hermeneutics apply to itself? Is it self-legitimating? Gadamer explicitly says,

[I]t is no refutation of the acceptance of this fundamental [historical] contingency [of all human thought] if this acceptance itself seeks to be true absolutely, and thus cannot be applied to itself without contradiction.[64]

The kind of contradiction which results from self-reference of a general theory simply does not bother Gadamer. If employing the logical rules and principles traditional "analytic" epistemology reveals the self-contradiction of relativism, then, Gadamer says, so much the worst for the logical rules and principles of epistemology.

However cogent they [arguments which demonstrate the "inner" contradiction of relativism] may seem, they still miss the point. In making use of them one is proved right, and yet they do not express any superior insight or value. That the thesis of skepticism or relativism refutes itself to the extent that it claims to be true is an irrefutable argument. But what does it achieve? The reflective argument that proves successful here falls back on the arguer, in that it renders the truthfulness of all reflection suspect. It is not the reality of skepticism or of truth dissolving relativism, but the claim to truth of all formal argument that is affected.[65]

Now Russell's theory of types, Gödel's proof of incompleteness and Tarski's semantic conception of truth have all served to teach us that truth does not mean provability in a formal system. Gadamer sometimes takes this "limitation" of logic and the natural sciences as a fatal flaw[66] while, at the same time, arbitrarily counting his philosophical hermeneutics of the human sciences as an *ad hoc* exception to the logical restrictions on internal inconsistency and self-referential paradox. However, as Weinsheimer puts it, "are not the human sciences stretched on this same rack [as the natural sciences]?"[67] One might agree with Gadamer that "human passions cannot be governed by the universal prescriptions of reason" and that "the possibilities of rational proof . . . [do] not fully exhaust the sphere of knowledge";[68] however, the move from these modest and reasonable claims to the claim that "formal refutability of a proposition does not necessarily exclude its being true"[69] is unfathomable and simply self-serving. Gadamer does consider the problem of the consistency of his theory and acknowledges that philosophical hermeneutics and historicism (since "it takes itself seriously") should "allow for the fact that one day its thesis will no longer be considered true, i.e., that people will think 'unhistorically'."[70] In other words, historicism might have its day and then come to an end and be replaced by some other theory—perhaps even the much-maligned epistemology and method. But how could this ever happen? Or, if it did happen, how would one ever be able to determine that it did?

Gadamer maintains that should historicism ever be replaced with another theory, it would not be because his claim that "all knowledge is historically conditioned" is self-referentially contradictory.[71] His theory is immune to such criticism, he thinks, since this is simply a "special problem".[72] However, what Gadamer ignores is that unless his philosophical hermeneutics is internally consistent, it cannot even be distinguished from other theories (or non-theories) much less compared with and replaced by them. Compare Gadamer's claim that "all knowledge is historically conditioned" with Quine's claim that "all statements are revisable" or with Kuhn's claim that "all paradigms are incommensurable". None of these general claims can avoid logical scrutiny and the requirement of logical consistency by simply pleading special privilege. Gadamer's problem of self-reference is the same as that encountered by Wittgenstein at the end of the *Tractatus;* Wittgenstein simply had the integrity to admit the difficulty and to admit that within the theory of language and the world developed in the *Tractatus* he had no way of dealing with the problem.

POSTMODERNISM

Lyotard's way of developing Gadamer's philosophical hermeneutics leads to what he calls the *postmodern condition* since science and philosophy (epistemology) cannot legitimize themselves by an appeal to some metadiscourse or grand "narrative".[73] Postmodernism, for Lyotard, means "incredulity toward metanarratives"—the abandonment of any attempt to arrive at a grand, universal, transcultural scheme for legitimizing knowledge. We are left with a condition characterized by a fundamental heterogeneity of "many different language games" whose differences result in the impossibility of any absolute knowledge. Pluralistic, postmodern knowledge is characterized only by differences which are fundamentally incommensurable; there is no common ground which allows for any general, universal knowledge. Any attempt at a general epistemology falls victim to "the inventor's paralogy".[74]

Knowledge, for Lyotard, is a much more broad notion than science, since scientific knowledge is essentially "narrative"—legitimized by appealing to a single, grand scheme which provides epistemological warrant. Scientists have never played the game of the legitimization of narratives fairly according to Lyotard. While scientists have examined other narratives which they have described as "fables, myths, or legends" characterized by ignorance, prejudice, and customs, they have failed to examine the underlying narrative which is supposed to provide warrant for science. Any "true science" must be legitimated; however, any attempt to legitimize science by applying the "rules of the science game" to itself always result in science becoming just an ideology.[75] Postmodern knowledge, by contrast, abandons any attempt to arrive at a single grand scheme for understanding or justifying knowledge; it is comprised of "an extensive array of competence-building measures" which are derived from culture and custom,[76] and any attempt at legitimization must be sociopolitical and ethnocentric. Thus, epistemology essentially becomes sociology. In the end, any serious justification of knowledge fails. As Lyotard says, "All we can do is gaze in wonderment at the diversity of discursive species, just as we do at the diversity of plant and animal species".[77]

LYOTARD AND LANGUAGE GAMES

Lyotard's brand of relativism greatly resembles Winch's in that it relies very heavily upon the use of Wittgenstein's notion of language games. It also has the same intrinsic weaknesses since Lyotard has the same convenient blind spot which so many epistemological relativists seem to have. Lyotard, like Quine, Goodman, Kuhn, Winch, and Gadamer, wants to eat his cake and have it too. Everything is relative to a multiplicity of language games except what Lyotard has to say about those language games. As I have argued above, surely Lyotard's analysis of knowledge is as much a narrative account as are any that he criticizes. For example, in his argument against Habermas's claim that people of different cultures might reach a consensus through discourse, Lyotard arbitrarily says that while the notion of a consensus is a "suspect value", justice is not.[78] According to Lyotard, we must assume a situation where we have a multiplicity of irreducible, limited language games *with the arbitrary stipulations that we rule out "terror" (the use of force) and that we agree that the rules for the various language games and the moves within those language games have local autonomy (they are agreed upon by their respective players).*[79] In other words, we must assume the basic, fundamental tenants of Lyotard's epistemological relativism. But what if one of the multifarious language games of which Lyotard is speaking is such that it is not willing to grant Lyotard's assumptions? What if some member of one of the heteromorphous groups insists that Lyotard prove his claims to the satisfaction of the members of that group? And what if the members of that group, or any other, refuse to admit the reasonableness of Lyotard's claim and treat it as a "paralogical" metanarrative? Neither Lyotard nor Gadamer has anything convincing to say to these questions since the statements of their relativistic theories are either arbitrarily immune from logical scrutiny or arbitrarily treated as a non-narrative. Everything changes except Lyotard's theory of the nature of change which is arbitrarily exempted from the theory itself. As Karl Popper so eloquently concludes his analysis of *The Poverty of Historicism,*

> It really looks as if historicists . . . [are] trying to compensate themselves for the loss of an unchanging world by clinging to the faith that change can be foreseen because it is ruled by an unchanging law.[80]

Beyond *Beyond Objectivism and Relativism*

The same sort of blind spot is evidenced by Richard Bernstein's attempt in *Beyond Objectivism and Relativism.* Bernstein emphasizes "the growing sense that there may be nothing—not God, Philosophy, Science, or Poetry—that satisfies our longing for ultimate foundations, for a fixed Archimedean point upon which we can secure our thought and action".[81] Bernstein aligns himself with Thomas Kuhn and Paul Feyerabend and describes those philosophers who still try and defend some transhistorical, transcultural basis for philosophy as arch reactionaries—"trying to hold on to what has been discredited and ought to be abandoned".[82] However, Bernstein insists that incommensurability of different "frameworks" does not mean that they cannot be compared. "We can recognize losses and gains," he says. "We can even see how some of our standards for comparing them conflict with each other".[83] Bernstein moves "beyond relativism" by advocating a return to "practical rationality" and "practical discourse and judgment" and "community" and "solidarity".[84] Implicit in Bernstein's position is the attempt to reinstate the Socratic virtues and to further "the type of solidarity, participation, and mutual recognition that is founded in dialogical communities."[85]

What is perplexing is Bernstein's additional claim that "the incommensurability thesis has *nothing to do* with relativism"[86] and his insistent denial of any methodological commitment to any ahistorical claims. Bernstein fails to recognize (or if he recognizes it, he fails to admit it) that if practical rationality is radically relative to the community, if there is no basis for ahistorical critique, there is no basis upon which he can reasonably advocate any particular *telos* for the process of dialogue.[87] Indeed, there are no compelling grounds upon which Bernstein can consistently advocate communities which value dialogue. Given Bernstein's rejection of any ahistorical standard for assessing a community and his adoption of Kuhn's claim that the only possible standard for assessing a community is "the assent of the relevant community",[88] Bernstein has no grounds upon which to advocate or prefer dialogue or philosophical argumentation or rhetoric—except relative to the assent of the members of his own community. As with Lyotard, what we find in Bernstein is the assumption that the various individual communities will play by his rules. Bernstein recognizes that this amounts to a move beyond relativism. What he fails to recognize is that it is a move back towards the modern notion of a universal and transhistorical basis for human rationality.

We see played out in the hermeneutical tradition the same issues and problems as we have earlier seen within the analytic tradition and traditional philosophy of science: the issue of objectivity of knowledge, the question of the universal or relativistic nature of knowledge, the problem of the commensurability of different schemes of knowledge, and the question of the consistency of the theory being advanced. There are also various positions regarding these issues within the hermeneutical tradition—as we have seen that there are within the analytic tradition. Gadamer and Lyotard represent the more radical, relativistic extreme, and the more moderating influence comes from Jürgen Habermas and E.D. Hirsch. Although we cannot explore the details of all of the subtle differences amongst these different figures here, it will be profitable to sketch a few of the most important points of comparison to see how the main epistemological issues resemble those we have examined earlier.[89]

HABERMAS AND LIMITED HERMENEUTICS

Perhaps the two most urgent matters to pursue here are the questions of the universal application of philosophical hermeneutics and epistemological relativism. Habermas, showing some sympathy with the kind of objections which I have raised concerning the more radical forms of relativism, departs from Gadamer on both of these crucial issues. His responses to Gadamer concerning these two issues are inter-related. Habermas recognizes the necessity of some general, metahermeneutical theory such as I have insisted upon. His search for some way of legitimating a hermeneutical critique of knowledge and method leads Habermas to appeal to principles and rules of reason which *transcend* the immediate, concrete situation. His search for rules which transcend the immediacy of any particular, historical situation leads Habermas to develop a theory of "communicative competence" according to which there are universal principles transcending "pure" hermeneutics and which function in a regulative, normative manner to explain how competent language speakers are able to formulate sentences and *to use them in appropriate ways in appropriate circumstances.* This theory of "universal pragmatics" imposes a limit on any attempt at a universal hermeneutics and becomes a "bridgehead" between individual discourses (in the sense claimed above by Hollis and Lukes), thereby forming a basis for the possibility of a general, universal discourse through which some agreement or consensus amongst various peoples becomes possible. As David Hoy describes Habermas's commitment to a general, universal theory of communicative competence, "[h]is philosophical concern is a transcendental one in searching for the underlying conditions for the possibility of thinking about history".[90] Habermas thus agrees with my insistence on the necessity for a metahermeneutical theory which legitimates and regulates hermeneutics in just the manner which Gadamer denies is possible. We might say, in a paraphrase of one of the popular hyperboles of the day, that Habermas "goes beyond hermeneutics". As we have seen in the cases of Gadamer and Lyotard, in the absence of such a metahermeneutical theory, philosophical hermeneutics is another illegitimate totality which is hoist by its own petard of self-reference.

HIRSCH AND INTERPRETATION

The radical relativism resulting from Gadamer's philosophical hermeneutics is further eroded by E.D. Hirsch. Hirsch insists that the process of interpretation is one of trying to determine the original meaning of the author. The role of the original meaning or intention is one of bridling the completely unchecked and free-wheeling process of interpretation of Gadamer according to which the meaning of any text is variable to the interpreter and the historical context of the interpreter. In *Aims of Interpretation,* Hirsch attacks the position that there is no original and stable meaning of a text which is trans-historical and trans-cultural—the position he describes as "cognitive atheism".[91] Positing the notion of the original intent of the author provides a framework within which sensible interpretation can take place, according to Hirsch. The original meaning of the author, even it is never known to the interpreters, provides a regulative, normative principle according to which hermeneutics can proceed. It is only because of the regulative force of the original meaning of the author that we are able to avoid the complete chaos of a hermeneutics with absolutely no criterion or warrant for different interpretations. Without some regulative, normative principle which functions epistemologically as a rule, it is impossible to speak meaningfully of validity amongst different interpretations. Hirsch says, "To banish the original author as the determiner of meaning . . . [is] to reject the only compelling normative principle that could lead to validity in interpretation."[92]

The debate about method between Hirsch and Gadamer and Lyotard parallels rather closely the debate between Kuhn and Feyerabend, on one hand, and Peirce on the other. Although I will treat this issue more thoroughly in Chapter 7, it is helpful to touch upon it briefly here. I understand Hirsch's insistence upon the notion of the author's original meaning as a necessary methodological posit in order for meaningful (or rational) hermeneutical interpretation to take place. Such a claim is a far cry from the imposition of a final authority, which some writers fear. For example, Hoy understands Hirsch's claims concerning the original meaning of the author as providing a basis for "the dogmatic assertion" that a particular interpretation is true.[93] But nothing of the sort follows. Hirsch's point is not that the notion of original meaning provides us with any authority to label any single interpretation as true; the point is that the notion of original meaning provides us with a mechanism for making intelligible any talk about the relative merits of different interpretations. In other words, Hirsch intends to provide a way of distinguishing between dogma and theory. Without some methodological rule or principle to function in a regulative capacity relative to the process of inquiry, any answer is just as good as any other answer—which simply means that, to paraphrase Wittgenstein, there is no answer. The parallel with Wittgenstein's argument against private language is obvious. As we shall see in the next chapter, without some criterion or standard to function to regulate the enquiry, there can be no meaningful distinction between right or wrong interpretations or even any intelligible distinctions amongst different interpretations. Such a criterion functions to provide a context within which the distinction between right and wrong answers becomes possible, as well as the distinction between right and wrong moves within the process of inquiry. Without such a rule or principle, whatever seems right is right; this leads, as Hirsch recognizes, to anarchy, where the strongest argument does not prevail but where the strongest prevail—where philosophical argumentation in whatever form gives way to terror. It would be comforting to think that in a world of cognitive anarchism we would end up with a situation where justice and Socratic virtues would prevail, as Lyotard and Bernstein claim. However, there is no reason to expect such a happy outcome without some criterion or principle to adjudicate amongst various interpretations, by providing a basis for comparative judgments amongst different interpretations.

— 6 —

QUINE ON NATURALIZED
EPISTEMOLOGY AND RELATIVISM

TRADITIONAL EPISTEMOLOGY AND NATURALIZED
EPISTEMOLOGY

In the Introduction to this book, I claimed that the failure of the positivists to succeed with their general program of the reduction of empirical claims to directly verifiable claims is a major contributing influence upon the current wave of relativism. Perhaps in no other place is this connection so explicit and so easily seen as in the case of Quine's attempt at the naturalization of epistemology. In his well-known and much-disputed article, 'Epistemology Naturalized', Quine notes the failure of the positivists generally (and that of Rudolf Carnap specifically in his *Der logische Aufbau der Welt*) to translate all meaningful language into language based upon immediate sense experience. He then cites this failure as a reason for abandoning the attempt to provide a general theory of knowledge, traditionally conceived by empiricists as being based upon and reducible to sense experience.[1]

Given Hume's attack upon what Quine calls the "doctrinal" side of epistemology—that aspect of epistemology which has to do with truth and justification of knowledge claims—what might have motivated Carnap to continue to pursue a *conceptual* logical and rational reconstruction of the *meaning* of knowledge claims? Quine identifies two possible motivations:[2] First, such a rational reconstruction would set forth explicitly the relationship between science and sense experience, and second, it would, through conceptual analysis, clarify the claims of science and provide for a deeper understanding of any claims about the world. Quine concludes that for Carnap (and empirical epistemologists generally) we must recognize the "hopelessness of grounding natural science upon immediate experience in a firmly logical way", and ultimately, we must "despair of any such reduction".[3]

Despite the failure of the empiricists' program of grounding science in sense experience, Quine maintains that the two surviving "cardinal tenets" of empiricism have escaped unscathed and still thrive in empiricist theories of epistemology. Quine's theory of naturalized epistemology is aimed at these two cardinal tenets. The first is that "whatever evidence there *is* for science *is* sensory evidence", and the second is that "all inculcation of meanings of words must rest ultimately on sensory evidence".[4] The intention of the empiricists is, of course, to *ground* epistemology and science in sense experience, and Quine insists that such a link between science and sense experience cannot be established. He calls for abandoning the "make-believe" attempts at rational reconstruction (such as Carnap's) in favor of "creative reconstruction"—simply replacing epistemology with psychology without any attempt at translation or reduction—in other words, abandoning the epistemological enter- prise altogether.[5]

Those who wish to naturalize epistemology view traditional epistemology as the attempt to provide some epistemological war- rant for our beliefs concerning the existence of an objective, indepen- dent external world. Given the epistemological position in which we find ourselves of having no immediate access to such a world (except for the naive realists), we must seemingly construct such warrant ac- cording to "immediately given" experience. For many philosophers, all such attempts are doomed to failure and must lead inevitably to skepticism. Of the various ways of trying to avoid such an outcome, those who advocate the naturalizing of epistemology argue that the whole epistemological enterprise is either unintelligible or hopelessly over-ambitious and that we should consequently abandon the entire endeavor of epistemology.[6] If we give up any attempt to explain or justify science in terms of sense experience and simply focus instead on how science in fact develops, we would do better, Quine says, to simply settle for psychology.[7] In abandoning epistemology for psy- chology, we would be, in fact, admitting the failure of the empiricists' program of reducing knowledge claims to claims based upon sense experience. Empirical meanings of individual statements about the physical world are theoretically inaccessible because individual statements are always embedded in some general *theory,* Quine reminds us. As we saw at some length in Chapter 2, Quine's holism insists that one must evaluate a theory epistemologically as a whole rather than evaluating an individual, particular statement which must be held up against experience for comparison.[8] Indeed, as we have seen, such reductionism constitutes the second "dogma" of empiricism. Given any sort of empiricist theory of meaning which embodies meaning in some verification procedure, what is to count as evidence for the truth of any particular claim will always be relative to some general theory in which that statement occurs. Various ways of translating particular statements of a theory might all preserve the "empirical" content of the general theory.

Quine thus commits epistemology to the same dustbin in which the logical positivists deposited metaphysics. Rather than the grand, sweeping, all-inclusive conception of knowledge represented in traditional epistemology and the view of the epistemological enterprise as primitive and basic, epistemology survives, according to Quine, only as "a chapter of psychology".[9] Abstract, theoretical epistemological theories give way to empirical psychology. Quine describes the "new" epistemology as follows:

> We are studying how the human subject of our study posits bodies and projects his physics from his data, and we appreciate that our position in the world is just like his. Our very epistemological enterprise, therefore, and the psychology wherein it is a component chapter, and the whole of natural science wherein psychology is a component book—all this is our own construction or projection from stimulations like those we were meting out to our epistemological subject.[10]

With epistemology thus naturalized, we should, according to Quine, abandon any notions about the priority of epistemological theories in comparison with "actual" physical sense stimulation. We are no longer to talk or think of epistemological theories as providing a framework for structuring or interpreting physical experience or as providing some epistemological grounding or warrant for science. Given Quine's holism, we must give up all considerations of epistemology as "first philosophy"[11] and recognize that epistemological claims, like analytic ones, are simply additional claims in the theory, along with (and on the same "level" with) psychological ones. Quine thus joins the ranks of those philosophers who would reduce epistemology to the social sciences. Whereas Peter Winch would reduce epistemology to sociology, and Hans Gadamer, to history, Quine would reduce it to psychology.

EVOLUTIONARY EPISTEMOLOGY

Quine's "naturalized epistemology", with its reduction of epistemology to psychology, has become the best-known theory of the various more recent developments in current philosophical theory about the relationship between epistemology and psychology. Other philosophers have also attacked the simplistic or "armchair" style of traditional, analytic epistemology and have similarly urged abandoning such inquiry in favor of empirical psychology.[12] Epistemology naturalized forsakes any attempt to conduct a presupposition-free inquiry into the nature of human knowledge and conducts its inquiry within the confines of "user-friendly" cognitive science. As a part of psychology, epistemology becomes simply an inquiry into the reliability of human cognitions given psychology's best estimation of the *actual* nature of human beings, their *actual* environment and how the two interact. For example, Alvin Goldman has advocated a "re-orientation of epistemology" and an "alliance of epistemology and psychology" in his theory of epistemics.[13] Donald Campbell and Karl Popper have also insisted that epistemology is inseparable from the evolutionary theories in biology and psychology.[14] Campbell's and Popper's 'evolutionary epistemology' treats epistemology (human knowledge) as continuous with animal knowledge and the process of epistemology as continuous with the trial and error processes which contribute to survival. Thus, Popper's well-known understanding of science as a series of conjectures and refutations can easily be explained by comparison to biological natural selection. When theories are in competition with other theories, the process of trial-and-error (of attempted refutation *in seriatim*) allows us to choose the theory which survives where the others fail—the one which proves to be the fittest.

Evolutionary epistemology also requires a re-orientation of traditional epistemology—Campbell calls it "a recentering of the epistemological problem", which he insists makes the *growth* of knowledge central to epistemology.[15] Such an emphasis means that an understanding of learning as well as perception will be essential to any theory of knowledge, an emphasis which both Campbell and Popper see as one shared by many of the major historical figures in traditional epistemology, including Plato, Descartes, Kant, Mill, Peirce, and Russell.[16] Although such a "recentering" of epistemology involves some significant re-ordering of the epistemological process, and, in some cases, complete departure from traditional epistemology (in particular, Popper and Campbell eschew any phenomenalistic basis for knowledge), evolutionary epistemology still maintains close ties with the mainstream of traditional epistemology.[17] For example, as we shall see in the next chapter, the view of knowledge as "rationally justified" or as the result of a reliable method is closely aligned with Charles Peirce's treatment of method. Although evolutionary epistemology emphasizes a shift of traditional epistemological problems to science and biology, it does not represent an abandonment of traditional epistemology in the manner in which Quine's naturalized epistemology does; nor does evolutionary epistemology introduce the possibility of radical epistemological relativism as naturalized epistemology does.

QUINE AND HUME ON EMPIRICAL JUSTIFICATION

We have already argued at some length in Chapter 2 against Quine's rejection of the analytic-synthetic distinction and the notion of logical relativism to which it has given rise, and I will not pursue those same considerations here. However, in our examination of Quine's attempted elimination of epistemology and its resulting epistemological relativism, we shall see that Quine's argument is based upon the rejection of the same distinction between content and structure. I will argue that Quine's attack upon traditional epistemology, like his attack upon analyticity, is internally inconsistent, and I will conclude that Quine's position, unlike Hume's, fails to address the traditional questions of epistemology and the philosophy of science.

Quine adopts and endorses most of Hume's famed attack upon induction and the scientific reasoning which is based upon induction, and he adopts the same rigorous standards for epistemology by insisting that grounding science in sense observation means "*deducing* science from observations" [my emphasis].[18] And again, Quine ties the reason for preferring psychology over any attempted "rational reconstruction" to the failure of any program where every sentence of science is "*equated*" with a sentence in strict observational and logical terms [my emphasis].[19] Naturalized epistemology replaces traditional epistemology when "we have stopped dreaming of *deducing* science from sense data" [my emphasis].[20] In Quine's account, Hume, Carnap, and the rest of the empirical epistemologists finally had to admit the "impossibility of *strictly* deriving the science of the external world from sensory evidence" [my emphasis].[21] It is evident from these descriptions of the process of epistemology that Quine has followed Hume in setting unreasonably high standards for epistemology, and his focus upon the attempts of the logical positivists ignores other programs of empirical epistemology.[22]

Quine's point of departure from Hume is illustrative and telling for understanding how Quine finally arrives at a theory of naturalized epistemology. Whereas Hume despaired of ever justifying induction (and hence, matters of fact and scientific reasoning) given the standards for justification which he had adopted, the story did not end there for him. Hume's natural beliefs—though not based upon reason—still provide an element of explanation of why we hold the fundamental beliefs which we do about the external world and induction. In particular, natural beliefs provide a framework within which epistemological inquiry can take place. In this way, Hume's position, though skeptical, is still an investigation into the problems of traditional epistemology. Quine turns all epistemological questions into "internal" questions, that is, questions internal to science and ultimately psychology. As we saw in Chapter 2, a major point of difference between Quine and Carnap is that while Quine treats the general question of the legitimacy of all knowledge as an internal one, Carnap treats it as an external one. That same difference now accounts for why Quine's naturalized epistemology is unable to address any of the traditional problems of epistemology.

THE IMPASSE OF NATURALIZED EPISTEMOLOGY

In 'The Significance of Naturalized Epistemology',[23] Barry Stroud has provided a strong case for the failure of Quine's naturalized epistemology to address traditional epistemological problems.[24] Stroud explores the relationship between Quine's new naturalized epistemology and the old epistemology which asked such questions as "How [is it that] any of us knows anything at all about the world around us?" and "[Is it possible for the world to be] quite different *in general* from the way it is perceived to be?" [my emphasis][25] Now despite some ambiguity about the matter, Stroud provides strong evidence that Quine intends for his naturalized epistemology to address these same fundamental issues of traditional epistemology. As evidence for his interpretation of Quine's intentions, he supplies a convincing array of quotations from a variety of different sources of the kinds of claims which Quine has made about traditional epistemology. However, it seems that the most compelling evidence that Quine intends for naturalized epistemology to supplant traditional epistemology is provided in 'Epistemology Naturalized' itself. Quine never indicates that the project which both Hume and Carnap undertook—trying to provide some justification of our scientific claims about reality through sense experience—is a different problem than the one which he is addressing. On the contrary, Quine says that "[t]he Humean predicament is the human predicament".[26] Attempting to provide some justification of such claims is a universal predicament, and Quine goes on to say that we are no further along in dealing successfully with that predicament now than was Hume.[27]

But does naturalized epistemology allow us to make any progress toward resolving this predicament? Stroud thinks not, and I agree.[28] When another person makes any claims about his or her surrounding world, that person, according to Quine, "posits bodies" and "projects his physics from his data". In order for us to make some assessment of those claims in terms of their truth or falsity, we must be in a position to make some assessment or judgment about those claims in addition to stating merely that certain facts are being asserted by those claims. Since we determine that some claims made by others are true while others are false, we must have some means of determining truth and falsity independently of simply examining what is said by other people. But notice carefully that Quine says that in carrying through on the enterprise of epistemology "we appreciate that our position in the world is just like his." [another subject's][29] But here a major difficulty arises for Quine. If we are to imagine ourselves in the same epistemological position as another subject, how are we to gain independent information about the world which will allow us to make any judgments about our own claims? As Stroud says,

> We could not compare our beliefs with the world they are about as we can in the normal experimental study of another person. Each of us would find himself with a set of beliefs and dispositions to assert things about the world, and we could of course undergo experiences that would strengthen or alter those dispositions, but those reinforced or newly acquired beliefs themselves would have to be seen in turn as at most some further "projections" from some new but still extremely meager "input". They could not be seen as a source of independent information about the world against which their own truth or the truth of the earlier beliefs could be checked.[30]

If all of our beliefs about the external world are mere "projections", then the belief that the "input" for those projections is the result of sense experiences must also be a projection as well as the belief that we have sense organs at all. As Stroud concludes, on Quine's naturalized theory of knowledge, "[M]y own 'output' would for me be no better than whistling in the dark".[31] In other words, without the epistemological underpinning according to which one's projections are based upon sensory inputs, Quine would have no reason to prefer science to any other method of inquiry and no reason to prefer psychology to theology. Without epistemology, there is no reason to prefer naturalized epistemology to theologized epistemology.

EPISTEMOLOGICAL ANARCHISM

This criticism brings into focus one of the major drawbacks in Quine's naturalized theory of knowledge. 'Epistemology Naturalized' provides a very straightforward and explicit line of attack according to which epistemology is either reduced to psychology or eliminated altogether. For instance, Quine mentions explicitly the notion of "justification". Now the difficulty which is implicit in Stroud's criticism (and which is made explicit by Hilary Putnam[32]) is that the notion of truth must be counted amongst those epistemological concepts which are eliminated or reduced to psychology. If the notion of truth is stripped of all its epistemological, normative content, then all that is left of truth for Quine is a Tarskian, semantic conception, according to which to say that 'p' is true is simply to assent to the assertion 'p'. As Putnam observes,

> What the [Tarski's] procedure does is to define 'true' so that saying that a statement is true is equivalent to *assenting* to the statement; truth, as defined by Tarski, is not a *property* of statements at all, but a syncategoramatic notion that enables us to 'ascend semantically', that is, to talk about sentences instead of about objects.[33]

The notion of truth adopted from Tarski by Quine carries with it no normative, epistemological import at all; it is only a semantic device which allows us to move from the object-language level to the meta-language level. Without an epistemological notion of truth, as we have seen above, we are unable to assess the claims of other people or even those that we make ourselves. There is no notion of "rightness" by which to make such assessments. As Putnam laments, "[I]f all notions of rightness . . . are eliminated, then what are our statements but noise-makings? . . . The elimination of the normative is attempted mental suicide."[34]

The success of Quine's attempted elimination of the distinction between epistemology and psychology and the attending reduction of epistemology to psychology hinges upon the possibility of eliminating completely any notion of epistemological justification for all of our knowledge or of accounting for epistemological justification solely in psychological terms. In a certain respect, we have arrived at a new formulation of Hume's old problem or deriving 'ought' from 'is'. Psychology tells us what *is* the case, i.e., how humans *do* arrive at beliefs and knowledge while epistemology tells us how we *ought* to do this. Can psychology provide us with any justificatory scheme for assessing beliefs? Is psychology even *relevant* to the process of *assessing* beliefs? It seems clear that the concerns of psychology and epistemology are concerned with different spheres of inquiry. If we understand epistemological justification to be concerned with the problem of providing *reasons* for beliefs and knowledge claims, then, as Harvey Siegel says, "a psychological claim can never be genuinely justificatory, can never be an epistemologically justificatory claim, because it can never by itself offer good reason for taking some knowledge-claim to be true."[35] Since psychology simply *describes* the processes by which we arrive at beliefs, it cannot tell us what beliefs are "good" ones (true ones). As Siegel concludes, "psychology cannot be relevant to [traditional] epistemology."[36] Psychology cannot provide any explicandum for such notions as 'justified' and 'true' unless we are willing to count whatever people actually think as justified or true, and conduct epistemological inquiry simply by observing and tabulating what people say and do. But such a method eliminates all content from the notion of justification and reduces it solely to a factual question. In other words, this approach leads to exactly the extreme epistemological nihilism which Quine wants to avoid. Such *carte blanche* permissibility regarding beliefs and knowledge claims amounts to the complete denial of epistemology and results in epistemological anarchism.

THE CIRCULARITY OF NATURALIZED EPISTEMOLOGY

Naturalized epistemology is thus unable to offer any way of making any significant progress towards resolving the Humean and human predicament of gaining some warrant for our claims about the external world. Indeed, it is difficult to see how naturalized epistemology even addresses the same problems. Quine explicitly attempts to avoid the "epistemological nihilism" which he thinks threatens the abandonment of old style epistemology. We cannot resort to observation as a means to anchor our beliefs since, as Quine says, "[o]ne man's observation is another man's closed book or flight of fancy".[37] Since what counts as an observation statement varies with the speakers of a particular language, the best that we can do, according to Quine, to arrive at something like an objective and absolute standard for assessing our beliefs is to survey "all speakers of the language, or most".[38]

Saying that all we have to do is to survey all the speakers of a language initially sounds simple enough; however, it obscures the fact that we must be in a position to make some judgments about what these different speakers have to say. In other words, one must be in a position to make judgments about the judgments while, at the same time, one is simply to imagine one's self in the same epistemological position as everyone else. So, it seems, we are not even in a position to get the enterprise started. We apparently wind up in an epistemological *cul de sac*. At best, a radical relativism is the result, and, at worst, an extreme skepticism.

Quine's naturalized epistemology simply turns what was an external question for Hume and Carnap into an internal one—for Quine, all questions about the justification of epistemology and science must be raised within some theory. As we have seen in Chapter 2, such an internal approach to epistemological problems is an integral part of Quine's holism. Quine summarizes the move from the external view of justification of the "old" epistemology to the internal view of the "new", naturalized epistemology in the following manner:

> The old epistemology aspired to contain, in a sense, natural science; it would construct it somehow from sense data. Epistemology in its new setting, conversely, is contained in natural science, as a chapter of psychology. But the old containment remains valid too, in its way. We are studying how the human subject of our study posits bodies and projects his physics from his data, and we appreciate that our position in the world is just like his. Our very epistemological enterprise, therefore, and the psychology wherein it is a component chapter, and the whole of natural science wherein psychology is a component book—all this is our own construction or projection from stimulations like those we were meting out to our epistemological subject.[39]

According to Quine, if the problem of justification is treated as an internal problem of epistemology and science, "the old threat of circularity" is no longer a problem since we will have given up the notion of "deducing" science from sense data.[40] The "illegitimate" circularity of the old epistemology arose supposedly from trying to validate knowledge of the world by using that very knowledge. But are we in any better position with naturalized epistemology? Supposedly, the "friendly" or benign circularity of Quine's naturalized epistemology is different since, according to Stroud's understanding of Quine, "naturalized epistemology is to be seen as itself part of psychology and hence part of the very science of nature the sources of which it seeks to understand, but there is nothing viciously, or even unpleasantly, circular about that".[41] Quine's claims for allowing the particular brand of circularity involving naturalized epistemology fit into what has now become a familiar pattern. It is reminiscent of the special case pleading we have found earlier in the cases of Goodman in Chapter 3, Kuhn in Chapter 4, Gadamer in Chapter 5, and Quine himself in Chapter 2. In each case, we have seen that the attempt to exempt whatever the particular, privileged theory is under consideration at the moment from general constraints and requirements has failed. It fails in the present case as well.

QUINE AND NEURATH'S BOAT

The circularity involved in the case of naturalized epistemology is neither friendly nor benign. Quine quotes with approval Otto Neurath's tale of the mariner at sea who manages to successfully rebuild his boat while managing to stay afloat.[42] The obvious application of this parable is supposed to be that through naturalized epistemology, according to which epistemology is just a part of psychology, we are able to examine and validate or justify different epistemological claims "plank by plank", without involving ourselves in what Quine regards as the illegitimate task of trying to validate the entire enterprise. By examining and validating each claim *in seriatim,* we are presumably supposed to avoid any illegitimate circularity or inconsistency. However, when Neurath used this story, it was with a very different understanding of epistemology than Quine's. Neurath was still committed to the positivists' account of knowledge according to which the structure and content of a theory are qualitatively and epistemologically different—a claim which Quine has abandoned. How can Quine embrace this parable when, for him, analytic statements—logical rules and laws included —are "in the same boat" (so to speak) as synthetic ones, that is, observation statements?

Imagine how one would go about making the replacement of one part of the boat for another and gradually rebuilding the boat. The situation would be strictly analogous to the one which I described in Chapter 2 regarding the process of evaluating beliefs and "redistributing truth-values" over statements in a network of beliefs such as the one Quine describes. Some principle for evaluation and validation must be invoked. Let us recall Quine's principle from Chapter 2:

(Q) If some recalcitrant experience E occurs which causes a subject to regard as true (hold on to) statement S1, and if S1 and some other statement S2 are incompatible, then S2 must be regarded as false (given up or 'revised'). Furthermore, if holding on to S1 or the revision of S2 causes some other inconsistency with some other statement S3, then S3 must also be revised.

In we now invoke this principle and make the appropriate changes in order to continue with the analogy of completely refurbishing a boat while keeping it afloat, we could invoke the following principle (let us call it FB for "floating boat"):

(FB) Each part (P1–Pn) of the floating boat is examined and evaluated. If some evidence is available which allows us to validate a part, we keep it. However, if some evidence or experience causes us to regard a part as unwarranted or undesirable, we discard it and make whatever adjustments are necessary to the other parts to keep the boat afloat— either by replacing it with a new part or by re-arranging the remaining parts.

The logical isomorphism of the two procedures is obvious. Now the difference between Neurath and Quine can be clearly shown. The principle or rule FB sets forth a logical procedure for examining the parts of the boat (or theory) and deciding what to do with them. Such a process must presuppose some principle(s) as well as normal rules of inference (modus ponens). To understand this, just think of what would actually be necessary to physically replace some parts while not replacing others while keeping the boat afloat. Laws of physics (including Archimedes's Law—he did indeed discover something!) and laws of logic must be rigorously observed. For Neurath, FB, the laws of physics, and the rules of inference are not parts of the boat; these rules and principles and laws cannot be evaluated, revised or replaced (not if we want to keep the boat afloat). For Quine, FB, Archimedes's Law, as well as all the laws of logic and rules of inference are just "other parts of the boat"; however, if such were the case, the boat would surely sink. Neurath's analogy of the boat is useful only if one makes an epistemological distinction between descriptive statements (which provide the content) and logical ones (which provide the structure)—a distinction which Quine has abandoned. It is only because of such rules and principles that we would have any idea of the proper way to repair the boat, and there *must be a proper and an improper way* since we must repair it in a particular way in order to keep the boat afloat. It is these rules and principles which provide the basis for the introduction of some normative, evaluative aspect into the process of assessing our beliefs. Without such rules and principles, it seems, anything goes, and the circularity is not only vicious but pernicious. The "old threat of circularity" will then sink Quine's boat.

THE FAILURE OF THE BOOTSTRAP METHOD

Next, let us focus explicitly upon the question of validating "scientific" claims. If naturalized epistemology makes any progress in this regard over the "old" epistemology, it must be by the "bootstrap" method—naturalized epistemology must lift psychology from the general epistemological quagmire by using only psychology itself. In other words, the warrant for empirical psychology must derive from within psychology itself rather than from any more general epistemological claims. Again, vicious circularity raises its ugly head. How could this be possible? What gives physical psychology such privileged status? If we begin with the general epistemological inquiry into the relationship between our beliefs and the external world, what special condition would make psychology immune from such an inquiry? And how would it be possible to construct a theory of epistemology within psychology unless the general epistemological problems are dealt with first? Stroud argues convincingly that such a bootstrap approach will not work:

> Suppose we have asked how any knowledge at all of the physical world is possible, and suppose that we have asked it because of what we take at the outset to be true about the physical world—in particular about the processes of perception. If we then arrived by *reductio* at the general skeptical conclusion which Quine thinks is at least coherent, we would find all our alleged knowledge of the physical world suspect. . . . At that point in our investigation surely no scientific "knowledge" could then be unproblematically introduced to meet the skeptical challenge.[43]

Minimally, what we need is an argument for the special status of scientific psychology which gives it immunity from the general epistemological problems concerning justification and truth and establishes it as context within which all inquiry will take place. We have examined Quine's attack against the foundationalism of much of contemporary epistemology; however, if his attempt to naturalize epistemology is successful, the claims of empirical science come to occupy that epistemologically privileged position which provides a foundation for all justification.

Although Quine wishes to relocate epistemology within psychology, he does not wish to give up all epistemological notions completely; he particularly wants to continue to talk about the notions of evidence and observation. Quine maintains that once we abandon talk about consciousness and awareness and concentrate exclusively upon what he regards as the completely scientific question of "the stimulation of our sensory receptors", we are freed from the traditional epistemological entanglements. He then takes as given whatever the current, most approved theories of empirical psychology and perception happen to be, and these theories are immune to the usual epistemological questions. Quine thus neatly "brackets off" empirical psychology and arbitrarily avoids the fundamental epistemological problems which have beset traditional epistemologists.

Now it may be the case that Quine finds such general, fundamental epistemological problems somehow basically confused or logically inconsistent, but he gives us no arguments to that effect. Consider, for example, his rather summary claim that "[w]hat to count as observation now can be settled in terms of the stimulation of sensory receptors".[44] With this remark, Quine intends to have settled the whole matter of the epistemological problems of evidence and how evidence is related to theory. Admittedly, if one chooses empirical psychology, some issues in the philosophy of mind regarding consciousness might be easily "bracketed" and set aside. However, the fundamental epistemological issues are not so easily dismissed. Questions concerning the status and role of the sense organs have long been part of the common body of literature in epistemology on perception and result in some of the major points of issue between Locke and Berkeley. Quine takes refuge in "the stimulation of sensory receptors", but notice how completely packed with epistemological baggage this innocent-sounding little phrase really is. "Stimulation" presupposes some causal theory of perception, and, as Berkeley might be quick to demand, "How do we know that we have 'sensory receptors' except by other 'stimulations' of our 'sensory receptors'?" Psychology is, after all, psychology; it cannot do the work of philosophy.

The Human Being as a Black Box

Even Richard Rorty, who is certainly as anxious to hasten the demise of epistemology as is Quine, goes to great lengths to show "how very remote any psychological discovery of the sort he [Quine] envisages will be from any concern with the foundations of science or with the relation between theory and evidence".[45] Any supposed connection between psychology and epistemology comes, according to Rorty, from Quine's "loose use" of the basic, key epistemological terms.[46]

Quine sees the dilemma of epistemology as one of trying to distinguish between causal stimulus and awareness. Once we have converted to naturalized epistemology, we have the advantage, according to Quine, of not having to worry about when or how of even if consciousness arises. He says,

> We can look upon man as a black box in the physical world, exposed to externally determinable stimulatory forces as input and spouting externally determinable testimony about the external world as output. Just which of the inner workings of the black box may be tinged with awareness is as may be.[47]

However, surely this position simply conveniently ignores the fundamental epistemological question concerning causality or arbitrarily assumes an answer to it. Quine condenses all epistemological problems into problems of consciousness and awareness, but this amounts to a self-serving distortion. As Rorty observes,

> We may talk about irradiated patches on a two-dimensional retina or pulses in the optic nerve, but this will be a matter of *choosing* a black box [my emphasis], not of discovering touchstones for inquiry. Quine dissolves a dilemma only by changing the motive of inquiry. If one were only interested in causal mechanisms, one would never have worried one's head about awareness. . . .
>
> If there are indeed no experimental criteria for where the real data come, then Quine's suggestion that we give up the notion of "sense data" and speak causally of nerve endings and epistemologically of observation sentences does not resolve a dilemma which has plagued epistemology. Rather it lets epistemology wither away.[48]

THE ROLE OF OBSERVATION SENTENCES

Rorty parts company with Quine at this juncture because he thinks that Quine does not go far enough with the process of the deconstruction of epistemology. He is particularly concerned that Quine wishes to retain the notion of an observation by defining it in terms of the intersubjective agreement of the members of the language community. As we have already seen, Quine says that "an observation sentence is one on which all speakers of the language give the same verdict when given the same concurrent stimulation".[49] Since Quine wants to eat his cake and have it too (a condition which, as we have seen, is common to Goodman, Kuhn, Winch, and Gadamer), he wants and needs some sort of anchor or "tether" to tie epistemological claims to sensory stimulation. As he says, "what we want of observation sentences is that they be the ones in closest causal proximity to the sensory receptors."[50] In terms of Quine's "network" of beliefs, which we discussed in Chapter 2, we are to understand an observation sentence as "situated at the sensory periphery of the body scientific" and as "the minimal verifiable aggregate" which wears its empirical content "on its sleeve".[51] Now it is easy to understand why Rorty, given his very strong relativistic tendencies, complains that Quine does not follow the implications of his positions to their logical conclusions. Quine develops what should lead to a complete dismantling of epistemology, and then at the very end, at the most crucial point, he turns away from the process and re-introduces, or simply refuses to part with, the notion of an observation sentence. Quine recognizes the importance of some such notion to any attempt to ground language and epistemology in our experience, and he sounds like a member of the old empiricist school of epistemology when he says, "Its [the observation sentence's] relation to . . . our knowledge of what is true, is very much the traditional one: observation sentences are the repository of evidence for scientific hypotheses."[52]

By "holding on to" the notion of an observation sentence and grounding that notion in our experience and intersubjective agreement about experience, Quine cautiously avoids throwing the epistemological baby out with the relativists' bath water. He explicitly admonishes those people who "accentuate cultural relativism" and "discredit the idea of observation", and he offers the "absolute" standard of community agreement for observation sentences instead.[53] However, the notions of observation sentence and community agreement are surely *ad hoc* exceptions to Quine's general program. Quine is faced with the same choice which Carnap faced when he tried to develop the notion of protocol sentences. Carnap's move from a completely phenomenalistic interpretation of protocol sentences to a public, intersubjective one was necessitated by the same kind of concerns which now beset Quine. All of the epistemological problems of verification, truth, and evidence surely arise in the process of trying to determine intersubjective, community agreement. Indeed, as we have already seen, some way of handling all of those problems is necessary for us even to determine that there *is* a community to agree or disagree. If we try and imagine how this process would actually take place, we can easily understand the difficulties involved here. The agreement of the community is supposed to provide an "absolute standard" for observation statements which means that we must survey, observe, record and compare the reactions of various different members of the language community to the same sensory stimulations under the same conditions. This process is supposed to provide us with a rough description of empirical psychology and a basis for epistemology. But examine closely how this process is supposed to be conducted and look at the fundamental epistemological questions which are being begged. What is to count as a member of the language community? What is to count as the "same" sensory stimulus? What is to count as the "same" conditions? How do we know that people agree or disagree? At any given point, how are we to trust our records of our earlier interviews with other members of the community? Without some answers to these questions, the "new" epistemology cannot count as an improvement over the old, and psychology cannot count as an improvement over epistemology.

No Escape from First Philosophy

Quine must recognize the difficulties which he faces here because he takes a completely uncharacteristic position in his answer. An observation sentence must have empirical content in order to provide any evidence at all for scientific theories, but how are we to settle on this empirical content? Are not all of the same old problems of verification which Quine has highlighted as the major stumbling blocks of the old epistemology still present in the case of his use of observation sentences? His answer is simply that in the case of the empirical content of an observation sentence, an observation sentence "wears it on its sleeve".[54] The empirical content of observation statements is supposed to be something so obvious that we all "see" it and agree what it is *simpliciter,* but how does such a claim represent any real advance over Descartes's notion of "clear and distinct" ideas? And does this admission of such a need not mark a remission to traditional empiricist epistemology of the first order?

Quine thus retains an element of empiricism and realism in order to avoid a completely relativistic position. The holism and the new epistemology both operate on the level "above" the level of observation sentences. Individual sentences have no meaning, Quine reiterates, "once we get beyond observation sentences".[55] In other words, psychology replaces epistemology once we have psychology; however, we need observation sentences (with all of the attending epistemological issues and problems) to develop psychology. Quine has tried to steer between the Scylla of relativism and the Charybdis of the old epistemology, and he seems doomed to disaster in one direction or the other. As Rorty correctly concludes,

> So he [Quine] should either let Polanyi, Kuhn, and Hanson [the relativists] say that "observation" is just a matter of what we can agree on these days, or he should show how psychological discoveries can make something more of this notion. If they cannot, then defining "dependence on present sensory stimulation" in terms of intersubjectivity will just be invoking an old epistemological honorific to no psychological purpose.[56]

One way of possibly understanding these criticisms of Quine is to see the main points of dispute as semantical ones involving how certain terms are used and with what meanings. There is considerable evidence for such an interpretation in Quine's reply to Stroud. "In what way do I see the Humean predicament as persisting?" Quine asks rhetorically. "Only in the fallibility of prediction: the fallibility of induction and the hypothetico-deductive method in anticipating experience," he answers.[57] And who in the recent history of Western epistemology—except for a few recalcitrant skeptics—would disagree? Such an understanding of Hume's predicament seems to place Quine squarely in the middle of the mainstream of current epistemology—except that he wants to call it science instead of epistemology.

On the one hand, Quine claims that "the furniture of our world"—things which occupy our world such as sticks and stones, electrons and molecules—are merely "manners of speaking". On the other hand, he says that these same sticks and stones and electrons and molecules are "real".[58] The way to resolve the apparent tension between such extreme claims, according to Quine, is to see that through naturalized epistemology, we come to deal with such issues *within* science rather than within epistemology. As we have seen, Quine treats all meta-theoretical and meta-methodological questions as internal ones—internal to the theory or method. The major differences, Quine suggests, are merely semantical:

> They [the semantical considerations] concern questions not of reality but of method and evidence. They belong not to ontology but to the methodology of ontology, and thus to epistemology. And here still I recognize no first philosophy prior to science.[59]

However, the main issue at dispute here is not simply a semantical one. It is not simply the case that what other people have called epistemology Quine now calls science. There are serious questions of substance at stake.

Quine simply cannot develop the general theory of naturalized epistemology without doing "first philosophy"—exactly what naturalized epistemology is supposed to eliminate. Consider the general principle of naturalized epistemology which maintains something such as the following:

(NE) Meaningful epistemological endeavors can only be pursued within empirical psychology (epistemology is a part of psychology).

Now consider the status of (NE). Is this claim a claim of empirical psychology? Of course it is not. (NE) is a meta-scientific, meta-theoretical claim which cannot be reduced to or made a part of any scientific theory; however, surely (NE) is supposed to be a rationally held position. Indeed, naturalized epistemology is a *philosophical theory* of interest to philosophers—not scientists. Quine offers a detailed rationale for (NE) which is supposed to constitute an *argument* or *reason* for our preferring (NE) to the old-styled epistemology. He accepts Hume's critique of induction, and he uses his rejection of the analytic-synthetic distinction and the resulting collapse of analytic statements into synthetic ones to broaden the scope of Hume's attack to include all of our knowledge claims; however, both of these arguments are philosophical arguments within traditional epistemology. At the same time, Quine has explicitly denied that there is a "first philosophy" within which such questions as the justification of induction and the viability of the analytic-synthetic distinction can arise—this is the main point of naturalized epistemology.[60] Either, it seems, (NE) must be completely unjustified or it is self-refuting. It is this aspect of naturalized epistemology which places it in the same awkward dilemma as Goodman's theory of worldmaking and Kuhn's theory of paradigm-based science. If all epistemological matters of justification and warrant are supposed to be internal to the theory being put forth, it is impossible to justify or give any reasons or evidence—compelling or otherwise—for the theory. Unless there are extra-scientific criteria for epistemologically evaluating (NE), there are no grounds upon which we could say that it is a good theory, or that it is to be preferred to any competing theory, or that there is any reason at all for adopting it. Simply put, (NE) is not a claim of empirical psychology, and if all evidence and reasons occur only within empirical psychology, then there can be no evidence or reasons for (NE). To the extent that (NE) is a justified theory which commands considered assent, it is also inconsistent and self-defeating. So, paradoxically, for the advocates of naturalized epistemology, good reasons for (NE) are also good reasons against it.

As Siegel observes,

> a rational embrace of naturalized epistemology involves accepting that some metascientific theses are justified on the basis of extrascientific reasons . . . but this recognition forces the rejection of naturalized epistemology, which renounces that sort of justification.[61]

Thus, naturalized epistemology "*presupposes,* rather than eliminates, first philosophy".[62]

The inability to justify naturalized epistemology as a scientific theory has, of course, not gone unnoticed by those who support some version of a naturalized epistemology. For example, Paul Roth argues that it is Quine's ambiguous use of the term 'theory' which might lead one to think that naturalized epistemology is itself a scientific theory.[63] Since naturalized epistemology is a meta-scientific theory about the nature of science, it cannot be justified by any appeal to natural science. In other words, Quine's theory about the nature of epistemology is part of his rationale for adopting naturalized epistemology and hence cannot be a part of naturalized epistemology itself. As Roth says, "since Quine's arguments with regard to the *a priori* limits to theoretical knowledge are what are to convince us to accept the new epistemological project [naturalized epistemology], the relevant arguments cannot assume the prior acceptance of that epistemological stance."[64] The only alternative seems to be to understand Quine's theory about naturalized epistemology as an *a priori* claim about the nature of knowledge;[65] however, given Quine's criticisms of traditional epistemology, surely it would be the ultimate irony for him to be forced to have to justify his claims about the nature of knowledge as *a priori* ones. Minimally, resorting to *a priori* claims as a way out of the difficulty of justifying (or at least providing some rationale for) naturalized epistemology means that we are back to doing traditional epistemology ("first philosophy") once again.

We have seen that not only is epistemology not reducible to psychology, it cannot be. It may well be the case that epistemology stands to learn a great deal from psychology; however, this is an epistemological claim, not a psychological one.

— 7 —

PEIRCE ON METHOD AND RATIONALITY

A NINETEENTH-CENTURY REPLY TO POSTMODERNISM

It is somewhat ironic that one of the best avenues to approach an attempt at providing some response to the post-modernist critique concerning the nature and role of reason and scientific method is through the works of a nineteenth-century philosopher. In attempting to straighten out what he took to be Kant's mistakes, Charles Sanders Peirce delved as deeply into the foundations of science and the methodology of science (which Peirce called "the experimental habit of mind") as anyone before or since. However, plunging directly into Peirce's claims about science and rationality is not very profitable unless we lay some foundation for what he has to say; therefore, our route to Peirce's treatment of method and rationality is circuitous and takes us through much of Peirce's epistemology and some of his metaphysics.

For Peirce, all knowledge begins with experience, and it is only through experience that a person gains knowledge. There has never been a more scathing and devastating attack upon the intuition of Cartesian rationalism than Peirce's,[1] but the subjectivism of twentieth-century sense-data theory would have equally incurred Peirce's wrath. No experience comes stamped with the Good Housekeeping Seal of Approval saying that this is a basic experience which can be used as a foundation for all knowledge. It is true that there are distinctions amongst different objects of consciousness—for example, between objects of imagination and sensation—but none of these comes with its own label and designation as basic (5.241 and 5.242). The legitimacy of any claim to knowledge is not to be found in its beginning point but rather in the method used to attain it. The beginning points are many and are constantly changing since they are always open to further scrutiny and future revision (fallibilism). Knowledge is grounded in experience, but it is grounded in the shifting sands of experience. The bedrock of knowledge is in experience; however, there is no bedrock in experience. All of this means that the knower is actively involved in the pursuit of knowledge in a manner which is foreign to both Cartesianism and traditional science.

Peirce then would certainly have been sympathetic with Gadamer's claim, which we examined in Chapter 5, that "all understanding inevitably involves some prejudice".[2] We can never completely overcome such "prejudices" and take refuge in "pure" reason as some traditions in Western epistemology have claimed. Rather, while embracing our prejudices, we must make them explicit and subject them to the scrutiny of investigation. And, according to Peirce, we cannot simply adopt some cute little principle or maxim such as "I am going to doubt everything which can be doubted" in order to overcome our prejudices. Peirce says:

> We cannot begin with complete doubt. We must begin with all the prejudices which we actually have when we enter upon the study of philosophy. These prejudices are not to be dispelled by a maxim, for they are things which it does not occur to us *can* be questioned. (5.265)

Therefore, we must trace the development of a theory of knowledge, science and rationality in Peirce's writings according to which *method* is the final arbiter and judge.

PEIRCE'S CATEGORIES

It is impossible to understand Peirce's analysis of experience, method, and rationality without using his treatment of the *categories*.[3] For our purposes, *Firstness* is not the most important of the categories, but metaphysically for Peirce, it is primary. Firstness involves the *pure* qualitative aspect of things. It is "[t]he unanalyzed total impression made by any manifold not thought of as actual fact, but simply as a quality, as simple positive possibility of appearance" (8.329). It is "the quality itself, independently of its being perceived or remembered" (8.329). Although Peirce regularly revised his notion of Firstness, as he did the other categories, it is consistently a monadic, non-relative notion.[4] It is the pure possibility of quality. Of more interest to us here is the notion of *Secondness*. Secondness is a dyadic relation, and whereas Firstness provides us with the 'whatness' of a thing, Secondness provides us with the 'thisness' of a thing.[5] Secondness provides us with *haecceity* through the "resistance", "shock", and "compulsion" in and by experience (1.334–

1.336). Secondness provides us with a "sense of externality" (1.334). It is not by perceiving the qualities of a thing that we are allowed to talk about its existence, but by "feeling" its haecceity, by "hefting its insistency then and there" (6.318). *Reality* does not consist in haecceity, but existence does (5.503), as does experience (5.613). Both existence and experience essentially involve the notion of Secondness, of relationship to or interaction *with* something else. "There is nothing at all that is absolutely confrontial," Peirce tells us, "although it is quite true that the confrontial is continually flowing in upon us" (7.653). Finally, *Thirdness* is that category which involves signs and is essentially triadic. Signs stand for something to someone, and since all thinking involves signs, all thinking involves the element of Thirdness (1.343), as does all *meaning* according to Peirce. Since Thirdness is not a reducible category, thinking and meaning are not reducible to quality (whatness) and reaction (thisness). Consider Peirce's example of the act of one person *giving* something to someone else:

> Take, for example, the relation of *giving*. A *gives* B to C. This does not consist in A's throwing B away and its accidentally hitting C, like the date-stone, which hit the Jinnee in the eye. If that were all, it would not be a genuine triadic relation, but merely one dyadic relation followed by another. There need be no motion of the thing given. Giving is a transfer of the right of property. Now right is a matter of law, and law is a matter of thought and meaning. (1.345)

Since all signs are conventions, then the category of Thirdness essentially involves the notions of rules, laws and conventions. As Richard Bernstein points out, "What is characteristic about giving is that there are some conventions, rules, or customs by virtue of which an act is *giving* and not just physical displacement."[6] Thinking is also a matter of thirdness since all thinking involves signs. As Peirce tells us,

> The only thought, then, which can possibly be cognized is thought in signs. But thought which cannot be cognized does not exist. All thought, therefore, must necessarily be in signs. (5.251)

PEIRCE'S THEORY OF BELIEF

Peirce's treatment of Thought and his theory of signs involve the crucial notions of belief, doubt, habit, logic and rationality. We cannot explore here all of the details of Peirce's theory of thought except to give a very rough sketch for the purpose of laying the ground work to discuss rationality and the scientific method. "[A] belief," Peirce says, "is itself a habit of mind by virtue of which one idea gives rise to another" (7.354). And "an inference is the process by which one belief *determines* another" (7.354 my emphasis). The general rules which regulate inferences are what Peirce scholars recognize as "leading principles", and critical logic is primarily a study of these "leading principles".

For Peirce, belief (which is itself a habit) gets "fixed" by inference which is determined by leading principles. Beliefs get "fixed" by becoming hardened and resistant to doubt. Logic enables our reasonings to be secure (2.1) and further enables us to act upon our beliefs; while doubt prevents our beliefs from becoming fixed and inhibits our ability to act (2.242).

All of these processes—belief, habit, doubt, inference, logic, leading principles, and action—involve signs and are therefore matters of Thirdness; and, as such, they all involve rules, conventions, and principles. So significant are these rules, habits and conventions that Peirce uses them to differentiate objects from other objects. "What we call a Thing is a cluster or habit of reactions" (4.157). Therefore, the very definition of a thing (or the meaning of a concept) involves not the possession of a quality or characteristic by an individual (Secondness) which would be determined by the familiar process of verification, but rather it is the "habit of conduct" (Thirdness) which essentially involves the notions of rules and conventions which defines a concept for pragmaticism. This is one of the key reasons why Peirce felt it necessary to distinguish pragmaticism from pragmatism. Peirce emphasizes this point:

> To say that I hold that the import, or adequate ultimate interpretation, of a concept is contained, not in any deed or deeds that will ever be done, but in a habit of conduct, or general moral determination of whatever procedure there *may come to be,* is no more than to say that I am a pragmaticist. (5.504)

In terms of understanding how Peirce would fit into the current dispute concerning the notion of rationality and scientific method, it seems very clear that Peirce would agree with the disputants who emphasize that reason and rationality are conventional. Thought, beliefs, habits, inference, and logic are all "conventional" for Peirce in the sense that they all involve signs (hence, Thirdness) which are essentially governed by rules or principles which give rise to habits and, eventually, action. At the same time, Peirce emphatically insists that these habits, conventions and principles are not subjective. He would be concerned to separate himself from the subjectivists and the relativists which we have discussed earlier. Peirce is undoubtedly a realist and sees realism as an essential part of pragmaticism (See 5.453, 5.470).

PEIRCE ON REALITY

We must turn then to an examination of Peirce's notion of reality[7] to examine how his treatment of reality can be used as a starting point for attempting to resolve many of the main disputes in the present discussion concerning rationality and relativism. In particular, Peirce's treatment of reality serves to protect scientific and epistemological methodology from the attacks of the subjectivists and relativists.

The most important place to begin is with what is perhaps one of the best known passages from Peirce:

> The real, then, is that which, sooner or later, information and reasoning would finally result in, and which is therefore independent of the vagaries of me and you. Thus, the very origin of the conception of reality shows that this conception essentially involves the notion of a COMMUNITY, without definite limits, and capable of a definite increase of knowledge. And so those two series of cognition—the real and the unreal—consist of those which, at a time sufficiently future, the community will always continue to re-affirm; and of those which, under the same conditions, will ever after be denied. (5.311)

Compare this essentially public and social aspect of reality with Descartes' "Cogito". Descartes conducts his famed enquiry in the privacy of his study. The enquiry itself is subjective and intuitive. There are no protections against the "vagaries" of the individual, and there is no criterion for assessing either the result or the method. Peirce himself has successfully attacked the Cartesian enterprise far better than I can here. It remains to be pointed out, however, that much of philosophy since Descartes has not escaped the same kind of subjectivism and foundationalism. Descartes's "light of reason" and Russell's "knowledge by acquaintance" are in the same leaky boat. Descartes's notion of clear and distinct ideas was supposed to provide him with some criterion—some standard by which ideas could be assessed. The difficulty is, as Peirce has pointed out, that no ideas—including supposedly clear and distinct ones—provide a magical, private, and subjective beginning point or end point to enquiry. Peirce concludes that any investigation of "internal" (subjective) matters must proceed by inference from external facts, and there is no such faculty of introspection as Descartes supposed (5.249).

The Private Language Argument

In Peirce's argument against Descartes there is more than just a hint of Wittgenstein's famous argument against the possibility of a private language. Although I will not recount Wittgestein's argument here, and although there is, admittedly, some disagreement about the argument,[8] the conclusion of the argument is important and relevant for our present considerations. The main thrust of Wittgenstein's attack on private language is to eliminate the logical possibility of a private language—a language which is theoretically accessible to only one person, in which the names for sensations are learned ostensively, and which is used to describe subjective, internal experiences (sensations). In the famous passages of the 'beetle in the box' and 'the diary keeper' Wittgenstein claims that the absence of some public and external criterion makes this whole enterprise impossible.

> Now someone tells me that *he* knows what pain is only from his own case!—Suppose everyone had a box with something in it: we call it a "beetle". No one can look into anyone else's box, and everyone says he knows what a beetle is only by looking at *his* beetle. —Here it would be quite possible for everyone to have something different in his box. One might even imagine such a thing constantly changing. —But suppose the word "beetle" had a use in these people's language? —If so it would not be used as the name of a thing. The thing in the box has no place in the language-game at all; not even as a *something:* for the box might even be empty. —No, one can 'divide through' by the thing in the box; it cancels out, whatever it is.
> That is to say: if we construe the grammar of the expression of sensation on the model of 'object and designation' the object drops out of consideration as irrelevant.[9]

The situation of the diary keeper also dramatically illustrates what Wittgenstein argues is the philosophically absurd situation of any theory which must rely upon the notion of a private language.

> Let us imagine the following case: I want to keep a diary about the recurrence of a certain sensation. To this end I associate it with the sign 'S' and write this sign in a calendar for every day on which I have the sensation. —I will remark first of all that a definition of the sign cannot be formulated. —But still I can give myself a kind of ostensive definition. —How? Can I point to the sensation? Not in the ordinary sense. But I speak, or write the sign down, and at the same time I concentrate my attention on the sensation—and so, as it were, point to it inwardly. —But what is this ceremony for? For that is all it seems to

be! A definition surely serves to establish the meaning of a sign. —Well, that is done precisely by the concentrating of my attention; for in this way I impress on myself the connexion between the sign and the sensation. —But "I impress it on myself" can only mean: this process brings it about that I remember the connexion *right* in the future. But in the present case I have no criterion of correctness. One would like to say: whatever is going to seem right to me is right. And that only means that here we can't talk about 'right'.[10]

It will not do, of course, for one to simply concentrate a little more carefully or to simply pay more careful attention to the private, subjective sensation or to focus upon the memory of earlier sensations in order to ensure that one is correct. Such attempts do not allow one to distinguish between what is right and what seems to be right and are like reading different copies of a newspaper in order to verify a news story.[11] An external and public criterion creates the possibility of error and correct and incorrect usage. Any meaningful use of language must take place against the context of a rule-governed situation within which there are recognizable proper and improper "moves". Otherwise, of course, anything one might say is just as correct as anything else one might say—which, according to Wittgenstein, simply means that the whole business would then be nonsense.

Something of a very similar argument lies behind Peirce's criticism of Cartesian subjectivism and introspection. When Peirce develops the notion of a community, he adopts a position which embodies a public criterion in a manner which is very similar to the argument which lies behind Wittgenstein's rejection of a private language. Peirce says:

And what do we mean by the real? It is a conception which we must first have had when we discovered that there was an unreal, an illusion; that is, when we first corrected ourselves. Now the distinction for which alone this fact logically called, was between an *ens* relative to private inward determinations . . . and an *ens* such as would stand in the long run. (5.311)

The "*ens* such as would stand in the long run" he makes clear is that which finally comes from the community, sooner or later, given enough information and reasoning. The concept of the real first originates only because we discover that upon occasions we make mistakes and that there is such a thing as the unreal. But consider Wittgenstein's diary keeper. He could never make a mistake because when he introspects and examines his sensations and focusses upon his memory whatever he decides will always "seem" right to him; so, he will never be in the position of having to correct or being able to correct himself. If we are ever to correct ourselves, Peirce tells us, the distinction between the subjective, private *ens* of the individual and the objective, public *ens* of the community is "logically" required.

PEIRCE'S ANTI-FOUNDATIONALISM

Peirce thus simultaneously undermines both the subjectivism of Cartesianism (and some forms of empiricism) and its foundationalism. There is no subjective reality about which we can be indubitably certain; therefore there is no fundamental and primitive foundation of human knowledge which is theoretically immune to mistakes and which can serve as the fountainhead for all knowledge. There is no knowledge which is known immediately and directly. As Peirce puts it, we have no faculty of intuition according to which we are able to have cognitions which are not determined by other cognitions but are determined directly by some transcendental (subjective) object (5.213ff). So there is no foundation of knowledge which we are able to know in some qualitatively different way from the way in which we know all other knowledge claims.

Neither then are any of our knowledge claims infallible. Peirce's well-known theory of fallibilism is rooted in the fact that all cognitions involve signs as does all inference. Cognition and inference—thought and reason—are thus essentially grounded in habits, rules and principles. Although these habits and principles may serve as the beginning point of enquiry, they themselves are not absolute but are constantly open to scrutiny and review. The process of enquiry is a process of continual self-correction and adjustment, and any result of the process may prove to be fallible and, in Quine's term, "revisable" in the face of some future changes or adjustments by the community. It is only through this process that we could ever correct ourselves or even determine that we have made a mistake.

However, in terms of dealing with the current disputes concerning rationality and relativism, the most important issues are still unresolved. Initially, it appears as if we could add Peirce to the group of those discussed earlier who are responsible for the precipitation of the current crisis regarding traditional science. If Peirce is successful in undermining both the supposed *foundations* of knowledge and the *results* of inquiry as legitimizing factors, or as epistemic warrant guarantors, then what is left? How does Peirce avoid the skepticism and relativism in which some of the modern detractors of rationality and method have taken refuge?

PEIRCE AND METHOD

Peirce takes his stand in the method itself. It is the method which becomes the guarantor of the results of inquiry and knowledge. Bernstein puts this point clearly:

> Our claims to knowledge are legitimized not by their origins—for the origins of knowledge are diverse and fallible—but rather by the norms and rules of inquiry itself.[12]

Others have also recognized Peirce's relevance to the present dispute. Ian Hacking points out, for example, that

> Peirce tried to replace truth by method. Truth is whatever is in the end delivered to the community of inquirers who pursue a certain end in a certain way. Various aspects of Peirce's philosophy, especially the fallibilism and the revolutionary epistemology, have by now amply been compared to Popper. But the greater novelties in Peirce's thought are seldom recalled: the idea that man is language, that the world is not deterministic, and that there is *an objective surrogate for truth to be found in methodology*.[13]

Peirce's commitment to method provides us with an alternative to the current resurgence of naturalism and relativism as ways of responding to the criticisms raised against traditional understandings of science, rationality and method. One way to respond to the skeptic is to resort to naturalism. Hume, of course, is the recognized master of this craft. He determined that it is not possible to give a sound theoretical response to the skeptic. Nature does not permit us to actually believe the *conclusions* of the skeptic, but the *arguments* of the skeptic are unassailable logically. As we have seen in the preceding chapter, the naturalistic response to the skeptic has recently been raised to new heights in the face of the attacks on science and epistemology in this century.[14] But, as we have seen, such a response to the skeptic amounts to "throwing in the towel". The naturalist admits that it is not possible to appeal to reason and arguments to deflect the attacks of the skeptic and the relativist and takes refuge in "good, old Mother Nature". The arguments of the skeptic are invulnerable to counter-argument, but Nature renders them inconsequential.

Most of the threads in the fabric of modern epistemology seemed to have passed through the eye of the needle of relativism. If the naturalist is correct and there is not a theoretical response to the skeptic, and if the blatant *ad hoc* and *deux ex machina* of Nature is not appealing as a solution, then we are left with precious few alternatives. How are we to avoid the conclusion of Richard Rorty that epistemology is dead[15] or the equally pessimistic claim of Paul Feyerabend that science is just another ideology, along with magic and astrology, against which society needs to be defended?[16]

Peirce undoubtedly has a certain sympathy with the naturalist because the notion of haecceity given in Secondness is a feeling—not a concept which is the result of a deliberative process of reasoning. Indeed, Secondness as a mode of being is supposed to correspond to the external world.[17] Secondness gives us the feeling of "active oppugnancy" in our experience (8.291), of something being forced upon us (2.138), of reaction with the environment (5.503). From Secondness we "naturally" get the notion of existence, and this notion is "nonrational" in the sense that it is immediately experienced; thus, haecceity is given not by perceiving any qualities or as the result of any inference, but ostensibly, "in hefting its insistency then and there" (6.318). Bernstein compares the feeling of externality we get from Peirce's category of Secondness with the "over-againstness" or facticity of experience to be found in existentialist thinkers.[18] But Secondness gives us no guarantee of *externality* or *reality* which must be inferred and is thus the result of Thirdness and the use of signs. To explain and justify our notions of externality and reality, Peirce goes beyond Secondness (and beyond naturalism) to Thirdness, semiotics, habits, rules, principles, inference, and method. Otherwise, there would be no *response* to the skeptic and certainly no response to the relativist. Exploring Peirce's defense of method provides us with an avenue of response to the skeptic and the relativist which has been neither properly understood nor properly appreciated.

SCIENCE AND PRIVATE LANGUAGE

Let us imagine a scientist in a position similar to the one which Wittgenstein describes concerning the diary keeper and ask some of the same questions of the scientist that Wittgenstein asks of the diary keeper. Think about what would be involved is such a scientist conducting an experiment completely "privately". For example, consider a biologist who imagines looking through a microscope at different pieces of tissue. She imagines observing certain characteristics and mentally notes certain features. She makes mental, imaginary comparisons between different kinds of tissues, and then on the basis of her memories of those differences forms a hypothesis which she further "tests" in a similar manner. At some point, she finally announces to the world that she has discovered the cause of a certain kind of cancer. Obviously, other scientists would not take such an announcement seriously nor would we even regard the activity involved as one of practicing science. Surely the scientist in this example is in exactly the same position as is Wittgenstein's diary keeper. There is no standard of correctness here—no theoretical possibility of error or even an understanding of what error would mean—which means that whatever is going on here it is not a rational process about which we can make any epistemological claims. Even the individual involved is not in a position to make any such claims. Whatever seems right will be right to her.

Similarly, consider the example of a geologist making a map. He imagines a landscape—perhaps even a landscape which he has actually visited before. He then begins to mentally "draw" a map of the landscape. He carefully concentrates on every exact detail of the landscape—the topography, bodies of water, coast line, and so on. Finally, he finishes the map. Is the map an accurate one? Initially, it seems that no one but the individual involved can sensibly answer this question. Certainly none of us would be in a position to try and answer the question. But is even the individual in a position to answer the question? He may give us an answer by again imagining the landscape and then comparing his imaginary map to his imagined or remembered landscape. But again, whatever the outcome of this process, it seems to be epistemologically completely empty. In the absence of any Wittgensteinian-styled public and external criterion, there is no standard of correctness, no possibility of error—even theoretically. Whatever the final determination of the map maker, it will be right simply because it seems right. Not only then can the imaginary mental map maker not answer the question about the accuracy of the map, the question cannot even sensibly be asked.

Science and the scientific method are essentially public just as Wittgenstein argued that language is essentially public. One can no more play a completely private game with oneself or perform essentially private inferences than one can use a private language. What would it be like to win or lose? Or even to make a proper or improper move? What guarantor would there be of correct inference? In each instance, one would be in the same position as the diary keeper. Science and inference and method are as much in need of some public standard and criterion as is language, and the community provides that standard according to Peirce. Critics of Peirce have focussed too much upon the question of what guarantee we have that the community provides us with the correct standard of truth or reality. They have ignored the fact that the community provides us with the only possible kind of standard of truth and reality and method. It is only within the public and social context that the further question concerning the correctness of the method or the results of the method can be raised.

If Tarot Card reading and astrology were to have some *public* mechanism for assessing their methods and for determining when and how mistakes are possible, only then would they become rivals to science. To the extent that one can make sense of anything like a commonly accepted standard for the correct way of practicing such alternative methods for fixing beliefs (such as reading Tarot Cards), that method must and does approximate the scientific method—depending upon public observation and repeatable events—not just upon Tarot Card reading itself. In other words, reading Tarot Cards is neither self-regulating, nor self-correcting, nor self-justifying.

SCIENCE AND THE POSSIBILITY OF ERROR

It is exactly this feature which gives rise to the very possibility of mistakes and fraud in science. Recently, the occurrence of fraud within scientific research has been of great concern to scientists.[19] Of course, there have been very important and much celebrated cases of fraud in science. Perhaps the most famous hoax is the case of the Piltdown Man whose remains were alleged to have been found in Sussex, England, between 1909 and 1915. For almost 40 years, human evolutionists took the Piltdown fossils as evidence of asymmetrical evolution until fluorine dating demonstrated the bones to be modern. The misrepresentation survived decades of scrutiny by physical anthropologists and the general public until the hoax was finally revealed. Numerous other mistakes and deliberate frauds are generously sprinkled throughout the history of science. In 1969, we witnessed the "discovery" of "polywater" (a supposed allotrope of ordinary water) by a Russian chemist, and there was fear that once this polywater was loosed upon ordinary water in an unsuspecting world, there would be a chain reaction and all regular H_2O would be converted into the sticky, dense polywater. The "discovery" turned out to be the result of poor, contaminated samples used in the experiment.

Even more recently, and even into the 1980s, cases of fraudulent research being represented as "genuine" science continue. A well-known case which was adjudicated by the National Institute of Mental Health involved the "research" of Stephan Breuning whose theories advocating the use of stimulants for the treatment of mental retardation were widely adopted by people in the field of mental health until they were revealed to be based upon fraudulent research. Similarly, Robert Slutsky was regarded as one of the leaders in cardiac research until it was discovered that over 60 of his articles that were published in leading biomedical journals around the world were based on fraudulent data. In another celebrated case, Wilbert Aronow, one time Chief of the Cardiovascular Section of the Veterans Administration Hospital, Long Beach, California, finally admitted to falsifying data submitted to the Food and Drug Administration on the effects of drugs which were being tested.[20]

As such cases of fraud multiply, much of the attention of both the scientific community and the general public has focussed upon the causes of fraud in science, and a certain distrust of science has resulted. Now fraud in science is certainly a legitimate cause for concern. For example, much attention has justifiably been given to the extreme competition amongst scientists for the recognition and financial rewards which come from success. There is also legitimate cause for concern over the great pressure upon scientists in some positions to generate the funds for their research through various grants, and there is also the problem of the additional pressure upon scientists in academic institutions to produce research quickly for tenure and promotion decisions. The mounting concern is one of how science and scientific research can maintain their integrity in the face of ever-increasing pressures and rewards for cheating.

There is no doubt that science would be much better off if the incentives for fast, sloppy, and fraudulent research were reduced. But the most crucial *theoretical* point is that it is the unique nature of scientific methodology which even allows for *the possibility of fraud.* It is only against the backdrop of legitimate research and legitimate scientific methodology that the notion of fraud or hoax even makes sense, and it is of the very nature of scientific method to try to disprove its own findings. Scientific methodology is the only methodology of which this is true. After all, what would fraudulent astrology be except simply astrology? It is of the very nature of the scientific method to question the results of its own method, and it is of the very nature of the scientific community to question the findings of its own members. In other situations, such enquiry is left to the initiative and energy of different individuals, but, in the case of science, publicizing the results of one's experiments and subjecting them to the scrutiny of other members of the community of enquirers is a part of the method itself. Consequently, the scientific community is constantly on vigil, and though mistakes are made and frauds perpetrated, the scientific community is never "unsuspecting" but is rather skeptical by nature.

Consider the recent controversy which raged over the claims of Stanley Pons and Martin Fleischmann concerning "cold fusion"— (what has been called "fusion in a jar"). A storm of controversy within the scientific community followed the claim that fusion has been produced by the two chemists in a test tube at room temperature, and numerous attempts were made to duplicate the experiment —although Pons and Fleischmann have still not revealed all of the details of their experiment. Much of the usual restraint and decorum of scientific research were lost while various groups of scientists rushed to make announcements before the news media, and there is some evidence that Pons and Fleischmann rushed their original announcement in order to "beat" a physicist, Steven Jones, with the discovery; so there is certainly much to lament about the way in which the whole affair has been conducted. However, the main issue for this discussion should not be lost amongst the sensational headlines. Whether the report of Pons and Fleischmann concerning cold fusion eventually stands or falls, whether it is accepted or rejected, whether it is found to be fact or mistake (or even worse, fraud) will result from the most intense scrutiny and testing imaginable within the scientific community. Hundreds or thousands of chemists and physicists will spend as much time as it takes to try and prove Pons and Fleischmann wrong. This is an excellent example of the self-correcting mechanism at work within the scientific method. If there is a mistake in the application of the method, it will be detected by the application of the same method, and though mistakes and frauds do occur, they can only be detected and corrected within the framework created by the method which provides the very notion of legitimate results. A counterfeit piece of currency can occur only within a monetary system which provides the framework for the meaning of legitimate tender.

Peirce explicitly recognizes the necessity of an external criterion and its resulting effect of creating a context within which right and wrong usage become possible. He says, for example, that "it is necessary that a method should be found by which our beliefs may be determined by nothing human, but by some external permanency— by something upon which our thinking has no effect" (5.384). Because of this "external permanence", science is the only method "which presents any distinction of a right and a wrong way" (5.385). The other methods considered—the method of tenacity, the method of authority, and the a priori method—provide no possibility of critical examination of the method and no possibility of error. In a claim which could well serve as the conclusion of Wittgenstein's argument against private language, Peirce says that with methods other than science, one is left "to think as one is inclined to think" (5.385). Only science provides even the possibility of making mistakes and correcting the mistakes by using the method. Whatever the "external permanency" is which guarantees the method of science over all other methods, it cannot be "restricted in its influence to one individual" (5.384). So, not only is Descartes's intuition ruled out, but Russell's sense data and Carnap's protocol language are as well.

> The test of whether I am truly following the [scientific] method is not an immediate appeal to my feelings and purposes, but, on the contrary, itself involves the application of the method. Hence it is that bad reasoning as well as good reasoning is possible. (5.385)

ROBINSON CRUSOE AND SCIENCE

If this point is put within the context of Wittgenstein's argument against private language, we might say that Peirce has not demonstrated simply that science is the *best* method for fixing beliefs, but that it is the only method. This point can be put more sharply in focus by raising some of the same questions about science which participants in the private-language debate have raised about language. Let us imagine a Robinson Crusoe who is left on his deserted island while he is a mere infant. He is raised in the wild by some animal until he finally becomes a mature adult,[21] and we then raise the question of whether such a person could invent a language. Could he invent a language with which he could keep a diary similar to the one attempted by Wittgenstein's diary keeper? Well, in one sense he could. He could certainly invent symbols and write them down. In one way, the results of such a Crusoe's diary-keeping efforts would appear no different from yours or mine. But in another sense, such a Crusoe's diary is meaningless gibberish. Rush Rhees makes this point very clearly:

> What is it that he [Robinson Crusoe] cannot do? What is it that I can do and he cannot? There seems to be nothing logically absurd in supposing that he behaves just as I do. To a large extent I agree. But it is absurd to suppose that the marks he uses mean anything; even if we

might want to say that he goes through all the motions of meaning something by them.[22]

Language is a social phenomenon and requires a social context within which rules, patterns of use, principles and a community of language speakers create standards of correct usage and within which incorrect usage becomes possible.

> The point is that no one could invent just *language.* Language goes with a way of living. An invented language would be a wallpaper pattern; nothing more.[23]

Let us now focus upon some of the issues concerning the public aspect of science by raising some of the same questions which have been asked concerning Robinson Crusoe and language. Could Robinson Crusoe, raised in the wild from infancy in complete isolation from other intelligent beings, invent science? What *additional* issues are raised by the consideration of the possibility of Crusoe inventing science? This way of putting the issue takes us right to the heart of what Peirce considered to be the essentially public and social aspect of science and the scientific method.

Even if we imagine that Crusoe's attempt to invent science involves only external, publicly observable objects, we are still led to an immediate recognition of the necessity of some sort of public *community* for Crusoe to develop any understanding of such notions as laws, theories, and experiments. The considerations which hold for language hold *a fortiori* for science. For example, suppose that Crusoe makes observations about the flora and animals on the island, forms hypotheses about possible explanations for certain phenomena, and tests those hypotheses by making further observations using his private science. In one sense, what he does would be no different from what you or I might do. But is it science? I think decidedly not! The results of Crusoe's attempts at science are scientific gibberish in a manner completely analogous to the way in which Crusoe's attempts at language are gibberish.

Although this extended claim about science may not be as readily apparent, consider the methodological questions which might be raised about Crusoe's attempts at science, methodological questions which parallel the questions raised about Crusoe's attempts at language. What would it be like for Crusoe to make a mistake? What would it be like for Crusoe to make a mistake not just about some observation but about some rule or law or principle which he invents and then invokes in his investigation? Even if he pays very careful attention to whatever consideration is at stake, even if he goes over his memories of the designs of his experiments time and time again, what is to prevent him from making the same mistake each time? Without a public, empirical criterion by which the results of such an investigation can be assessed, memory is no better than imagination, and Crusoe would be in no better position epistemologically than our biologist and geologist with their imaginary experiments. Scientific theories, laws, principles, designs of experiments, and so on, are essentially social phenomena—just as language is. To do science and to hold certain scientific beliefs or to maintain certain scientific theories does not mean simply to arrive at certain results. Science and scientific theories are not characterized simply by their content but also by the process by which they are derived. It is not simply that Crusoe's *results* must be available in a form which makes them accessible to other people in order to be scientific; it is rather that the scientific language, theories, laws, and experiments by which the results are obtained are a part of a community in the sense that they are available for public scrutiny. Otherwise, the private scientist is in the position of having invented a game in which he or she is simultaneously the only player and umpire, the only judge and defendant, and in which there are no right and wrong moves.

There is some evidence that Wittgenstein (perhaps even influenced by Peirce) recognized that this claim applied with even more force to science than to language since he seems to take the essentially non-private nature of science to be a paradigmatic case for language to follow. He says, "Looking up a table in the imagination is no more looking up a table than the image of the result of an imagined experiment is the result of an experiment."[24] To which we might add that looking up a table solely in the memory fares no better.

SCIENCE AND SOLITAIRE

The epistemological position of a normal, mature adult placed in an isolated situation is, of course, quite different, and it is not all that different epistemologically from the position in which many of us might find ourselves some time. The mature Robinson Crusoe who finds his way to the deserted island as a normal adult with a language and an understanding of science already in place can, I maintain, practice science. His position would not be all that different from a scientist practicing science in a private, isolated laboratory. For example, an individual living alone can surely form hypotheses and test them, and such an individual can surely make mistakes and correct them in very much the same way that you or I can play a game of solitaire. But even with an apparently simple case such as this one, we must be careful. What about the game of solitaire I played *yesterday* for which there are no records or other public accounts? Did I make a mistake in that game? If our only access to the game of solitaire which we played yesterday is our memory, then our best recollection will necessarily be the right answer since it is the only possible answer. Now undoubtedly we are in such a situation many times with respect to our own memories, and the epistemological difficulties attending such situations are notorious. I will not address those problems here. The important issue here is that we impose higher epistemological standards for science than we do for individual beliefs. In order for the beliefs of an individual to be scientific, those actions must not only be theoretically assessable, they must also be *empirically* assessable as well. If we think of the example of playing solitaire again, we might be inclined to say something such as, 'Well, if another person had been present when I was playing solitaire yesterday, then that person could have observed my mistake.' This is true, and it illustrates that playing solitaire is certainly on a much better epistemological footing than claims regarding one's essentially private, mental states. However, unless there are records, accounts, video tapes, or some other publicly assessable accounts which the parties agree are an accurate record of the earlier event, then, I maintain, *science* cannot be involved. An ideal observer kind of theory is not adequate for providing the kind of public access needed for science. The adult Robinson Crusoe, living in isolation, can form and test hypotheses scientifically, but only if there are empirical accounts of some sort for him and others to consult. This is exactly what we mean by requiring that an experiment be *repeatable,* and it is this condition which provides the epistemological mechanism for assessing correct and incorrect applications of the method. Without such a requirement, Pons and Fleischman would have slipped quietly and easily into the annals of the history of science without causing a ripple of dissent.

THE IDOL OF THE CLOSET

The essentially public aspect of science and scientific methodology requires that Francis Bacon's famous list of idols be extended.[25] Bacon's idols are those negative influences upon one's thinking which lead to biases, confusions and mistakes which threaten science. To Bacon's list of idols of the tribe, cave, market-place and theater, we must now add the Idol of the Closet. The Idol of the Closet is that idol of the mind which leads one to attempt to pursue the life of a private scientist. To the degree to which one is successful in becoming *essentially* private in one's activities, in separating oneself *essentially* from the scientific community, one succeeds in becoming something other than a scientist. Essential privacy guarantees only epistemic emptiness. This is why Descartes's notion of clear and distinct ideas cannot serve as the criterion that he intends. A clear and distinct idea is supposed to be something which the subject never mistakes for anything else. It is supposed to bear its own guarantee "on its sleeve" so that one is able to determine its veracity simply at "face value". But what would it be like for a person to be mistaken about a claim involving clear and distinct ideas? What standard can one impose to make sure that one's judgment about a clear and distinct idea is correct? Since all of this is completely internal and subjective for Descartes, attempting to make judgments about clear and distinct ideas seems to place one in exactly the same untenable epistemological position as Wittgenstein's diary keeper. And the only way to avoid this epistemological cul-de-sac is to avoid the Idol of the Closet.

A clear example of failing to avoid adequately the Idol of the Closet is the history of astronomy in ancient China. Although very extended and exact astronomical observations were made by ancient Chinese astronomers, astronomy never developed to the level of a mature science there because of the influence of "the secret science of priest-kings".[26] Given a powerful and well-organized central government with leaders who regarded "scientific" information from the state astronomers as vital state secrets and an official, ancient "state secrecy act" which prohibited the state astronomers from collaborating with each other, from working with their own subordinates, or from even telling anyone else about their findings or theories at all,[27] it must be questionable whether astronomy as practiced by the ancient Chinese was really scientific at all. This example illustrates how the practice of science requires the existence of an external and public scientific community. Notice that the accuracy of the observations or the gathered data is not the issue here. One might well make what turns out to be accurate observations or even accurate predictions based upon those observations, as the ancient Chinese actually did, but how are we to know whether a person's data are simply the result of sheer happenstance or luck or fraud if the methods for arriving at those data are not recorded and made public? Gettier's counter-examples to the justified true belief theory of knowledge[28] have taught us the necessity for some epistemic connection between the reason a person holds a belief and whether the belief can qualify as knowledge. In this case, the mere accuracy of certain beliefs on the part of ancient Chinese astronomers does not make those beliefs scientific ones.

It is not the *content* of beliefs but the *fixation* of beliefs which is scientific. The *content* of beliefs may first come from dreams, hallucinations, hunches or indigestion. Scientific beliefs are those which are the result of a particular method according to which one belief produces another. Consequently, the method is more fundamental and logically primitive than the beliefs it produces, and theoretically the method is neutral in terms of the content of the beliefs which it produces. The young boy in D.H. Lawrence's "The Rocking Horse Winner", who consistently and unerringly predicted the winners of horse races by rocking himself into a frenzied state on a rocking horse, serves as a good example. The accuracy and precision of the boy's predictions might well be the envy of every scientist; however, the boy is clearly not "doing science", and the commitment of the scientist and the rational person is to the method—not to the results.

METHOD AND THE HISTORY OF SCIENCE

Such a commitment to method has direct consequences for dealing with two important aspects of the history of science highlighted by Kuhn. The primitive nature of scientific method and its essentially public nature allows one to explain the phenomena of simultaneous discoveries in the history of science by appealing only to what Imre Lakatos characterizes as *internal* reasons. The public method and community act as forces which, if not directing scientific inquiry and history, can be used to explain the particular events in the history of science. Such a commitment to method, however, requires one to look at the "revolutions" in the history of science in a different manner from the way in which Kuhn describes them. As we have seen in Chapter 4, changes in paradigms—revolutions—for Kuhn are a dramatic, cataclysmic, and ultimately, nonrational process. One cannot conceptually "stand" within one paradigm and "reason" oneself into the new one. A change in paradigms is not simply a re-interpretation of the data.[29] Something much more drastic takes place—something requiring a Gestalt-like change which occurs in a "lightning flash" or in "flashes of intuition".[30] This is why paradigms are supposed to be "incommensurable" with one another and why one cannot use "normal science" to move from one paradigm to another.

Peirce (and, following him, Lakatos) is intent upon denying the irrational and cataclysmic nature of these changes, and exploring Peirce's argument for denying these irrational interruptions in the history of science leads us into the final issue in Peirce's characterization of scientific method. Since the initial and ultimate commitment of the scientist qua scientist is to method, then truth and reality become secondary—but inevitable and ultimate—byproducts of continual and never-flagging commitment to that method. If scientific method acts as the ultimate guarantor of the content or result, then how are we to demonstrate that the beliefs fixed by science are true or that there is any progress in the history of science? What good reason is there to believe in the convergence of science? Peirce believes that though there may be some dead ends and setbacks, and though the way may be circuitous at times, the developments and changes in the history of scientific enquiry must be viewed as a gradual convergence toward the ideal end. But why, one might ask, is there any reason to believe that enquiry converges? Peirce has frequently been criticized for holding an unfounded commitment to the idealized state with no good argument or reason to support it. I maintain that, on the contrary, there is a compelling reason for maintaining that scientific inquiry not only does but *must* converge.

SCIENCE AND CONVERGENCE ON TRUTH

The place to begin in trying to provide an explanation for and a defense of the claim that scientific enquiry converges is to remind ourselves of how enquiry begins for Peirce. No enquiry is possible without doubt. This is "real" inquiry which Peirce is interested in—not some hypothesized, artificial or "academic" Cartesian pursuit. It is only the "irritation of doubt" which causes the struggle to reach some resolution to the irritation—some belief. Indeed, Peirce tells us, "The irritation of doubt is the only immediate motive for the struggle to attain belief" (5.375). So we are talking about *real* enquiry here. As such, enquiry begins with doubt so it ends with the cessation of doubt. The purpose of enquiry "is the settlement of opinion" (the fixation of belief) (5.375), and we are led inexorably toward this final end by the nature of the method itself. The

Community of Inquirers settles upon a single understanding of reality when all doubt has been satisfied, when all irritation has led through enquiry to the satisfied state of belief. But why must anyone admit that what the community of enquirers settles upon is the right or only understanding of the nature of reality?

Anyone who ever engages in enquiry must admit that there is a single understanding of the nature of reality which has a legitimate claim to the title of truth; otherwise, doubt would and could present no irritation and no dissatisfaction. *Any* enquiry, and hence the commitment to *any* method of fixing beliefs must arise from some apparent conflict between different claims; hence, even in the *attempt* to appease doubt, in the pursuit of enquiry itself, there "already is a vague concession that there is some *one* thing which a proposition should represent" (5.384). So, the "hypothesis" of some reality upon which scientific inquiry converges is one which every inquiring mind must admit (5.384). As Peirce describes the process: "When we busy ourselves to find the answer to a question, we are going upon the hope that there is an answer, which can be called *the* answer, that is, the final answer. . . . [This is the answer which] sufficient inquiry will compel us to accept" (4.61).

It does seem that Peirce's point here captures a commonsense notion which occurs rather frequently in ordinary discourse. Consider an investigation into something like a plane crash. When an airliner crashes and there is an investigation to determine the cause of the crash, there is an implicit commitment to the hypothesis that there is theoretically some *one* correct explanation for the crash and that given enough time and information (and, of course, enough money) it would be theoretically possible to provide *the* account of the cause of the crash. We may say something like, "Well, we will never know the complete truth of what happened here," but the mere pursuit of the investigation commits us to the theoretical belief that there is a single, objective, "complete truth" to be known—perhaps by no single individual enquirer, but certainly theoretically by the Community of Inquirers. Once we admit even the *possibility* of the reality about which enquiry takes place, then given the nature of scientific inquiry, the ultimate, idealized state of the end of enquiry which converges upon this reality follows.

There does remain the additional question, *"What guarantees that the method will converge to one single theory or understanding of reality?"* James puts the matter very clearly when he says: "There is nothing improbable in the supposition that an analysis of the world may yield a number of formulae, all consistent with the facts".[31]

Rorty also asks very poignantly, "What guarantees that our changing theories of the world are getting better rather than worse?"[32] The most important, and frequently overlooked, point to make in response to James and Rorty is to look at what even allows this sort of question to be raised. What would count as an answer? How would one even determine what would make a theory "better" rather than "worse"? Indeed, how would one even determine that our theories are "changing"? It is only within the context of the scientific method that answers to these questions become intelligible. One can detect different or changing theories only because one theory explains different facts, or is compatible with different facts, or is supported with different facts from another theory. For this supposed challenge to scientific method to even get off the ground, the method must be presupposed.

Given Peirce's commitment to the scientific method, the response to the implied criticism is obvious. First, we must ask if enquiry has come to an end. Has all doubt been appeased and is the Community of Inquirers satisfied at this point in the inquiry? If the answer is, 'No', then the enquiry must continue. If the answer is, 'Yes', which seems to be what is intended by James's criticism, then it is important to remember Peirce's commitment to the pragmatic theory of meaning. People generally ignore the important role played by Peirce's theory of meaning in his theory of the fixation of belief. So important is the pragmatic theory of meaning that Peirce claims that commitment to it is essential to being a pragmatist. So, given that "our idea of anything *is* our idea of its sensible effects" (5.401) to determine the meaning of any word or theory, we must look to the practice or habit it produces in us. Peirce says:

> [W]hat a thing means is simply what habits it involves. Now, the identity of a habit depends on how it might lead us to act, not merely under such circumstances as are likely to arise, but under such as might possibly occur, no matter how improbable they may be. What the habit is depends on *when* and *how* it causes us to act. As for the *when,* every stimulus to action is derived from perception; as for *how,* every purpose of action is to produce some sensible result. Thus, we come down to what is tangible and conceivably practical, as the root of every real distinction of thought, no matter how subtle it may be; and there is no distinction of meaning so fine as to consist in anything but a possible difference of practice. (5.400)

James's suggestion that enquiry could ultimately end in such a manner that the enquirers could be genuinely torn between two or more different conceptions of reality poses no problem for Peirce. If the two different conceptions of reality are really different, if they have different meanings, then they must lead to differences in practice—differences in how we act. If there are no such differences, then the two conceptions are identical and really have the same meaning; that is, one could not sensibly distinguish between the two in terms of any differences in the practices of people who hold the different beliefs.

Peirce explains the connection between belief and practice is the following way:

> The essence of belief is the establishment of a habit; and different beliefs are distinguished by the different modes of action to which they give rise. If beliefs do not differ in this respect, if they appease the same doubt by producing the same rule of action, then no mere differences in the manner of consciousness of them can make them different beliefs, any more than playing a tune in different keys is playing different tunes. (5.398)

There may well be a period—even a very prolonged period—when the community is not able to settle upon a single theory in a particular field. This simply means that one must remind oneself of the long-term, comprehensive view of the nature of scientific inquiry as it essentially resides in the Community of Inquirers. If anything is ever to resolve the dispute between competing theories it will be by the accumulation of more data through more experiments by more researchers over a longer period of time. Finally, notice that the only way that one could ever determine that two theories are equally compatible with all of the known data is by adopting the exact method of enquiry which is being challenged. In other words, the only way one can tell whether two different theories are equivalent or different is by examining what happens when they are tested during the process of confirmation. Since, as we have seen, science is the only method to provide us with a context within which correct and incorrect applications of the method become possible, then science provides us with the only possible mechanism for testing theories and for distinguishing one theory from another.

SCIENCE AND SELF-CORRECTION

The essential nature of science which ultimately guarantees it is the unique fact that it is self-correcting: the method has a built-in mechanism for catching and correcting its own mistakes. This is, Peirce tells us, "one of the most wonderful features of reasoning and one of the most important philosophemes in the doctrine of science" (5.575). Not only is science the only method within which it even makes sense to talk of mistakes, it is, additionally, the only method which purifies itself by eliminating those mistakes. Science is the only method of fixing beliefs where the very practice of the method itself does not give rise to doubts about the method. This is a feature, Peirce maintains, of induction, deduction and retroduction (See 5.576–5.579), but primarily and essentially, it is a feature of induction. Given this "wonderful feature" of being self-correcting, the only thing one needs, in theory, to arrive at truth and reality is an unswerving commitment to the theory and an unflagging Will to Learn (5.583).

> [Self-correction] is a property so deeply saturating its [inquiry's] inmost nature that it may truly be said that there is but one thing needful for learning the truth, and that is a hearty and active desire to learn what is true. (5.582)

Consequently, Peirce is led by this process of reasoning to what he identifies as the "fundamental hypothesis" of science:

> There are Real things, whose characters are entirely independent of our opinions about them; those Reals affect our senses according to regular laws, and, though our sensations are as different as are our relations to the objects, yet, by taking advantage of the laws of perception, we can ascertain by reasoning how things really and truly are; and any man, if he have sufficient experience and he reason enough about it, will be led to the one True conclusion. (5.384)

Reality and truth both become the ultimate end of enquiry. Continual pursuit of science by a public and external community of inquirers not only *will* but *must* arrive at the truth. It is the scientific method which guarantees progress in science. This is the crux of Peirce's theory and the heart of his genius. It is something like the Reverse Pinocchio Syndrome: The longer the story is told, and the longer the enquiry goes on, and the more data which are added, the closer we get to the truth, and the shorter the distance grows between our current state and the Truth. So, we can conclude along with Peirce, that science is a method "which, if duly persisted in, must, in the very nature of things, lead to a result indefinitely approximating to the truth in the long run" (2.781) since it is dependent upon

induction," which *must* [my emphasis] generally lead to truth in the
long run (1.67).[33]

LAUDAN'S ATTACK ON PEIRCE

Recently, Larry Laudan has attacked Peirce's claims concerning both
the reliability (and self-correcting nature) of the scientific method
and the necessity of a convergent truth by insisting that such claims
amount simply to "a face-saving ploy" for scientists and philosophers[34] who must be satisfied with ever-closer approximations of
truth since they cannot justifiably lay claim to Truth itself. Peirce,
Laudan contends, sought to establish his arguments simply by "a
combination of bluster and repetition".[35] According to Laudan,
"Science is *essentially* a problem-solving activity." Laudan's characterization of science sounds very much like Kuhn's characterization
of *normal science* which we examined in Chapter 4. Laudan claims
that the most important considerations are "the maximization of the
empirical problems which we can explain and the minimization of
the anomalous and conceptual problems we generate in the process".[36] Furthermore, in the pursuit of this activity, scientists "do not
have any way of knowing for sure (or even with some confidence) that
science is true, or probable, or that it is getting closer to the truth."[37]
Indeed, he says, "Determinations of truth and falsity are *irrelevant* to
the acceptability or the pursuitability of [scientific] theories and
research traditions."[38] Laudan differs from Kuhn only in claiming
that the rationality of a scientific theory can be determined by
assessing its *progress,* and its progress is determined by the number of
important and interesting problems which it enables us to solve.[39]

Laudan's attack upon Peirce seems to closely resemble Kuhn's
attack upon the traditional understanding of epistemology and
science; however, Laudan is much less sophisticated and thorough
than Kuhn. In particular, Laudan continues to include *empirical*
problems amongst the "problems" which science is supposed to
solve.[40] Now Laudan is quick to add that what he calls "empirical"
problems are still relative to some conceptual framework and that
calling them "empirical" is simply a convenience since we still *treat*
these problems as if they are really matters of fact, but, surely this is
an inadequate explanation. Laudan still maintains that empirical
problems are *qualitatively different* from other problems because we
treat them by examining "the objects in the domain".[41] It is clear that
empirical facts *function* for Laudan just as they do for the realist;

consequently, he has the same problem as Kuhn of explaining how, if facts are indeed relative to a conceptual framework, anomalies can ever arise. From whence comes the efficacy of a fact to be anomalous if facts are relative to theories (or paradigms)? Must not a fact have some objective, independent epistemological standing if it is to force a re-examination of the theory within which it occurs? Laudan criticizes Kuhn for focussing exclusively upon the number of anomalies without considering their epistemological importance;[42] however, Laudan blindly follows Kuhn by uncritically accepting and using the notion of anomalous facts without addressing the theoretical problem of how such anomalies could consistently occur within scientific theory as he has described it. So, Laudan still clearly has a notion of objective reality operating within his theory. If empirical facts are indeed relative to theories, then empirical problems cannot force themselves upon us.

Secondly, Laudan also clearly still has a notion of objective truth operating within his theory. He says, for example, that Peirce's claim that science is self-correcting is "simply incorrect", and he then proceeds to give an argument, including several historical examples, to the effect that Peirce's theory is simple false based upon the history of science and Western thought.[43] It is patently impossible to use "facts" from the history of science to attack theories about the nature of science if determinations of truth and falsity are, as Laudan claims, "irrelevant" to those theories. In attacking the decision in a much celebrated federal court case from Arkansas concerning the academic status of creationism, Laudan argues incongruously that the decision which ruled that creationism is not a science and hence does not have to be taught in public schools was in error because creationism *is an empirical theory which has been falsified.*[44] This is indeed a bizarre claim, and it is very difficult to know what to make of it if facts are relative to theories and determinations of truth are irrelevant to theories since whatever facts are regarded as falsifying for creationism are not those which are relative to creationism. Laudan's theory is wrecked on the reefs of objective fact and truth.

REALISM AND IDEALISM IN PEIRCE

There is a significant remaining issue to be dealt with concerning Peirce's theory of Reality and Truth. There is a real tension between the idealistic and realistic aspects of Peirce's thought.[45] Reality and Truth are somehow the products of thought, and Peirce himself indicates his own idealistic tendencies (1.42 and 6.25). His idea of reality is antithetical to the possibility of "a thing existing independent of all realtion to the mind's conception of it" (5.311). However, there are several considerations which ultimately push Peirce into the camp of the realists.

The thought upon which all reality and Truth are dependent essentially involves the use of signs and is an example of Thirdness. Thirdness is a primitive category which cannot be explained in terms of or reduced to Firstness and Secondness, and the principles, laws, and rules which "guide" thought are *given* and exist independently of thought. Thirdness is actually perceived. *General* truths are real, and this leads Peirce to a realist commitment (6.610). The laws, principles, and rules of thought given in Thirdness are independent of "any particular collection of minds" which is partially why we can never be sure that any actual community will ever settle upon a definitive answer to any particular given question (6.610); however, Reality and Community are independent of any actual collection of minds. It is only because the habits, rules, and principles given in Thirdness are *real* that things can continue to exist. "Continuity," he tells us, "represents Thirdness almost to perfection" (1.337). Things are what they are only becuase they manifest a unique set of habits. "What we call a Thing is a cluster or habit of reactions" (4.157).

The habits, rules, and principles which govern enquiry and act as "leading principles" are real and given in Thirdness, and thus, science and scientific enquiry are provided with a realistic underpinning—which is the method itself. The method of science is intrinsically rational and inevitably leads to Truth if pursued to its ideal limit. Since progress is a natural consequence of the self-correcting mechanism of the method of science, Peirce's commitment to that method and its basic, realistic, self-justifying nature allow him to deal with the troublesome issue of relativism in a rather straightforward way which is unavailable to people like Kuhn.[46] Peirce provides the "theory-independent" way of explaining and assessing claims concerning reality which Kuhn despairs of ever finding.[47]

Peirce thus would certainly agree with Gadamer's claim that all knowledge involves some "prejudice". Peirce would probably even insist that this point be put even more strongly: All knowledge *must* involve some prejudice. However, there is no difficulty, for Peirce, in explaining what this means and there is no threat to the epistemological enterprise. Knowledge only occurs within a certain context since it is only the scientific method which allows justifiable knowledge claims to be made. Consequently, prejudices are unavoidable, and certainly not negative or to be avoided. The "prejudice" of method is to be embraced since it is the only possible route to knowledge. Commitment to the method also involves us in commitment to our fellow enquirers, the members of the enquiring community. The way to avoid the skepticism and relativism which we have been discussed earlier is to take refuge in method and numbers. And here is where we take our stand along with Peirce. Grounding scientific method in Thirdness also provides Peirce with an answer to Rorty's question, "What guarantees that our changing theories of the world are getting better than worse?"[48] and provides epistemology with the "common ground" which ideally unites people in a "common rationality".[49] The demise of epistemology has thus been greatly exaggerated, and we do not yet have to pass from epistemology to hermeneutics.

— 8 —

MODERN SCIENCE AND FEMINISM

SCIENCE AND ITS PROGRESS

It is very illuminating that the phrase 'modern science' is redundant. Unlike modern art, modern literature, or modern music, modern science *is* science. One might easily hear someone say, indeed, one often does hear people say, "I just don't like *modern* art", with the implication that classical or some other kind of art is preferable. But think of our reaction if someone says that he or she does not like *modern* science, saying it in such a manner as to imply that science in some earlier period—say the sixteenth century—was preferable. It is even more illuminating to realize that the same overwhelming preference for whatever form of science is currently *modern* characterizes each period in the history of science—again, in contrast to art, music, and literature.

Science is what scientists currently *do,* and what scientists currently do (on a grand scale) is overwhelmingly preferable to what scientists have done in the past. It is much more difficult to defend or even make plausible such a claim for any other field of human endeavor. As Hilary Putnam observes, for those who first tried to deal with the question of *progress* in science, the grounds for claiming that Newton was a better scientist than Aristotle seem to be much clearer and stronger than any grounds for claiming that Shakespeare was a better poet than Homer.[1] Surely, the ordinary person in the street would agree that the scientists of today are much further along in understanding natural phenomena and in providing theories for predicting and influencing natural phenomena than they have been at any other time in human history. Consider the phenomenal advances in modern chemistry, physics, and astronomy, and the technological implications of these advances in modern medicine and space exploration.

Upon more reflection, however, it becomes clear that such a simple view of the nature of science and of scientific progress simply will not do. Serious and fundamental issues concerning the notions of the scientific community and scientific progress remain unresolved. For example, as we shall soon see, the feminist critique of modern science raises serious allegations concerning male bias in science. Indeed, the history of science is a checkered one, and even if one believes (as I described in the last chapter) that progress in science is asymptotically approaching a more complete picture of "reality", the journey has been anything but a straight, linear one. There have been pitfalls, dead ends, regressions and wild fluctuations. How are we to maintain that *science* is what scientists currently do *qua* scientists given the sometimes bizarre and foolish things which scientists have done at different periods in the history of science?

Many writers, including, most notably perhaps, Kuhn and Laudan, have chronicled the extremely circuitous route of scientific explanation. As we saw in Chapter 4, Kuhn insists that shifts in the history of science such as the one from Ptolemaic to Copernican astronomy, from the phlogiston theory to Lavoiser's theory of oxygen and from the ether theory to Maxwell's theory of electromagneticism can only be explained by his paradigm-based view of science.[2] And, as we saw in Chapter 7, Laudan insists that one can adequately account for the complicated and divergent path of "progress" in the history of science only by understanding the maximization of progress as the *raison d'être* of science and by abandoning, at the same time, the pretension of any connection at all between a rational or preferable scientific explanation and truth.[3] I have argued that Laudan's theory of science as progress invites the same sort of criticism concerning self-reference which I have raised concerning the theories of Kuhn, Quine, and Goodman. As a meta-scientific theory about the nature of science, but without the notion of truth (or even any fallibilistic, close approximation to truth), it is impossible to imagine any reason for adopting Laudan's view. He has, however, managed to bring to the forefront several questions about the nature of the scientific community which have been lurking in the background in our earlier treatment. If the nature of science and the scientific method are essentially tied to some sort of scientific community, then we certainly need to say more about the nature of this community than we have managed to say thus far.

THE SCIENTIFIC COMMUNITY

In the preceding chapter, while exploring the connections between scientific method and the notion of rationality, I made much use of the notion of a scientific community, but I have been very vague about any characterization of the community itself. In this final chapter, I will focus upon the nature of the community of enquirers and investigate questions about relativism arising from criticisms raised by feminist critics concerning the composition of the community of enquirers and the possibility of male bias in the community of enquirers. Since I have argued that the notion of an objective and universal method of enquiry is essentially public and essentially involves a community of enquirers, the feminists' claims of bias in the scientific community and in the scientific method must be addressed. Peirce was notoriously vague about the specifics of the notion of a community of enquirers. What are the rules for membership in the scientific community? Who are the members of the scientific community? How do theories become accepted (or not accepted) by members of the scientific community? Upon what grounds and for what reasons do theories become accepted or rejected?[4] Currently, feminist critics of traditional science, as well as others who focus on the sociology of science, have generated a great deal of controversy over these questions and a correspondingly great volume of recent literature concerning these issues.[5]

At the very beginning of our attempt to clarify the notion of the scientific community and to answer the very difficult issues surrounding this notion, it is necessary to make an important distinction between two different kinds of scientific communities. First, there is the community of practicing scientists—both natural and social—whose activities, *qua* scientists, involve experiments and theories about whatever phenomena are particular to the science in question (leaving aside now questions about the *nature* of the phenomena). So, for example, biologists are concerned with experiments, observations and theories which take as their argument living things, and sociologists are concerned with experiments, observations, and theories which take as their argument various aspects of human societies. I shall call this scientific community SC1. Let us say that SC1 is on the "object level"—the theories, laws, and statements used by members of SC1 are on the "lowest level" and take as their arguments what the members of SC1 understand to be natural phenomena. It is tempting to call this first scientific community the "primary" scientific community; however, as we shall soon see, there are several controversial issues concerning the relationship between SC1 and the second kind of scientific community. Secondly, there is the scientific community (whose membership includes a great number of philosophers and partially overlaps with the membership of SC1) whose members' main interests involve the experiments, observations, theory construction, and other activities of the members of SC1, again *qua* scientists. This much larger, meta-scientific community includes philosophers of science, sociologists of science, politicians, and those scientists from SC1 who are, upon occasion, concerned with meta-scientific questions about the theories, methods, and results of the practices of members of SC1. For ease of reference, I shall call this meta-scientific community SC2.

While philosophers of science routinely distinguish between scientific theories and meta-scientific theories and recognize the importance of this difference, far fewer of those philosophers of science concerned with the kind of general epistemological issues in science which I have tried to address have recognized the importance of distinguishing between SC1 and SC2. In order to address properly the fundamental epistemological controversies in science and the role of the scientific community in these controversies, it will be very helpful to be much more explicit about the differences between SC1 and SC2 and what these differences entail. As we pursue answers to the questions raised concerning the grounds and reasons for the beliefs and actions of the members of "the scientific community", the distinction between SC1 and SC2 will allow us to get a much clearer picture of the relationship between the scientific community and the return to reason.

It will also be crucial to keep in mind the distinction, which we have made repeatedly in earlier chapters, between reasons which are internal to a theory and those which are external. Using this standard nomenclature will allow us to identify the different categories into which the answers to the questions about grounds and reasons for the beliefs of scientists fall. On the one hand, the grounds and reasons for accepting a theory may be held to be "internal" to the scientific method and to the scientific community—that is, theories are thought to be adopted and to survive because of scientific evidence and rational argument. On the other hand, the motives for the actions of scientists, including the actions of adopting and maintaining a particular theory may be seen to be functions of causes which are "external" to the scientific method—that is, theories are thought to be adopted and to survive because of a variety of social and personal factors such as social pressure, the desire for fame and fortune, or various prejudices and biases.[6]

With the distinctions between SC1 and SC2 and between internalism and externalism firmly in place, let us now attempt to address some of the thorny issues which have been raised concerning the nature of the scientific method and the scientific community, and progress in science. I argued at some length in the previous chapter that the scientific method is inseparable from a public scientific community. We shall now see how this understanding of the scientific community actually works out in practice and how it allows us to accommodate and respond to the criticisms which have been raised against science.

THE FEMINIST CRITIQUE OF SCIENCE

It is interesting to see how the concept of the scientific community actually operates in practice by examining some of the controversies currently raging concerning the rationality of science and membership in the scientific community; so, let us begin our examination of the current feminist critique of science.[7] One of the most significant and general criticisms raised against science by contemporary feminist critics is the charge that traditional science is gender-biased. This criticism can be made in several different ways and is manifested in several different contexts. For example, Sandra Harding says:

> The radical feminist position holds that the epistemologies, metaphysics, ethics, and politics of the dominant forms of science are androcentric and mutually supportive; that despite the deeply ingrained Western cultural belief in science's intrinsic progressiveness, science today serves primarily regressive social tendencies; and that the social structure of science, many of its applications and technologies, its modes of defining research problems and designing experiments, its ways of constructing and conferring meanings are not only sexist but also racist, classist, and culturally coercive.[8]

Evelyn Fox Keller echoes this general attack upon the fundamental method of science as sexist when she describes what she calls the " 'genderization' of science".[9] Similar criticisms have been raised concerning the epistemological and methodological underpinnings of the traditional view of science. Perhaps one of the currently best-known forms of this kind of attack is Susan Bordo's criticism of what she identifies as the masculinization of human thought brought about by Cartesianism. Bordo specifically attacks the distinction between the knowing subject and the known object, which is so fundamental in Descartes's epistemology and modern thought, by characterizing it as a "flight to objectivity"—a flight from subjectivity, infantilism, and feminism.[10] Carolyn Merchant provides one of the most thorough treatments of the development of modern science and the changes which took place in the accompanying epistemological and metaphysical views.[11] Merchant's characterization of the development of modern science also involves the replacement of a feminine perspective by a masculine one. According to Merchant, during the changes in human thought which took place in the sixteenth and seventeenth centuries, "the organic conception of the cosmos gave way to a mechanistic model".[12] In Merchant's view, abandoning the organic view of nature paved the way for technological excesses and abuses and for the exploitation of our natural resources, and the foundations for a responsible ecological attitude toward nature are to be found in an organismic world view.[13]

If there is anything like a consensus amongst these various different current feminist critics of science, it is that the structure and methodology as well as the membership and activities of the members of SC1 have a masculine bias. Now it is important to note, at the very beginning of our investigation of the feminist critique of science, that the main issue at stake is not simply the relative absence of prominent women in SC1 in the history of science or in contemporary science. The relative paucity of women in SC1 might well be an issue of historical, social, and political interest in itself, but it is not the main focus of the feminist critique of science. Many of the intellectual fields in Western culture (including art and literature) have been dominated by men without the activity itself becoming identified as masculine. As Keller observes, what we need to explain is why "scientific thought is male thought", and we will then understand why most scientists have been and are male.[14]

In other words, the main issue is not simply that men have dominated the membership of SC1; the main general criticism is that, in some sense, male thought has dominated the *content and method* of the observations, laws, and theories of the members of SC1 as well. Thus, this feminist critique challenges the claims which have been made for the objective and universal character of scientific thought and *the* scientific method. The question becomes one of whether *the* scientific method of traditional science is simply the scientific method of white, middle-class males—one amongst perhaps many different scientific methods. Or, alternatively, is there such a thing as a uniquely feminist science?

There is much in this feminist criticism of traditional science with which I greatly sympathize. There is no doubt that many of the activities of scientists in SC1 have been and are sexist, but it is important to be clear about exactly what is sexist in science and the extent of the sexism; and the feminist critics are themselves divided over this issue. Harding says, for example, that the "modes of defining research problems and designing experiments" are sexist.[15] Now this is indeed a serious charge, and, depending upon exactly what it means, it could be a charge which undermines the entire program of SC1. On one level, this charge sounds very much like Kuhn's claim (which we have examined in detail in Chapter 4), that the search for facts and even the existence of facts are relative to a paradigm; however, the issues are quite different.

The biased interests of the members of SC1 can account for one way in which the research problems and experiment designs of SC1 have been and continue to be sexist (and racist). It is easy to theoretically characterize SC1 as being on the "object level" and involving theories and experiments about phenomena; however, in practice the particular theories and experiments of SC1 which receive the most time, attention and resources always reflect the particular interests and choices of particular members of SC1— interests in and choices about the relative scientific importance of one particular body phenomena as opposed to another. As the feminist critics remind us, to a large extent, these interests and choices are frequently not made on simply scientific grounds.

ALLEGED GENDER BIAS IN MEDICAL RESEARCH

The recent revelations concerning the possible sexual bias in medical research provide a good example of how scientific research is male biased in the selection of experiments and their designs. Frequently, medical research focuses on diseases which, for all practical purposes, afflict "males only". For example, in several recent, very significant research projects designed to explore different health problems and possible treatments, researchers conducted the studies by using only male experimental subjects.[16] A study to determine the correlation between taking aspirin regularly and reduced heart attacks involved 22,071 men and not a single woman, and another study to try and determine the correlation between the lack of exercise, smoking and high cholesterol and heart disease involved 12,866 men and, again, not a single woman.

Now there is no doubt that there is some cause for concern in such revelations, but it is important to be clear about what the legitimate cause for concern really is.[17] Were these studies "unscientific"? Do these revelations prove that science is male biased? Well, the answer to these questions depends upon how the scientists represent these studies and what conclusions they draw from them. If they represent the studies as providing some scientific basis for medical evidence for the correlation in *human beings* between regular ingestion of aspirin and the rate of heart attacks or between lack of exercise, smoking and high cholesterol and heart disease, then the studies are obviously biased. Such studies would also exemplify poor science *on the level of SC1 and by members of SC1* because of the lack of a representative sample. On a very rudimentary level, this is an example of what moderate feminist critics describe as "bad" science resulting from a clear male bias. I consider this claim to be obvious and beyond serious debate.

On the other hand, if the studies are represented as providing some medical evidence about the health of men only, then the situation is completely different and is more complicated and much more controversial. Is the choice to study only males or males' diseases a biased choice? If so, what kind of bias is it? And does this bias mean that the resulting studies are somehow deficient *as scientific experiments on the level of SC1?* I think not. Consider for a moment how we would regard two different medical studies which have to do with breast cancer and prostate cancer. Surely, we would want to say that it is completely scientifically justified to use only female subjects in one study and only male subjects in the other. Indeed, such a practice would be not only permissible but a sign of "good" science. A completely separate question is whether medical studies involving breast cancer receive their "equal due" with those involving prostate cancer. This is an issue about the priorities for the allocation of resources for conducting scientific research in a particular society—an issue on the level of SC2. There are certainly serious issues of societal fairness and equity involved here, but these are not issues which threaten to undermine the basic rationality of the scientific method.

Suppose that one begins to investigate this issue by raising the question concerning the fairness of distributing the resources in a society in such a manner as to encourage, support, and reward certain activities of certain members of SC1 rather than other activities of other members of SC1. For example, why support the study of heart disease in men by male researchers rather than support the study of heart disease in women by female researchers? This is a question which occurs within and is arguable on the level of

SC2. Now there is an obvious, important sense, it seems, in which this question is a question of fairness. It may not be a scientific question at all but rather a moral, social or political question. In other words, there is a sense in which this question is simple a particular instantiation of the much more general question of how a particular society decides to distribute its resources. At the same time, it seems as though this is also a question about science since it involves the way in which scientists choose and design certain experiments rather than the way in which members of some other group in a society, such as philosophers, practice their profession. However, in contrast to a situation in which a non-representative sample is used, this is a question on the level of SC2 and not a question about the nature of science at all.

IS THERE A FEMINIST SCIENCE?

There is no doubt that social and cultural values significantly influence *the practice of science;* however, the connection between the social and cultural choices about how to distribute resources which occur on the level of SC2 and *the nature and method of science* on the level of SC1 is far from obvious, and I maintain that the connection has not been made by feminist critics. Focussing our attention upon the question of the influence of broad, social and cultural values upon scientific inquiry is certainly an important and valuable contribution of the current feminist critique of science. However, the additional claim that the methods and nature of science are male biased on the level of SC1 is another matter altogether.

Once we focus our attention upon the interplay between the meta-scientific values and scientific inquiry, the most prominent question quickly becomes the one of whether or not the social and cultural values shape and determine the nature of scientific inquiry, scientific reasoning itself—on the level of SC1. In other words, the main question of the feminist critique of traditional science and epistemology becomes: "Are the traditional scientific method and the traditional criteria of knowledge on the level of SC1 themselves male-biased?" So important and fundamental is this question to our way of life that some feminists envision a revolution, based upon a feminist science and feminist epistemology, which will transform "all Western consciousness and civilizations".[18] If the answer to this question is in the affirmative, then we must examine and determine the possibility of male and female science and male and female epistemology. Donna Haraway poses the following questions as the crucial ones for the feminist critique of science:

> Is there a specifically feminist theory of knowledge growing today which is analogous in its implications to theories which are the heritage of Greek science and of the scientific revolution of the seventeenth century? Would a feminist epistemology . . . be a family member to existing theories of representation and philosophical realism? Or should feminists adopt a radical form of epistemology that denies the possibility of access to a real world and an objective standpoint? Would feminist standards of knowledge genuinely end the dilemma of the cleavage between subject and object or between noninvasive knowing and prediction and control? Does feminism offer insight into the connections between science and humanism? Do feminists have anything new to say about the vexed relations of knowledge and power?[19]

Haraway's questions are both about the ways in which the members of SC1 conduct their activities and about the ways in which the members of SC2 conduct their activities (as well as how members of society at large conduct their activities). Her implied suggestion is that women are in the position of deciding what strategy is best from a feminist point of view and that the process of deciding whether to "adopt a radical form of epistemology" or "feminist standards of knowledge" is a voluntary one. To focus sharply upon the differences between these questions and to pursue what feminist critics have to say about the nature of scientific inquiry, it is necessary to separate and isolate the questions concerning *the nature* of scientific inquiry on the level of SC1 from the more general meta-scientific questions which arise of the level of SC2.

Several feminist writers have argued in a variety of different ways that the very nature of feminist scientific reasoning is unique and different from the traditional scientific method as practiced on the SC1 level.[20] For the most part, feminist critics have attempted to avoid the pitfall of radical relativism which results from Kuhn's thesis of incommensurability, but there is still a pervasive tension amongst feminist critics of traditional science and epistemology concerning exactly how much of the traditional method and theories to hold onto and how much to abandon. This is certainly the single most significant unresolved issue in contemporary feminist theory. It appears that political pressure pushes in the direction of a more radical stance, and philosophical good sense pushes in the direction of a more moderate one. The tension between the more moderate and more radical positions have resulted in serious ambiguities in the positions of feminist critics. For example, Helen Longino argues explicitly, in her early writings, that social and cultural values actually influence the nature of science enquiry, that is, scientific reasoning itself. In her treatment of the kind of problem which we have considered above concerning the question of bias in medical research, Longino distinguishes between what she calls "constitutive values" and "contextual values":

> Constitutive values, internal to the sciences, are the source of the rules determining what constitutes acceptable scientific practice or scientific method. The personal, social and cultural values, those group or individual preferences about what ought to be, I call contextual values, to indicate that they belong to the social and cultural context in which science is done.[21]

Traditionally, Longino tells us, philosophers of science have maintained a strict dichotomy between constitutive and contextual values and have attempted to sustain a "value-free" notion of science by denying any influence of contextual values upon the nature of scientific reasoning. However, Longino argues that constitutive values alone do not determine the nature of scientific inquiry and that contextual values also influence the essential nature of—the very structure of—scientific inquiry.[22] Longino concludes that the notion of a value-free science is "pernicious"[23] and that "both the expression of masculine bias in the sciences and feminist criticism of research exhibiting that bias are—shall we say—business as usual".[24] So, according to Longino, scientists should abandon their notion of a value-free science, make their political and social commitments clear, and commit themselves to the particular brand of science which is a result of their commitment to a more basic "interpretative model" composed of contextual values.[25]

Such an understanding of feminist science amounts to an explicit reversal of Francis Bacon's doctrine of the Idols, those influences upon a person's thinking which Bacon thought lead to bias and confusion.[26] Whereas I have suggested, in the previous chapter, that we expand Bacon's list of idols to include the Idol of the Closet, Longino seems to suggest that we simply abandon Bacon's attempt to free scientific thinking from bias and prejudice altogether and, instead, that we simply make our biases and prejudices explicit. Longino's feminist strategy is thus quite different from the feminists who try to bring male bias to public attention and then to eliminate it. According to Longino, seeking an unbiased, value-free science might easily go awry by harboring hidden values which differ from the ones which the feminists might prefer. Instead, Longino claims, "we can acknowledge our ability to affect the course of knowledge and fashion or favor research programs that are consistent with the

values and commitments we express in the rest of our lives."[27] Being
"up front" and explicit about our political and social commitments
and acknowledging the way in which those commitments influence
the way we do science, gives us a choice as scientists between doing
"establishment science" or feminist science.[28] I shall use the phrase
"feminist science" (in contrast to 'feminist philosophy of science') to
identify a position according to which supposed gender differences in
members of SC1 result in supposed differences in the nature and
method of scientific inquiry—theory formation, experiments, observations, and other related activities of members of SC1.

I find several things about the suggestion of a program of feminist
science particularly disturbing. First of all, it is not clear that
Longino completely understands and appreciates just how radical
her proposals are. Since Longino's version of feminist science is a
form of *externalism,* the reasons for accepting scientific claims or
adopting scientific theories are external to the method of science
itself and consequently external to SC1. The ultimate consequent of
her suggestions is a Hobbesian war, on the level of society at large, of
all ideologies against all. Apparently, Longino assumes a democratic
setting with a free exchange of ideas with a fair market place where
each person—misogynist and feminist alike—receive equal time
and opportunity to influence the course of human knowledge and
science. However, as the feminist critics are too painfully aware and
as they repeatedly try to bring to the attention of society at large,
such a view does not accurately describe any contemporary Western
society (although some may well fare better than others). Ours is still
a male dominated society as are both SC1 and SC2. Consequently, so
far as possible public advocacy of their position is concerned, radical
feminists who advocate feminist science seem to be in the same
position as the ethical egoists. If ethical egoists really believe that
people generally are selfish and ought to act in ways of furthering
their own self-interests, then it seems they ought never to tell anyone
about their theory since it would be against their own self-interests to
have everyone else acting on an enlightened basis of such a theory.
Also, an intelligent ethical egoist would not publicly announce his or
her commitment to egoism since then other people would be placed
on guard against the egoist. Similarly, if the feminists who advocate
feminist science are right and if they really believe that they are right
about the influence of general social and cultural values on the level
of SC2 (contextual values) upon the nature of scientific inquiry on
the level of SC1, then surely they ought not to publicly advocate their
position in a male-dominated society. If it is true that our general

social and cultural commitments are primary, as Longino claims, and if these social and political commitments shape and determine our way of reasoning and our way of doing science, then the only reasonable strategy of the radical feminists would seem to be an attack upon the dominant male social and political beliefs on the level of SC2. The real battle, if there is such a thing as feminist science, will be fought between feminist contextual values and masculine contextual values—which will not be a battle about science at all, and if "science" on the level of SC1 is understood broadly enough to include epistemology and rationality (as some feminist critics have suggested), then, in such a battle, there could be no possibility of a peaceful or reasonable resolution based upon some common ground of evidence.

THE FEMINIST SCIENCE CIRCLE

One of the major liabilities of an externalist position is that one cannot consistently use reason and evidence, which are *internal* to the method, to justify the externalist account. For example, Bleier points out that the absence of fossil data which might support claims about anatomical differences between men and women weighs heavily against the claims of sexual division of labor,[29] but given a radical feminist science, there could be no "objective" data for feminists to point to in support of their argument against a male-dominated, sociobiological theory of sex differences since facts and data (including fossil data) would then be relative to a particular brand of science. Any dispute about the scientific data would have to be waged and won or lost on the more general level of social and political beliefs.

In a similar vein, if Longino is right, then surely what she claims for the natural sciences would be true *a fortiori* for the social sciences—including political science. Consequently, when the radical feminists do concentrate their attention and effort upon the political issues rather than the scientific ones, it seems that the approaches which are available to them to persuade or coerce other people to share their point of view are very limited. In particular, it seems that normal persuasion and argumentation based upon evidence or observations of any kind (such as the statistics involving the medical research mentioned above) would not be a viable option if, according to feminist science, a person's observation and experience and reasoning (the constitutive values of SC1) are all shaped by the prior commitment to the underlying social and cultural values (the contextual values of SC2). In such a world, the only plausibly effective measure would be to line up the economic and political forces to do battle against the competing ideologies. Attempts at serious scholarly works and persuasion based upon evidence and argumentation would have to give way to propaganda and "epithet slinging". Genetic fallacies and *ad hominem* fallacies[30] would become the order of the day.

Finally, it seems that Longino underestimates, in particular, the significance of her claim that constitutive rules cannot prevent the contextual rules from influencing the nature of scientific inquiry and hence, the very notion of reason itself. Longino claims that scientific reasoning always takes places within a *context* wherein *background assumptions* determine the way in which a person reasons by determining the way in which a person treats evidence in relation to a hypothesis.[31] Thus, according to Longino, we should not be concerned with the question of rationality but by the question of *rationality in a context.*[32] Feminists must recognize that the background assumptions which have been operative in science are those from "capitalist and male supremacist societies" and set about constructing their own new social context with its unique contextual values.[33]

Now Longino is explicit about wishing to avoid what seem to be the radical consequences of her position, but she focusses her attention upon avoiding radical subjectivism.[34] She argues that scientific reasoning is objective since scientific inquiry is a *social practice* and is hence, non-arbitrary and non-subjective.[35] Now I have argued at length in the preceding chapter that science is, indeed, social, but I have argued that it is a social practice amongst those practitioners united by commitment to a particular common method —not by those united by sex or race or commitment to a particular common ideaology. Being a social practice rescues science from being arbitrary in the sense of being subjective, but it does not rescue it from being arbitrary in the sense of being radically relative. If it is possible to have both Masculine Science and Feminist Science which can justifiably lay claim to be objective and non-arbitrary, then are we to expect the same of Black Science, or Hispanic Science, or Aryan Science?

From Longino's claim that background assumptions (or simply, contextual values) on the level of SC2 can shape and influence the very nature of scientific reasoning on the level of SC1, it would clearly follow that contextual values would have the ability to alter the constitutive rules themselves. And if the contextual rules can alter and determine the constitutive rules to some small degree, then there seems to be no possibility of placing any limit on the degree to which this can be done without begging the question. Then, it seems, "all bets are off" and it would be every man and woman for himself or herself. It appears that we would then have arrived at the state of intellectual anarchy, which Paul Feyerabend describes, where no one method is preferable to any other.[36] There would be no real distinction between questions of fact or scientific questions about nature and questions about ideology and political belief. The philosophy of science would simply become an arena for a political and ideological war, reducing us to a position where might makes right.

Although the suggestion of a unique feminine epistemological perspective upon which a unique feminist science might be based might initially sound plausible, the ultimate, extreme relativistic consequences are evident if we develop fully the implications of such a suggestion fully. For example, some feminists have suggested that a feminist science would incorporate certain unique aspects of "female sensibility or cognitive temperament" such as "complexity, interaction and wholism".[37] These feminine characteristics might plausibly make a feminist, ecological science preferable since it might, for example, contain a more accurate depiction of "the true character of natural processes".[38] Consider, however, the complete implausibility of such claims. The "scientific" characterization of the different unique traits of the "female sensibility and cognitive temperament" —from psychology or biology—would itself be tainted by the social and cultural commitments of the psychologists or biologists; therefore, such a characterization cannot be the foundation of a feminist science. Suppose, for example, that the chosen unique traits of female cognitive faculty were to be those of the familiar masculine propaganda—the traits which male-dominated societies have used to prevent women from entering science—traits which make women inferior and deficient as scientists. Then, of course, a feminist science, based upon such unique aspects of "female sensibility and cognitive temperament" would hardly seem to have anything to offer at all. Feminist critics have successfully waged a long and ultimately effective campaign against such sociobiological characterizations of women; however, the notion of a feminist science once again puts the sociobiologists and the feminists on the same footing. If the general cultural and social values of scientists on the level of SC2 are epistemologically fundamental and if scientific data and reasoning from SC1 are filtered through and colored by those general cultural and social values, then so are all of the scientific data and theories on the level of SC1 about the similarities and differences of the characteristics of the sexes. Thus, we arrive at the feminist science circle, and surely it is a vicious one. In other words, even if we grant that the feminist critics who advocate a feminist science are clear enough about what, in their different estimations, makes feminist science *feminist,* the question which must be answered is, "What makes it science?" What I have argued is that feminist science throws the scientific baby out with the masculine bath water.

Radical feminist critics of science who argue for a unique feminist science are in the same position as the sociobiologists who desperately search for some "objective" scientific facts to support a general theory which has the effect of tainting all facts. As Bleier points out, the attempt by sociobiologists to link some innate human nature to a particular genetic configuration is hopelessly mired in a circular argument:

> Sociobiologists themselves, as well as geneticists, agree that it is not possible to link any specific human behavior with any specific gene or genetic configuration. The only evidence for such a link is that which is provided by Sociobiologists' circular logic. This logic makes a *premise* of the genetic basis of behaviors, then cites a certain animal or human behavior, constructs a speculative story to explain how the behavior (*if* it were genetically based) could have served or could serve to maximize the reproductive success of the individual, and this *conjecture* then becomes evidence for the *premise* that the behavior was genetically determined.[39]

Feminist science would seem to be in the same boat as sociobiology in the sense that it is a meta-scientific theory on the level of SC2, but it is a theory according to which the evidence, facts, and reasoning on the level of SC1 are relative to the values or "background assumptions" of SC2. Consequently, the process of supplying any supporting "evidence" for radical feminist science mirrors exactly the circular argument which Bleier describes for sociobiology. Feminist science makes a premise of the theory of the gender-based differences for members of SC1, then points to these gender-based differences as explanations for differences in behavior of members of SC1 (which would be the case if radical feminist science were to be true), and then offers these explanations as evidence that feminist science is true. However, these "facts" from SC1 concerning sex differences, upon which the claims of feminist science is based, would, according to feminist science itself, be relative to different general social and political values on the level of SC2, that is, feminist science.

Feminist writers are aware of this problem of circularity. Sandra Harding, for example, explicitly recognizes the issue of circularity and the threatened specter of self-refutation.[40] Since she is aware of the kind of difficulties caused by self-reference, illegitimate totalities, and circularity which I have attributed earlier to theories of Quine, Goodman, Kuhn and Winch, Harding attempts to avoid the threat of circularity. The reluctance of feminists critics to jump on the bandwagon of radical relativism is responsible, according to Harding, for the differences amongst feminists concerning the possibility of a uniquely feminist science.[41] Harding is admirably cautious in advocating a new, feminist epistemology. She explicitly tries to avoid "the leap to relativism" and maintains that feminist philosophy of science can attack the distortions of traditional science caused by male bias "on traditional objectivist grounds".[42] However, at the same time, Harding maintains that modernist epistemologies still incorporate "distinctively masculine" concepts and practices and that a fully developed and coherent feminist science must await the political and social changes which will lead to a feminist society,[43] a claim which suggests that Harding also wants to have her cake and eat it too. She wishes to hold open the possibility of a unique feminist science and feminist epistemology without committing herself to the kind of radical relativism which results from Kuhn's incommensurability thesis and which I have argued follows from a commitment to feminist science. The current and obvious tensions, ambiguities, and contradictions in contemporary feminist theory are accounted for, according to Harding, by the fact that feminist epistemology and philosophy of science are still in a "transitional" stage[44]—awaiting the completion of the development of a uniquely feminine social context. I have argued that whatever further developments take place in feminist theory there is a theoretical limitation upon how these can affect our view of the nature of scientific inquiry and human reason. If I am correct, then the current tensions, ambiguities, and contradictions in contemporary feminist theory are much more deeply seated and much more serious than previously noted.

MALE BIAS AND THE SLOW BUT SURE PROGRESS OF SCIENCE

Feminist literature is replete with examples of male bias in Western culture—in science, philosophy, psychology, history, and the arts.[45] The force of such evidence is compelling, but only because we regard the evidence as counting against claims for universal and objective theories. In other words, bias can be recognized and weighed only within a framework according to which rules for proper theory construction, validation and confirmation have force. As we saw in the preceding chapter, the scientific method creates the framework within which fraud can take place, be identified, and be corrected. Similarly, the scientific method creates the framework within which mistakes and bias can take place, be identified, and be corrected. Feminist critics of modern science are certainly correct in their accusation that the rule of reason in Western science has been tyrannical, but the tyranny of reason is its *repressive tolerance,* reason's willingness to accommodate any and all objections from any and all comers.

The feminist criticisms of modern science are re-affirmations of the *fallibilism* with which all beliefs based upon warrant and evidence are held. No belief whose warrant is supplied by the method of science is epistemologically privileged to the point that it is immune to being overturned. This same fallibilism must also extend to the claims of feminists who defend a unique feminist science based upon gender-differentiated cognitive abilities. There must be an arena where the claims to such a science receive what warrant they can muster and are subjected to the same scrutiny to which the identified, male-biased claims were subjected. And it is *the same method and the same use of reason* which permits this scrutiny to take place. For example, as Jean Grimshaw points out,

> The experience of gender, of being a man or a woman, inflects much if not all of people's lives. . . . But even if one is always a man or a woman, one is never *just* a man or a woman. One is young or old, sick or healthy, married or unmarried, a parent or not a parent, employed or unemployed, middle class or working class, rich or poor, black or white, and so forth. . . . Experience does not come neatly in segments, such that it is always possible to abstract what in one's experience is due to "being a woman".[46]

For example, the only way in which feminists can even explore—much less begin to resolve—the problems created by what Harding calls the "fractured identities"[47] of women as black women, white women, yellow women, working class women, married women, heterosexual women, homosexual women, Marxist women, libertarian women, and so forth, is by appealing to a method which provides a common ground upon which argument, rejoinder, and resolution can take place. In this regard, if we recall the debate between Galileo and the Catholic Church of the sixteenth century, which I discussed at length in Chapter 1, surely it is the stance of Galileo and the elevation of reason by the Enlightenment of the eighteenth century which now provides the avenue for protest and the vehicle for dissent for feminist critics of science.

The feminist critique of modern science and the accusation of male bias in science serve to focus our attention once again upon the question of the role which the Community of Inquirers plays in scientific enquiry. We have seen that scientific enquiry is an essentially public, communal, co-operative endeavor, and the feminist critics have brought to our attention the fact that, in the history of Western science, a large segment of our society has regularly been excluded from membership in this community. Not only have women been denied access to the community of enquirers on both levels SC1 and SC2, but because they have not been counted as members of this community of enquirers, scientific enquiry has also been denied the benefits of their membership. There is no doubt, also, that some members of the community have been and still are sexist, and there is no doubt that such sexism has contributed to much "bad science". For example, as Jane Roland Martin points out, as a result of male bias,

> Time after time key questions that should have been asked and key experiments that should have been performed were not. . . . Furthermore, data are used selectively and overgeneralizations are frequently drawn from available data. . . . Overgeneralizing from the data, selective use of data, a failure to ask key questions; these are mistakes in scientific procedure and method that beginning science students are taught to avoid.[48]

Martin correctly focusses our attention upon the kind of issues which need to be addressed. Her accusations, if true, raise serious questions about the results of much scientific investigation. However, possible mistakes are identifiable only because of the context created by the scientific method and the arena of free enquiry created by this method. Without the presupposition of such a method, the accusation of sexist bias in science could not reasonably be made. I have maintained that it is *the method* of scientific enquiry and not *the results* of the enquiry which is distinctively scientific. Any results of scientific enquiry must receive whatever warrant they have by an appeal to the method by which we finally came to arrive at those results, and as we have seen in the last chapter, the Community of Inquirers is absolutely essential in this regard. Scientific enquiry cannot be a solitary process or even a process severely limited to a small, select group of enquirers. Scientific enquiry has been limited to the extent that women have been excluded from membership in the Community of Inquirers. In some cases, this has meant that "the scientific view" has been limited and incomplete, and in others, it has meant that the results of the enquiry have been blindly biased or even grossly distorted.[49] Feminists critics have confirmed this appraisal repeatedly by focussing upon the way in which women have been excluded from traditional science.

As we have seen, science is an activity. It is an activity conducted by a co-operative community of fellow enquirers who, as scientific enquirers, pursue knowledge in an unbiased manner—"independent of the vagaries of me and you".[50] We are able to identify the rules and principles which determine correct and incorrect application of the method only because of the unbiased nature of scientific enquiry. Because we are able to correct science, we are able to explain progress in science when progress in other areas of human endeavor is so ambiguous and controversial. It is because both the method of science and its results are, *by their very nature,* systematically scrutinized, evaluated and corrected that progress in science is not only possible but necessary. It may be that what we learn from history is that we never learn from history, but what we learn from science is that we do learn science. In science, we thus have a "criterion of progress" by which we are able to determine *in advance of testing a particular theory* whether it would represent an advance upon existing theories.[51] Without such a cornerstone of objectivity and bias-free enquiry, science becomes like art or music, with different sciences for different communities of people with different tastes based upon differences in sex, race, or culture. Science and the nature of scientific enquiry would then simply become matters of social, political, and, perhaps, aesthetic preferences, but, as I have shown throughout this book, such *laissez faire* relativism in the case of human rationality and scientific inquiry is not possible.

The existence of a criterion for measuring progress in science and the intrinsically rational structure of the method of science explain why we regard modern science so differently from the way in which we regard modern art and modern music. Things do get settled in science. Controversies, so essential to the very nature of science, do get resolved. In the short run, disagreements and controversies *must* rage in science because the very nature of science requires a public hearing for every new discovery and every new theory. So, whereas we can easily understand and tolerate a person who prefers only Baroque music or early Renaissance art, we cannot easily understand or tolerate a person who prefers alchemy or Nostradamus to modern science.

ALL THINGS CANNOT BE RELATIVE

Paul Feyerabend's anarchistic attack upon the notion of a systematic, rational method for human knowledge and human inquiry has become the rallying point for the radical relativists who reject such a notion of scientific progress. It was this kind of attack upon rationality and the abandonment of any systematic method for fixing belief which prompted this investigation into the various different forms of radical relativism and the defense of method. Feyerabend says:

> [T]he idea of a fixed method, or of a fixed theory of rationality, rests on too naive a view of man and his social surroundings. To those who look at the rich material provided by history, and who are not intent on impoverishing it in order to please their lower instincts, their craving for intellectual security in the form of clarity, precision, 'objectivity', 'truth', it will become clear that there is only *one* principle that can be defended under *all* circumstances and in *all* stages of human development. It is the principle: *anything goes.*[52]

However, as we have seen repeatedly during the course of our investigation, such a claim—though melodramatic and grandiose—is ultimately nonsense. Feyerabend's anarchism is intellectually, politically and practically self-referentially inconsistent. Feyerabend advocates getting rid of all of the rules which supposedly restrict free inquiry, and he proceeds to give us a reasoned view of why we should agree with him. He writes lengthy treatises on why we should prefer total intellectual anarchism to traditional understandings of rationality and method, and, in doing so, he confirms the very method against which he rails. A game with no rules is not a game. Science with no rules is not science. Meta-science with no rules is not meta-science. Philosophy with no rules is not philosophy. Feyerabend regularly appeals to the use of detailed and careful (though usually grossly exaggerated) arguments for his cause, and by doing so, he demonstrates just how tolerant method really is. As we have seen, method allows for its own inspection and correction. Feyerabend contends that *"all methodologies, even the most obvious ones, have their limits."*[53] We have seen that this claim is certainly true. The limits of method are the limits of rationality, and the limits of rationality are the limits of relativism.

NOTES

INTRODUCTION: FROM THE AGE OF ENLIGHTENMENT TO THE AGE OF RELATIVISM

1. Paul Feyerabend, *Farewell to Reason* (New York: Verso, 1987), 25.

2. Sandra Harding, *The Science Question in Feminism* (Ithaca: Cornell University Press, 1986), 23 and 121.

3. John Lough, *The Encyclopédie*, (New York: McKay, 1971), 215ff.

4. Peter Gay, *The Enlightenment: An Interpretation*, vol. 2, *The Science of Freedom* (New York: Knopf, 1969), 27.

5. I certainly am not claiming that the epistemology of the Enlightenment *entails* any particular view of social and political philosophy. I am claiming that as a result of the Enlightenment human beings were encouraged to enquire into such matters and that they were empowered with a view of and a role for human reason according to which human beings could understand, on their own and *qua* human, both natural and social phenomena. The context for general, intellectual, and philosophical inquiry was set.

6. *Ibid.*, 5.

7. Gilbert Murray, *Five Stages of Greek Religion* (New York: Columbia University Press, 1935), 123.

8. Gay, 6.

9. John Locke, *Some Thoughts Concerning Education*, ed. John W. and Jean S. Yolton (Oxford: Clarendon, 1988), 83.

10. David Hume, *An Enquiry Concerning Human Understanding*, edited with an introduction by L.A. Selby-Bigge (Oxford: Clarendon, 1961), sec. 8, 83.

11. Feyerabend, *Farewell to Reason*, 8.

12. For a discussion of some of the problems of the various formulations of the principle of verification, see R. W. Ashby, 'Positivism', in *A Critical History of Western Philosophy*, ed. D. J. O'Connor (New York: Free Press, 1964), 495–500; and Carl Hempel, 'Problems and Changes in the Empiricist Criterion of Meaning', in *Semantics and the Philosophy of Language*, ed. Leonard Linsky (Urbana: University of Illinois Press, 1952), 163–185.

13. Rudolf Carnap, *The Logical Structure of the World* (Berkeley: University of California Press, 1967), v.

14. See *The Philosophy of Rudolf Carnap*, ed. Paul Arthur Schilpp (La Salle: Open Court, 1963), 50–51.

15. *Ibid.*, 52.

16. Rudolf Carnap, *The Logical Syntax of Language* (New York: Harcourt, Brace, 1937), pt. 5A, sec. 73, 281–84.

17. See Rudolf Carnap, 'Intellectual Autobiography', in *The Philosophy of Rudolf Carnap,* ed. Paul Arthur Schilpp (La Salle: Open Court, 1963), 60–67. Also see Carnap's *Introduction to Semantics* (Cambridge: Harvard University Press, 1942); *Formalization of Logic* (Cambridge: Harvard University Press, 1943); and *Meaning and Necessity* (Chicago: University of Chicago Press, 1947).

18. See above, 4

19. Feyerabend, *Farewell to Reason,* 9.

20. *Ibid.,* 10.

21. *Ibid.,* 12.

1. A REPRIEVE FOR GALILEO

1. I will not discuss or explain here in any detail the nature of scientific theories. For a thorough description of the 'traditional' understanding of scientific laws, see Ernest Nagel, *The Structure of Science* (New York: Harcourt, Brace, 1961), 47ff.

2. This law figures prominently in keeping Neurath's and Quine's boat afloat while it is being repaired, in the example discussed in Chapter 7.

3. Alfred North Whitehead, *Process and Reality* (New York: Macmillan, 1929), 7.

4. See 'Three Views Concerning Human Knowledge', in Karl Popper, *Conjectures and Refutations: The Growth of Scientific Knowledge* (New York: Harper and Row, 1963), 97ff.

5. For further comparison of Galileo's realism and 'instrumentalism' see Joseph Agassi, *The Gentle Art of Philosophical Polemics.* La Salle: Open Court, 1988, 43ff.

6. Willard Van Orman Quine, 'Two Dogmas of Empiricism', in *From a Logical Point of View* (New York: Harper and Row, 1953), 44.

7. Nelson Goodman, *Ways of Worldmaking* (Cambridge: Hackett, 1978), 2.

8. Galileo Galilei, *Sidereus Nuncius,* translated by Albert Van Helden. Chicago: University of Chicago Press, 1989.

9. See William Wallace, *Galileo and His Sources.* Princeton: Princeton University Press, 1984, 264ff. and 282. There is considerable disagreement amongst historians of science as to the degree to which Galileo's commitment to experimentation might have been embellished by his early biographers. See, for example, William R. Shea, *Galileo's Intellectual Revolution.* New York: Science History Publications, 1972, 3ff.

10. Wallace, *ibid.,* 284ff.

11. Galileo, *ibid.,* 42ff.

12. *Ibid.,* 64ff.

13. See Thomas S. Kuhn, *The Copernican Revolution* (Cambridge: Harvard University Press, 1957), 222–23.

14. Shea, *ibid.,* 114.

15. Galileo Galilei, 'Letter to Madame Christine of Lorraine, Grand Duchess of Tuscany, Concerning the Use of Biblical Quotation in Matters of Science', in *Men of Physics: Galileo Galilei, His Life and His Works,* trans. Raymond J. Seeger (Oxford: Pergamon, 1966), 271.

16. See Shea, *ibid.,* 174ff and Wallace, *ibid.,* 308ff.

17. For a treatment of the attack upon scientific method which has come from analyses of historical achievements in science, see Larry Laudan, 'Progress or Rationality? The Prospects for Normative Naturalism', *American Philosophical Quarterly,* Vol. 24, No. 1, 1987, 19–31.

18. Kuhn, *The Copernican Revolution,* 227.

19. Thomas S. Kuhn, *The Structure of Scientific Revolutions,* 2d ed. (Chicago: University of Chicago Press, 1970), 151 and 158.

20. *Ibid.,* 122.

21. Paul Feyerabend, 'How to Defend Society Against Science', in *Scientific Revolutions,* ed. Ian Hacking (Oxford: Oxford University Press, 1981), 156.

22. Peter Winch, 'Understanding a Primitive Society', in *Rationality,* ed. Bryan R. Wilson (Oxford: Blackwell, 1970), 94, 97, and 99.

23. For a more detailed discussion of Bacon's famous theory of "the idols", see Chapter 7.

24. Other writers have identified additional aspects of the tradition which is traced to Galileo. See, for example, Popper, *Conjectures and Refutations,* 103ff. I will focus here only upon the issue of realism.

25. See Ludwig Wittgenstein, *Philosophical Investigations* (New York: Macmillan, 1953), sec. 1ff. I have earlier explored the epistemological assumptions of this view of language in 'Language, Language Games, and Ostensive Definition', *Synthese* 69 (October-December 1986): 41–49.

26. Harris, 'Language, Language Games, and Ostensive Definition', 43.

27. *Ibid.*

28. For further details, see Bertrand Russell, 'Facts and Propositions', in *Contemporary Analytic and Linguistic Philosophies,* ed. E. D. Klemke (Buffalo: Prometheus, 1983), 209ff.

29. I have earlier argued similarly in Harris, 'Language, Language Games, and Ostensive Definition', 43–44.

2. QUINE ON LOGICAL AND ONTOLOGICAL RELATIVISM

1. A pun on biologist Ernst Heinrich Haeckel's claim that "Ontogeny recapitulates phylogeny".

2. Willard Van Orman Quine, 'Two Dogmas of Empiricism', in *From a Logical Point of View,* Second Edition. (New York: Harper and Row, 1953), 20–46.

3. See, for example, H.P. Grice and P. F. Strawson, 'In Defense of a Dogma', *Philosophical Review,* Vol. 65, 1956; R.M. Martin, 'On "Analytic" ', *Philosophical Studies,* Vol. 3, 1952; J. Bennett, 'Analytic-Synthetic', *Proceedings of the Aristotelian Society,* N.S., 59, 1959; J.G. Kemeny, 'Review of Quine's "Two Dogmas" ', *Journal of Symbolic Logic,* 17, 1952.

4. See *ibid.,* 24–37. Quine explores the possibility of explicating the

notion of analyticity in terms of definition, semantical rules, interchangeability *salva veritate,* synonymy, and contradiction. In each case, Quine argues, the proffered explicandum either begs the question or is as much in need of explanation as the original notion of analyticity.

5. By "recalcitrant experience", Quine simply means one that cannot be 'explained away' or otherwise dismissed. A recalcitrant experience is one which the subject accepts as veridical.

6. *Ibid.,* 42.

7. *Ibid.,* 43.

8. *Ibid.*

9. William James, 'Pragmatism's Conception of Truth', in *Pragmatism* (Indianapolis: Hackett, 1987), 96.

10. *Ibid.,* 97.

11. *Ibid.,* 100.

12. William James, 'The Sentiment of Rationality', in *Essays on Faith and Morals* (New York: New American Library, 1974), 73.

13. *Ibid.,* 76.

14. *Ibid.*

15. James, 'Pragmatism's Conception of Truth', 96.

16. *Ibid.,* 95.

17. Lewis Carroll, 'What the Tortoise said to Achilles', *Mind* 4, n.s. (1895): 278–280. I have used this point against Quine earlier in 'Dogmas of "Two Dogmas"', *Southern Journal of Philosophy* 11, no. 4 (winter 1973): 286–87.

18. Willard Van Orman Quine and J. S. Ullian, *The Web of Belief* (New York: Random House, 1970), 10.

19. Quine, 'Two Dogmas of Empiricism', 43.

20. Willard Van Orman Quine, *Word and Object* (Cambridge: MIT Press, 1960).

21. Willard Van Orman Quine, 'Ontological Relativity', in *Ontological Relativity and Other Essays,* 2d ed. (New York: Columbia University Press, 1969).

22. Willard Van Orman Quine, 'On What There Is', in *From a Logical Point of View,* 2d ed. (New York: Harper and Row, 1953), 10.

23. Rudolf Carnap, *Logical Syntax of Language* (Harcourt, Brace, 1937), 51ff.

24. *Ibid.,* 52.

25. Rudolf Carnap, 'Empiricism, Semantics, and Ontology', in *The Linguistic Turn,* ed. Richard Rorty (Chicago: University of Chicago Press, 1967), 73.

26. *Ibid.*

27. *Ibid.*

28. *Ibid.,* 74.

29. Quine, 'Ontological Relativity', 47.

30. Willard Van Orman Quine, *Pursuit of Truth* (Cambridge: Harvard University Press, 1990), 33.

31. Quine, 'Ontological Relativity', 54.

32. *Ibid.,* 48.

33. *Ibid.,* 29ff.

34. *Ibid.,* 35.

35. *Ibid.,* 32.

36. *Ibid.*, 43.

37. *Ibid.*, 48.

38. *Ibid.*, 50.

39. *Ibid.*

40. Willard Van Orman Quine, 'Identity, Ostension, and Hypostasis', in *From a Logical Point of View,* 2d ed. (New York: Harper and Row, 1953), 79.

41. These questions have been raised by others in a much more thorough and sophisticated fashion than will be done here. See, for example, Donald Davidson and Jaakko Hintikka, eds., *Words and Objections: Essays on the Work of W.V. Quine* (Dordrecht: Reidel, 1969); Alonzo Church, 'Ontological Commitment', *Journal of Philosophy* 55, no. 23 (November 1958): 1008–1014; Richard L. Cartwright, 'Ontology, Relativity, and the Theory of Meaning', *Philosophy of Science* 21, no. 4 (October 1954): 316–325; and Charles S. Chihara, 'Our Ontological Commitment to Universals', *Nous* 2, no. 1 (February 1968): 25–46.

42. Charles S. Chihara, 'On Criteria of Ontological Commitment', *Ontological Commitment,* ed. Richard H. Severens (Athens, Georgia: University of Georgia Press, 1974), 70.

43. Donald Davidson and Jaakko Hintikka, eds., *Words and Objections: Essays on the Work of W.V. Quine,* 93.

44. Chihara, 'Our Ontological Commitment to Universals', 73.

45. Quine, 'Two Dogmas of Empiricism', 46.

46. Nelson Goodman, 'On Likeness of Meaning', *Analysis,* 10, 1949, and 'On Some Differences About Meaning', *Analysis,* 13, 1953.

47. Goodman, 'On Likeness of Meaning', p. 71. The page numbers here refer to the reprint in *Semantics and the Philosophy of Language,* edited by Leonard Linsky (Urbana: University of Illinois Press, 1952).

48. James F. Harris, 'Secondary Extensions, Meanings, and Non-Null Terms', *Notre Dame Journal of Formal Logic,* Vol. XIV, No. 3, 1973, 316–322.

3. GOODMAN ON WAYS OF MAKING WORLDS

1. Nelson Goodman, *Ways of Worldmaking* (Cambridge: Hackett, 1978), 94.

2. *Ibid.*

3. For Hume's well-known treatment of the problem of induction and causality see his, *An Enquiry Concerning Human Understanding,* edited with an introduction by L. A. Selby-Bigge (Oxford: Clarendon, 1961), sec. 4, 25–39.

4. Nelson Goodman, *Fact, Fiction, and Forecast,* Second Edition. (New York: Bobbs-Merrill, 1965), 62.

5. *Ibid.*, 82.

6. *Ibid.*, 63.

7. *Ibid.*, 64.

8. *Ibid.*

9. *Ibid.*, 74.

10. *Ibid.*

11. *Ibid.,* 82.
12. *Ibid.,* 75.
13. See Rudolf Carnap, 'On the Application of Inductive Logic', *Philosophy and Phenomenological Research* 8, no. 1 (September 1947): 133–147; Nelson Goodman's reply, 'On Infirmities of Confirmation-Theory', *Philosophy and Phenomenological Research* 8, no. 1 (September 1947): 149–151; and Carnap's 'Reply to Nelson Goodman', *Philosophy and Phenomenological Research* 8, no. 3 (March 1948): 461–62.
14. *Ibid.,* 83.
15. *Ibid.,* 86.
16. *Ibid.,* 87.
17. *Ibid.,* 94. A predicate 'Q' is said to be projected, according to Goodman when it occurs with an actually projected hypothesis such as 'All p's are Q's'.
18. *Ibid.,* 98.
19. See, for example, Frank Jackson, 'Grue', *Journal of Philosophy* 72, no. 5 (March 13, 1975): 113–131.
20. What were three rules in the first edition of *Fact, Fiction, and Forecast* and two rules in the second edition were later conflated by Goodman to one rule. Hence, where a certain hypothesis is said to be over-ridden by a contrary overhypothesis when the contrary overhypothesis contains better entrenched predicates, a hypothesis is finally defined by Goodman as projectible "if all conflicting hypotheses are over-ridden, *unprojectible* if over-ridden [by some other overhypothesis], and *nonprojectible* if in conflict with another hypothesis and neither is over-ridden." See Nelson Goodman, *Problems and Projects* (New York: Bobbs-Merrill, 1972), 390.
21. Goodman, *Problems and Projects,* 95.
22. I have earlier argued in a similar fashion. See James Harris and Kevin Hoover, 'Abduction and the New Riddle of Induction', *Monist* 63, no. 3 (July 1980): 334ff.
23. Abduction is also called, at various times by Peirce, hypothesis, retroduction, and presumption. I will consistently use abduction to refer to this third kind of reasoning.
24. All references to Peirce's writings are to his *Collected Papers,* ed. Charles Hartshorne, Paul Weiss, and Arthur Burks, vols. 1–8 (Cambridge: Harvard University Press, 1931–58). References are in the standard form which gives volume number, decimal point and paragraph number. (7.218).
25. Goodman, *Ways of Worldmaking,* 10.
26. Goodman, *Fact, Fiction, and Forecast,* 74.
27. For a more detailed comparison of Goodman's theory of projection and Peirce's theory of abduction, see Harris and Hoover, 'Abduction and the New Riddle of Induction', 335ff.
28. Goodman, *Fact, Fiction, and Forecast,* 88.
29. *Ibid.,* 119.
30. See Harris and Hoover, 'Abduction and the New Riddle of Induction', 339.
31. Nelson Goodman, *The Structure of Appearance* (Cambridge: Harvard University Press, 1951), 93.
32. *Ibid.,* xiii.

33. Nelson Goodman, 'The Way the World Is', in *Problems and Projects* (New York: Bobbs-Merrill, 1972), 30.

34. *Ibid.,* 30–31.

35. Goodman, *The Structure of Appearance,* 106.

36. Goodman, *Ways of Worldmaking,* 4.

37. *Ibid.,* 2.

38. *Ibid.,* 7–8.

39. *Ibid.,* 2.

40. *Ibid.,* 94.

41. *Ibid.,* 96–97.

42. Goodman explicitly warns us that we should not talk about *truth* here. "Truth is often inapplicable, is seldom sufficient, and must sometimes give way to competing critieria." *Ibid.,* 107.

43. *Ibid.,* 138.

44. See most recently, for example, Harvey Siegel, *Relativism Refuted: A Critique of Contemporary Epistemological Relativism* (Dordrecht: Reidel, 1987), 148–150.

45. Goodman, *Ways of Worldmaking,* 107.

46. Siegel, *Relativism Refuted: A Critique of Contemporary Epistemological Relativism,* 153.

47. *Ibid.,* 154.

4. KUHN ON SCIENTIFIC REVOLUTIONS AND RELATIVISM

1. James F. Harris, 'Language, Language Games, and Ostensive Definition', *Synthese* 69 (October-December 1986): 42ff.

2. Ludwig Wittgenstein, *Philosophical Investigations,* trans. G.E.M. Anscombe, 3d ed. (New York: Macmillan, 1953), sec. 1ff.

3. I am aware that some people do not believe that the concerns of general epistemology and science are as parallel as I take them to be. See, for example, Bas C. van Fraassen, 'Empiricism in the Philosophy of Science', in *Images of Science,* ed. Paul M. Churchland and Clifford A. Hooker (Chicago: University of Chicago Press, 1985).

4. Harold I. Brown, *Rationality* (New York: Routledge, 1988), 38.

5. *Ibid.,* 79.

6. Thomas S. Kuhn, *Structure of Scientific Revolutions,* 2d ed. (Chicago: University of Chicago Press, 1970), 23–34. Although much of the present discussion centers upon Imre Lakatos's notion of a 'research programme', it is instructive to pursue Kuhn's early treatment of the notion of a paradigm since it was that early discussion which prompted the controversial claims concerning the incommensurability of paradigms and the radical forms of epistemological relativism to which this discussion has given rise.

7. Kuhn's notion of a paradigm is notoriously controversial. For a full discussion of the notion, see Kuhn, *The Structure of Scientific Revolutions,* 174–190.

8. *Ibid.,* 10.

9. *Ibid.*

10. *Ibid.,* 10–11.
11. *Ibid.,* 103.
12. *Ibid.,* 122.
13. *Ibid.,* 120.
14. *Ibid.,* 120ff.
15. *Ibid.,* 122.
16. *Ibid.,* 151.
17. *Ibid.,* 158.
18. *Ibid.*
19. *Ibid.,* 199–200.
20. Larry Laudan, *Progress and Its Problems* (Berkeley: University of California Press, 1977), 3.
21. Richard J. Bernstein, *Beyond Objectivism and Relativism* (Philadelphia: University of Pennsylvania Press, 1985), 24.
22. Paul Feyerabend, 'How to Defend Society Against Science', in *Scientific Revolutions,* ed. Ian Hacking (Oxford: Oxford University Press, 1981), 156ff.
23. Robert F. Baum, 'Popper, Kuhn, Lakatos: A Crisis of Modern Intellect', in *Science and Culture In the Western Tradition: Sources and Interpretations* (Scottsdale, Arizona: Gorsuch Scarisbrick, 1987), 279.
24. Israel Scheffler, *Science and Subjectivity* (Indianapolis: Hackett, 1967), 84.
25. *Ibid.,* 84.
26. *Ibid.,* 85.
27. Thomas S. Kuhn, 'Objectivity, Value Judgment, and Theory Choice', in *The Essential Tension: Selected Studies in Scientific Tradition and Change* (Chicago: University of Chicago Press, 1977), 338–39.
28. This is the alternative which Goodman explicitly endorses. He admits that his "outline of the facts concerning the fabrication of facts is of course itself a fabrication". See Goodman, *Ways of Worldmaking* (Cambridge: Hackett, 1978), 107.
29. Kuhn, 'Objectivity, Value Judgment, and Theory Choice', 338.
30. Kuhn, *The Structure of Scientific Revolutions,* 109–110.
31. Kuhn, *Ibid.,* 101ff. and Thomas S. Kuhn, 'Reflections on My Critics', in *Criticism and the Growth of Knowledge,* ed. Imre Lakatos and Alan Musgrave (Cambridge: Cambridge University Press, 1970), 266.
32. Donald Davidson, 'On the Very Idea of a Conceptual Scheme', in *Post-Analytic Philosophy,* ed. John Rajchman and Cornel West (New York: Columbia University Press, 1985), 135.
33. *Ibid.,* 136.
34. *Ibid.,* 139–140.
35. *Ibid.,* 140.
36. For a general attack upon the theory of radical meaning variance, see Carl R. Kordig, *The Justification of Scientific Change* (Dordrecht: Reidel, 1971), Chapter 2.
37. *Ibid.,* p. 35.
38. I do not think that the terminology matters a great deal in this case.
39. *Ibid.,* 142.
40. Others have attempted to respond to criticisms of the notion of incommensurability but with very limited success. See, for example, Paul Feyerabend, 'Reply to Criticism', in *Boston Studies in the Philosophy of*

Science, edited by R.S. Cohen and M.W. Wartofsky (New York: Humanities Press, 1965), Vol. 2, 231–234. Feyerabend claims there that the notion of incommensurability is independent of the theory of meaning invariance. For a compelling response to Feyerabend, see Carl R. Kordig, *The Justification of Scientific Change* (Dordrecht: Reidel, 1971), 55–59. Also see Paul Feyerabend, *Against Method* (New York: Verso, 1988), Revised Edition, 220–226; and *Farewell to Reason* (New York: Verso, 1987), Chapter 10. For further criticism of Feyerabend, see Hilary Putnam, *Reason, Truth, and History* (Cambridge: University of Cambridge Press, 1981). 114ff.

41. *Ibid.,* 143.

42. See Chapter 4.

43. Kuhn, 'Reflections on My Critics', 234.

44. Kuhn, *The Structure of Scientific Revolutions,* 200.

45. *Ibid.,* 199.

46. *Ibid.,* 199.

47. *Ibid.*

48. Kuhn, 'Objectivity, Value Judgment, and Theory Choice', 331.

49. Richard Rorty, *Philosophy and the Mirror of Nature* (Princeton: Princeton University Press, 1979), 323.

50. See Dudley Shapere, 'The Paradigm Concept', *Science* 172 (1971): 707ff.

51. Harvey Siegel, *Relativism Refuted: A Critique of Contemporary Epistemological Relativism* (Dordrecht: Reidel, 1987), 58.

52. Kuhn, 'Objectivity, Value Judgment, and Theory Choice', 335.

53. Steven Lukes, 'Some Problems About Rationality', in *Rationality,* ed. Bryan R. Wilson (Oxford: Blackwell, 1970), 208ff.

54. Martin Hollis, 'The Limits of Irrationality', in *Rationality,* ed. Bryan R. Wilson (Oxford: Blackwell, 1970), 218.

55. See Kuhn, *Structure of Scientific Revolutions,* 112 and Norwood Russell Hanson, *Patterns of Discovery* (Cambridge: Cambridge University Press, 1961), chap. 1.

56. Siegel, *Relativism Refuted: A Critique of Contemporary Epistemological Relativism,* 59.

57. Kuhn, *The Essential Tension: Selected Studies in Scientific Tradition and Change,* xi–xii.

58. *Ibid.,* xii.

5. WINCH AND GADAMER ON THE SOCIAL SCIENCES, HERMENEUTICS, AND RELATIVISM

1. Peter Winch, *The Idea of a Social Science and Its Relation to Philosophy* (London: Routledge, 1958).

2. Hans-Georg Gadamer, *Truth and Method* (New York: Seabury Press, 1975).

3. Richard J. Bernstein, *Beyond Objectivism and Relativism* (Philadelphia: University of Pennsylvania Press, 1985), 27.

4. Peter Winch, 'Understanding a Primitive Society', in *Rationality,* ed. Bryan R. Wilson (Oxford: Blackwell, 1970), 93–94.

5. *Ibid.,* 92 and 100.

6. *Ibid.,* 98.

7. Winch, *The Idea of a Social Science and Its Relation to Philosophy,* 102.

8. I will not attempt to recreate this exchange here. See Winch, *The Idea of a Social Science and Its Relation to Philosophy* and 'Understanding a Primitive Society', in *Rationality,* ed. Bryan R. Wilson (Oxford: Blackwell, 1970), 78–111; and Alasdair MacIntyre, 'Is Understanding Religion Compatible with Believing?' in *Rationality,* ed. Bryan R. Wilson (Oxford: Blackwell, 1970), 62–77.

9. Winch, 'Understanding a Primitive Society', 86.

10. *Ibid.*

11. *Ibid.,* 88 and 91ff.

12. *Ibid.,* 94 and 99.

13. *Ibid.,* 97.

14. *Ibid.,* 86.

15. *Ibid.,* 91 ff.

16. *Ibid.,* 88.

17. *Ibid.,* 92.

18. *Ibid.,* 93.

19. *Ibid.,* 88.

20. See Martin Hollis, 'The Limits of Irrationality', and Steven Lukes, 'Some Problems about Rationality' in *Rationality,* ed. Bryan R. Wilson (Oxford: Blackwell, 1970). Also see Martin Hollis, 'The Social Destruction of Reality', and Steven Lukes, 'Relativism in Its Place', in *Rationality and Relativism,* ed. Martin Hollis and Steven Lukes (Cambridge: MIT Press, 1982). Robin Horton has similarly argued for a "logical bridgehead" amongst different cultures based upon what he calls "primary theory", which contains spacial and temporal relations for "middle-sized objects" of common human experience. See 'Tradition and Modernity Revisited' in Martin Hollis and Steven Lukes, *Ibid.,* pp. 227ff.

21. Hollis, 'The Social Destruction of Reality', 74.

22. Lukes, 'Some Problems About Rationality', 208.

23. Barry Barnes and David Bloor, 'Relativism, Rationalism, and the Sociology of Knowledge', in *Rationality and Relativism,* ed. Martin Hollis and Steven Lukes (Cambridge: MIT Press, 1982), 38.

24. *Ibid.*

25. Lewis Carroll, 'What the Tortoise Said to Achilles', *Mind* 4, n.s. (1895): 278–280.

26. *Ibid.,* 41.

27. *Ibid.,* 40.

28. James F. Harris, 'Achilles Replies', *Australasian Journal of Philosophy* 47, no. 3 (December 1969): 322–24.

29. Barnes and Bloor, 'Relativism, Rationalism, and the Sociology of Knowledge', 38.

30. *Ibid.,* 324.

31. *Ibid.,* 42.

32. A.N. Prior, 'The Runabout Inference-Ticket', *Analysis,* 21 (1960), 39.

33. *Ibid.,* 93.

34. *Ibid.,* 93–94.
35. *Ibid.,* 94.
36. Winch, 'Understanding a Primitive Society', 68.
37. *Ibid.,* 93–94.
38. Bernstein, *Beyond Objectivism and Relativism,* 106.
39. I cannot here, of course, attempt a thorough treatment of hermeneutics. I will only trace the line of development which I see as leading directly to a form of relativism concerning science, human reason, and rationality.
40. Gadamer, *Truth and Method,* 58.
41. *Ibid.,* 336.
42. Joel C. Weinsheimer, *Gadamer's Hermeneutics: A Reading of Truth and Method* (New Haven: Yale University Press, 1985), 5.
43. Richard Rorty, *Philosophy and the Mirror of Nature* (Princeton: Princeton University Press, 1979), 315.
44. Gadamer, *Truth and Method,* 311.
45. Hans-Georg Gadamer, *Philosophical Hermeneutics,* trans. David Linge (Berkeley: University of California Press, 1976), 54.
46. Weinsheimer, 8.
47. Mary Hesse, *Revolutions and Reconstructions in the Philosophy of Science* (Bloomington: Indiana University Press, 1980), 169.
48. Gadamer, *Truth and Method,* 311.
49. *Ibid.,* xi.
50. *Ibid.,* xii.
51. Weinsheimer, 64.
52. Gadamer, *Truth and Method,* 336.
53. *Ibid.,* p. 337. For further treatment of the controversy over the role of an original intention of the author, see E.D. Hirsch Jr., *Validity in Interpretation* (New Haven: Yale University Press, 1967); and David Couzens Hoy, *The Critical Circle: Literature, History, and Philosophical Hermeneutics* (Berkeley: University of California Press, 1978), 43ff.
54. *Ibid.,* 337.
55. See Gadamer, *Truth and Method,* xvi–xvii; Hoy, 48ff; and Weinsheimer, 32ff.
56. Gadamer, *Truth and Method,* xvi.
57. Rorty, *Philosophy and the Mirror of Nature,* 315–316.
58. Jean-François Lyotard, 'The Postmodern Condition', in *After Philosophy: End or Transformation,* ed. Kenneth Baynes, James Bohman, and Thomas McCarthy (Cambridge: MIT Press, 1987), 73.
59. *Ibid.,* 80.
60. *Ibid.,* 88–89.
61. *Ibid.,* 82.
62. *Ibid.,* 83.
63. *Ibid.*
64. Gadamer, *Truth and Method,* 406.
65. *Ibid.,* 308–09.
66. *Ibid.,* 410.
67. Weinsheimer, 58. For a discussion of Gadamer and the problem of internal consistency with comparisons with Russell, Gödel, and Tarski see *Ibid.,* 46–59.
68. Gadamer, *Truth and Method,* 23.

69. *Ibid.,* 309.
70. *Ibid.,* 483.
71. *Ibid.*
72. *Ibid.*
73. Lyotard, 73.
74. *Ibid.,* 74-75.
75. *Ibid.,* 83.
76. *Ibid.,* 78-79.
77. *Ibid.,* 80.
78. *Ibid.,* 89.
79. *Ibid.*
80. Karl Popper, *The Poverty of Historicism* (New York: Basic Books, 1957), 161.
81. Bernstein, *Beyond Objectivism and Relativism,* 230.
82. *Ibid.,* 7.
83. *Ibid.,* 92.
84. *Ibid.,* 230.
85. *Ibid.,* 231.
86. *Ibid.,* 92.
87. *Ibid.,* 206.
88. Thomas S. Kuhn, *The Structure of Scientific Revolutions,* 2d ed. (Chicago: University of Chicago Press, 1970), 94.
89. For a more detailed comparison of Gadamer and Habermas, see the following works by Habermas: *Knowledge and Human Interests,* trans. J.J. Shapiro (Boston: Beacon Press, 1971); 'A Review of Gadamer's *Truth and Method',* in *Understanding and Human Inquiry,* ed. Fred Dallmayr and Thomas McCarthy (Notre Dame: University of Notre Dame Press, 1977); and 'Der Universalitätsanspruch der Hermeneutik', in *Hermeneutik and Dialektik,* I, 73-103. Also see, by Gadamer, 'Rhetorik, Hermeneutik, und Ideologiekritik', in *Kleine Schriften,* I, 113-130. Gadamer, Habermas, and others contribute to *Hermeneutik und Ideologiekritik,* ed. Karl-Otto Apel, et al, (Frankfurt: Suhrkamkp, 1971).
90. Hoy, 122.
91. E.D. Hirsch, *The Aims of Interpretation* (Chicago: The University of Chicago Press, 1976), 36.
92. Hirsch, *Validity in Interpretation,* 5.
93. Hoy, 33.

6. QUINE ON NATURALIZED EPISTEMOLOGY AND RELATIVISM

1. Willard Van Orman Quine, 'Epistemology Naturalized', in *Naturalizing Epistemology,* ed. Hilary Kornblith (Cambridge: MIT Press, 1987), 18-20.
2. *Ibid.,* 18.
3. *Ibid.,* 18 and 20.
4. *Ibid.,* 19.
5. *Ibid.*

6. For an accounting of the various different forms of naturalized epistemology and their claims, see James Maffie, 'Recent Work on Naturalized Epistemology', *American Philosophical Quarterly,* Vol. 27, No. 4, 1990, 281–293.

7. *Ibid.,* 21.

8. *Ibid.,* 22.

9. *Ibid.,* 24.

10. *Ibid.*

11. *Ibid.,* 27.

12. See Maffis, *ibid.*

13. Alvin I. Goldman, 'Epistemics: The Regulative Theory of Cognition', *Journal of Philosophy* 75 (October 1978): 509–523. Reprinted in Hilary Kornblith, ed., *Naturalizing Epistemology* (Cambridge: MIT Press, 1985).

14. See especially Karl Popper, *Conjectures and Refutations: The Growth of Scientific Knowledge* (New York: Harper and Row, 1963); and D.T. Campbell, 'Methodological Suggestions from a Comparative Psychology of Knowledge Processes', *Inquiry* 2 (1959): 152–182. Also see more recent articles by Campbell, Popper, and others in *Evolutionary Epistemology, Rationality, and the Sociology of Knowledge,* ed. Gerard Radnitzky and W. W. Bartley III (La Salle: Open Court, 1987).

15. D.T. Campbell, 'Evolutionary Epistemology', *The Philosophy of Karl Popper,* ed. Paul Arthur Schilpp (La Salle: Open Court, 1974). Reprinted in Radnitzky and Bartley, eds., *Evolutionary Epistemology,* 51.

16. Campbell, 'Evolutionary Epistemology', 51–52 and Karl Popper, *The Logic of Scientific Discovery* (New York: Basic Books, 1959), 19 and 22.

17. For a further comparison of evolutionary epistemology with traditional epistemology, see Campbell, 'Evolutionary Epistemology', 53.

18. Quine, 'Epistemology Naturalized', 19.

19. *Ibid.,* 23.

20. *Ibid.,* 24.

21. *Ibid.,* 19.

22. However, in the case of Quine, given his rejection of the analytic-synthetic distinction and his insistence that logical laws and principles of inference are simple "additional statements" in any system, it is impossible to make out what even a deductive justification of science would be like. The fact that such a deductive justification apparently makes sense to Quine (though he rejects it) is further evidence in support of the arguments in Chapter 3 against Quine's holism.

23. Barry Stroud, 'The Significance of Naturalized Epistemology', in *Naturalizing Epistemology,* ed. Hilary Kornblith (Cambridge, MIT Press, 1985), 71–89. This paper is a revised version of 'The Significance of Skepticism', in *Transcendental Arguments and Science,* edited by Peter Bieri, R.P. Horstmann, and L. Kruger (Dordrecht: Reidel, 1979), and a revised version of this paper appears as Chapter 6 of Stroud's *The Significance of Philosophical Skepticism* (Oxford: Clarendon, 1984). The page numbers of the references herein refer to the Kornblith volume.

24. For a critical account of Stroud's criticism of Quine, see Roger F. Gibson, 'Stroud on Naturalized Epistemology', *Metaphilosophy,* Vol. 20, No. 1, 1989, 1–11.

25. *Ibid.*, 71.
26. Quine, 'Epistemology Naturalized', 24.
27. *Ibid.*, 17.
28. The following point follows Stroud very closely. See Stroud, 80–82.
29. Quine, 'Epistemology Naturalized', 24.
30. Stroud, 81.
31. *Ibid.*, 82.
32. See Hilary Putnam, 'Why Reason Can't Be Naturalized', in *After Philosophy: End or Transformation,* ed. Kenneth Baynes, James Bohman, and Thomas McCarthy (Cambridge: MIT Press, 1987), 240–41.
33. *Ibid.*, 240.
34. *Ibid.*, 241.
35. Harvey Siegel, 'Justification, Discovery, and the Naturalizing of Epistemology', *Philosophy of Science* 47, no. 2 (June 1980), 315.
36. *Ibid.*
37. Quine, 'Epistemology Naturalized', 27.
38. *Ibid.*
39. *Ibid.*, 24.
40. *Ibid.*
41. Stroud, 74.
42. Quine, 'Epistemology Naturalized', 24. See Otto Neurath, 'Protocol Sentences', in *Logical Positivism,* ed. A.J. Ayer (New York: Free Press, 1959), 201.
43. Stroud, 84–85.
44. Quine, 'Epistemology Naturalized', 25.
45. Richard Rorty, *Philosophy and the Mirror of Nature* (Princeton: Princeton University Press, 1979), 223.
46. *Ibid.*
47. Willard Van Orman Quine, 'Grades of Theoreticity', in *Experience and Theory,* ed. Lawrence Foster and J. W. Swanson (Amherst, Massachusetts: University of Massachusetts Press, 1970), 3.
48. Rorty, *Philosophy and the Mirror of Nature,* 225.
49. Quine, 'Epistemology Naturalized', 26.
50. *Ibid.*, 25.
51. *Ibid.*, 28.
52. *Ibid.*, 27.
53. *Ibid.*
54. *Ibid.*, 28.
55. *Ibid.*
56. Rorty, *Philosophy and the Mirror of Nature,* 227–28.
57. Willard Van Orman Quine, 'Reply to Stroud', in *The Foundations of Analytic Philosophy: Midwest Studies in Philosophy,* vol. 6 (Minneapolis: University of Minnesota Press, 1981), 474.
58. *Ibid.*
59. *Ibid.*
60. For further discussion of this point, see Harvey Siegel, 'Empirical Psychology, Naturalized Epistemology, and First Philosophy', *Philosophy of Science* 51, no.4 (December 1984): 667ff and 670ff and Robert Almeder, 'On Naturalizing Epistemology', *American Philosophical Quarterly,* Vol. 27, No. 4, 1990, 265ff.

61. *Ibid.,* 668.
62. *Ibid.,* 671.
63. Paul A. Roth, 'Theories of Nature and the Nature of Theories', *Mind* 89 (July 1980): 431–438.
64. *Ibid.,* 434.
65. *Ibid.*

7. PEIRCE ON METHOD AND RATIONALITY

1. Charles Sanders Peirce, 'Questions Concerning Certain Faculties Claimed for Man' and 'Some Consequences of Four Incapacities' in *Collected Papers,* ed. Charles Hartshorne, Paul Weiss, and Arthur Burks, vol. 5 (Cambridge: Belknap Press of Harvard University Press, 1934). All further references to the writings of Peirce are to these *Collected Papers.* References will be given in the text using the usual numerical designations for volume and paragraph numbers.
2. Hans-Georg Gadamer, *Truth and Method* (New York: Seabury, 1975), 239.
3. My examination of Peirce's categories here will be cursory. For a more detailed treatment, see Murray G. Murphey, *The Development of Peirce's Philosophy* (Cambridge: Harvard University Press, 1961) see especially 306–09, 312–14; Richard Rorty, 'Pragmatism, Categories, and Language', *Philosophical Review* 70 (April 1961); and Richard J. Bernstein, *Praxis and Action* (Philadelphia: University of Pennsylvania Press, 1971), 178ff.
4. See Murphey, 306.
5. Bernstein, *Praxis and Action,* 306.
6. Bernstein, *Praxis and Action,* 182.
7. As students of Peirce are aware, Peirce developed his notion of reality over some period of time and late into his final period of writing. I cannot here trace that development in detail. The main thrust of my treatment of Peirce's notion of reality is to attempt to resolve some of the current controversies about reality, rationality, and science.
8. See Saul A. Kripke, *Wittgenstein on Rules and Private Language* (Cambridge: Harvard University Press, 1982); and G.P. Baker and P.M.S. Hacker, *Skepticism, Rules, and Language* (Oxford: Blackwell, 1984).
9. Ludwig Wittgenstein, *Philosophical Investigations* (New York: Macmillan Publishing Co., 1953), sec. 293.
10. *Ibid.,* sec. 258.
11. *Ibid.,* sec. 265.
12. Bernstein, *Praxis and Action,* 175.
13. Ian Hacking, 'Lakatos's Philosophy of Science', in *Scientific Revolutions,* ed. Ian Hacking (Oxford: Oxford University Press, 1981), 131.
14. See, for example, P. F. Strawson, *Skepticism and Naturalism: Some Varieties* (New York: Columbia University Press, 1985) especially Chapter 1; and Hilary Kornblith, ed., *Naturalizing Epistemology* (Cambridge: MIT Press, 1985).

15. Richard Rorty, *Philosophy and the Mirror of Nature* (Princeton: Princeton University Press, 1979), 317.

16. Paul Feyerabend, 'How to Defend Society Against Science', in *Scientific Revolutions*, ed. Ian Hacking (Oxford: Oxford University Press, 1981), 156ff.

17. Murphey, 393.

18. Bernstein, *Praxis and Action*, 181–82.

19. See 'Is Science Really a Pack of Lies?' *Nature* 303 (June 1983): 361–62.

20. *Nature* 302 (April 14, 1983): 560. For accounts of similar incidents involving fraud in science, see *Nature* 301 (January 13, 1983): 101 and *Nature* 302 (April 28, 1983): 738.

21. See 'Can There Be A Private Language?' A. J. Ayer and Rush Rhees, *Proceedings of the Aristotelian Society,* Supplementary Volume 28 (1954): 63–94. Reprinted in *The Private Language Argument*, ed. O.R. Jones (New York: Macmillan, 1971) to which the page numbers here refer, 55.

22. *Ibid.,* 72.

23. *Ibid.,* 75.

24. Wittgenstein, sec. 265.

25. Francis Bacon, *Novum Organum,* edited with an introduction by Fulton H. Anderson (New York: Bobbs-Merrill, 1960), bk. 1, xxxviii–lxviii.

26. Daniel J. Boorstin, *The Discoverers* (New York: Random House, 1983), 74–75 and 332–35.

27. *Ibid.,* 74–75.

28. See Edmund Gettier, 'Is Justified True Belief Knowledge?' *Analysis,* Vol. 23, No. 6, 1963, 121–23.

29. Thomas S. Kuhn, *The Structure of Scientific Revolutions,* 2d ed. (Chicago: University of Chicago Press, 1970), 121ff.

30. *Ibid.,* 122–23.

31. William James, 'The Sentiment of Rationality' in *Essays on Faith and Morals* (New York: New American Library, 1962), 76.

32. Rorty, *Philosophy and the Mirror of Nature,* 296.

33. For more recent treatments of the claim that induction and science are self-correcting see Hans Reichenbach *Experience and Predication* (Chicago: University of Chicago Press, 1938) and Wesley Salmon, 'Inductive Inference', in *Readings in the Philosophy of Science,* edited by Baruch Brody (Englewood Cliffs: Prentice-Hall, 1970).

34. Larry Laudan, 'Peirce and the Trivialization of the Self-Correcting Thesis', in *Foundations of Scientific Method: The Nineteenth Century,* edited by Ronald Giere and Richard Westfall (Bloomington: Indiana University Press, 1973) p. 278.

35. *Ibid.,* 292.

36. *Ibid.,* 124.

37. *Ibid.,* p. 127.

38. *Ibid.,* 120.

39. *Ibid.,* 121ff.

40. *Ibid.,* 14ff.

41. *Ibid.,* 15.

42. *Ibid.,* 37.

43. *Ibid.,* 276ff.

44. Larry Laudan, 'Commentary: Science at the Bar—Causes for Concern', *Science, Technology, and Human Values,* Vol. 7, No. 41, 1982, 16.

45. See John E. Smith, 'Community and Reality', in *Perspectives on Peirce,* ed. Richard J. Bernstein (New Haven: Yale University Press, 1965), 99ff.

46. Kuhn, *The Structure of Scientific Revolutions,* 205–06.

47. *Ibid.,* 206.

48. Rorty, *Philosophy and the Mirror of Nature,* 296.

49. *Ibid.,* 318.

8. MODERN SCIENCE AND FEMINISM

1. Hilary Putnam, *Reason, Truth, and History* (Cambridge: Cambridge University Press, 1981), 176.

2. Thomas S. Kuhn, *The Structure of Scientific Revolutions,* 2d ed. (Chicago: University of Chicago Press, 1970), Chapter 7, 66–76.

3. Larry Laudan, *Progress and Its Problems* (Berkeley: University of California Press, 1977), 124 and 123.

4. Pursuing answers to such questions is deserving of a volume in itself, and I cannot reasonably hope to make much advance on these matters here. For more detailed discussion of these issues, see Robert J. Ackermann, *Data, Instruments, and Theory* (Princeton: Princeton University Press, 1985), 35–73; Joseph Grunfeld, *Method and Language* (Amsterdam: B.R. Gruner, 1982), 29–44; David L. Hull, *Science As A Process: An Evolutionary Account of the Social and Conceptual Development of Science* (Chicago: University of Chicago Press, 1988); and Robert K. Merton and Jerry Gaston, eds., *The Sociology of Science in Europe* (Carbondale: Southern Illinois University Press, 1977) as well as the related works cited in Chapter 7.

5. I cannot hope to treat adequately all of the issues—even all of the major issues—raised in this literature. See, for example, Ruth Bleier, *Science and Gender: A Critique of Biology and Its Theories on Women* (New York: Pergamon, 1984); Susan R. Bordo, *The Flight to Objectivity* (Albany: State University of New York Press, 1987); David L. Hull, *Science as A Process;* Larry Laudan, *Science and Values* (Berkeley: University of California Press, 1984); Sandra Harding, *The Science Question in Feminism* (Ithaca: Cornell University Press, 1986); Evelyn Fox Keller, *Reflections on Gender and Science* (New Haven: Yale University Press, 1985); and Carolyn Merchant, *The Death of Nature: Women, Ecology, and the Scientific Revolution* (New York: Harper and Row, 1980).

6. See, for example, Hull, 1–2. Hull explicitly uses the distinction between internalism and externalism while admitting that the use of this distinction gives some advantage to the internalists. Hull also implicitly recognizes the distinction between what I have called SC1 and SC2; however, he fails to explicitly use this distinction in his analysis of science as a process.

7. There is, of course, a plethora of different forms of feminist criticism of traditional science and these range from being rather moderate to rather radical. I cannot adequately represent or respond to each of these different

varieties in detail. I include here what I take to be the most challenging and difficult problems raised by feminist critiques.

8. Harding, *The Science Question in Feminism,* 9.

9. Keller, 76ff.

10. Bordo, 97ff.

11. Merchant, *The Death of Nature.*

12. *Ibid.,* 42.

13. *Ibid.,* 99–100.

14. Keller, 76.

15. Harding, *The Science Question in Feminism,* 9.

16. See *Journal of the American Medical Association* (Feb. 28, 1990).

17. I will not attempt a complete discussion of the relationship between science and values here. For a more complete treatment of these issues, see Bleier, *Science and Gender;* Harding, *The Science Question in Feminism;* Keller, *Reflections on Gender and Science;* Laudan, *Progress and Its Problems* (Berkeley: University of California Press, 1977) and *Science and Values;* and Merchant, *The Death of Nature.*

18. Bleier, 199.

19. Donna J. Haraway, 'In the Beginning Was the Word: The Genesis of Biological Theory', *Signs: Journal of Women in Culture and Society* 6, no. 3, 470.

20. I cannot treat the variety of different feminist theories in any detail here. However, see Bordo, *The Flight to Objectivity;* Harding, *The Science Question in Feminism;* Nancy M. Hartsock, *Money, Sex, and Power* (New York: Longman, 1983); Keller, *Reflections on Gender and Science;* Hilary Rose, 'Hand, Brain, and Heart: A Feminist Epistemology for the Natural Sciences', *Signs: Journal of Women in Culture and Society* 9, no. 1 (1983): 73–90. For a summary treatment of several of the different feminist theories, see Harding, *The Science Question in Feminism,* 141ff. Harding classifies the different feminist theories either as "feminist standpoint theories" or as "feminist postmodernist" theories. According to Harding, feminist standpoint theories "ground a distinctive feminist science in a theory of gendered activity and social experience", and try to "reconstruct the original goals of modern science". Feminist postmodernism is more radical and "more directly challenges [and rejects] those goals" (*Ibid.,* 141–42).

21. Helen E. Longino, 'Can There Be a Feminist Science?' *Hypatia* 2, no. 3 (Fall 1987): 51–64. Reprinted in *Women, Knowledge, and Reality,* edited by Ann Garry and Marilyn Pearsall (Boston: Unwin Hyman, 1989), to which the page numbers here refer, 206. Also see Helen Longino, 'Beyond "Bad Science" ', *Science, Technology, and Human Values* 8, No. 1, 1983, 7–17.

22. Longino, 'Can There Be a Feminist Science?' 206–08.

23. *Ibid.,* 212.

24. *Ibid.,* 208.

25. *Ibid.,* 213.

26. Francis Bacon, *New Organon,* edited with an introduction by Fulton H. Anderson (New York: Bobbs-Merrill, 1960), bk. 1, sec. xxxviii–lxviii.

27. Longino, 'Can There Be a Feminist Science?' 212.

28. *Ibid.,* 212–13.

29. Bleier, 143–44.

30. I am aware that some feminists consider the use of *'ad hominem*

fallacy' sexist. I am using it here to mean an argument directed against the *person*.

31. Helen Longino, 'Feminist Critiques of Rationality: Critiques of Science or Philosophy of Science?' *Women's Studies International Forum*, Vol. 12, No. 3, 1989, 264ff and *Science as Social Knowledge* (Princeton: Princeton University Press, 1990), Chapter 3.

32. Longino, 'Feminist Critiques of Rationality: Critiques of Science or Philosophy of Science', *ibid.*, 269.

33. *Ibid.*

34. *Ibid.*, 264.

35. *Ibid.*, 265.

36. Paul Feyerabend, 'How To Defend Society Against Science', in *Scientific Revolutions*, ed. Ian Hacking (Oxford: Oxford University Press, 1981), 156ff.

37. Longino, 'Can There Be a Feminist Science?' 204. Also see Bleier, 200ff; Harding, *The Science Question in Feminism*, 141ff; and Rose, 'Hand, Brain, and Heart: A Feminist Epistemology for the Natural Sciences', 73–90.

38. Longino, 'Can There Be a Feminist Science?' 204.

39. Bleier, 17.

40. Sandra Harding, 'Why Has the Sex/Gender System Become Visible Only Now?' in *Discovering Reality: Feminists Perspectives on Epistemology, Metaphysics, Methodology, and Philosophy of Science*, ed. Sandra Harding and Merill B. Hintikka (Dordrecht: Reidel, 1983), 316.

41. Harding, *The Science Question in Feminism*, 137.

42. *Ibid.*, 138.

43. *Ibid.*, 141.

44. *Ibid.*

45. See, for example, Bleier, chap. 1; Harding, *The Science Question in Feminism*, chaps. 1 and 3; Keller, chap. 4; Margaret W. Rossiter, *Women Scientists in America: Struggles and Strategies to 1940* (Baltimore: Johns Hopkins University Press, 1982).

46. Jean Grimshaw, *Philosophy and Feminist Thinking* (Minneapolis: University of Minnesota Press, 1986), 84–85.

47. Harding, *The Science Question in Feminism*, 163.

48. Jane Roland Martin, 'Ideological Critiques and the Philosophy of Science', *Philosophy of Science* 56 (1989): 8–9.

49. See, for example, Ruth Bleier's discussion of the history of the use of craniology to explain supposed sex and race differences in *Science and Gender*, 49ff.

50. Charles Sanders Peirce, *Collected Papers*, ed. Charles Hartshorne, Paul Weiss and Arthur Burks, 8 vols. (Cambridge: Harvard University Press, 1931–1958), 5.311.

51. Karl Popper, *Conjectures and Refutations: The Growth of Scientific Knowledge* (New York: Harper and Row, 1963), 217.

52. Paul Feyerabend, *Against Method* (New York: Verso, 1975), 19.

53. *Ibid.*, 53.

SELECT BIBLIOGRAPHY

ARTICLES

Almeder, R. 'On Naturalizing Epistemology'. *Pacific Philosophical Quarterly.* 27 (1990): 263–279.

Ashby, R. W. 'Positivism'. In *A Critical History of Western Philosophy.* Edited by D. J. O'Connor. New York: Free Press, 1964.

Ayer, A. J. and Rush Rhees. 'Can There Be A Private Language?'. *Proceedings of the Aristotelian Society.* Supplementary Volume 28 (1954): 63–94.

Barnes, Barry and David Bloor. 'Relativism, Rationalism, and the Sociology of Knowledge'. In *Rationality and Relativism.* Edited by Martin Hollis and Steven Lukes. Cambridge: MIT Press, 1982.

Baum, Robert F. 'Popper, Kuhn, Lakatos: A Crisis of Modern Intellect'. In *Science and Culture In the Western Tradition: Sources and Interpretations.* Scottsdale, Arizona: Gorsuch Scarisbrick, 1987.

Campbell, D. T. 'Methodological Suggestions from a Comparative Psychology of Knowledge Processes." *Inquiry* 2 (1959): 152–182.

———. 'Evolutionary Epistemology'. In *The Philosophy of Karl Popper.* Edited by Paul Arthur Schilpp. La Salle, Illinois: Open Court, 1974.

Carnap, Rudolf. 'On the Application of Inductive Logic'. *Philosophy and Phenomenological Research* 8, no. 1 (September 1947): 133–147.

———. 'Reply to Nelson Goodman'. *Philosophy and Phenomenological Research* 8, no. 3 (March 1948): 461–462.

———. 'Intellectual Autobiography'. In *The Philosophy of Rudolf Carnap.* Edited by Paul Arthur Schilpp. La Salle, Illinois: Open Court, 1963.

———. 'Empiricism, Semantics, and Ontology'. In *The Linguistic Turn.* Edited by Richard Rorty. Chicago: University of Chicago Press, 1967.

Carroll, Lewis. 'What the Tortoise said to Achilles'. *Mind* 4, n.s. (1895): 278–280.

Cartwright, Richard L. 'Ontology Relativity and the Theory of Meaning'. *Philosophy of Science* 21, no. 4 (October 1954): 316–325.

Church, Alonzo. 'Ontological Commitment'. *Journal of Philosophy* 55, no. 23 (November 1958): 1008–14.

Chihara, Charles S. 'Our Ontological Commitment to Universals'. *Nous* 2, no. 1 (February 1968): 25–46.

———. 'On Criteria of Ontological Commitment'. In *Ontological Commitment.* Edited by Richard H. Severens. Athens, Georgia: University of Georgia Press, 1974.

Davidson, Donald. 'On the Very Idea of a Conceptual Scheme'. In *Post-Analytic Philosophy*. Edited by John Rajchman and Cornel West. New York: Columbia University Press, 1985.

Fraassen, Bas C. van. 'Empiricism in the Philosophy of Science'. In *Images of Science*. Edited by Paul M. Churchland and Clifford A. Hooker. Chicago: University of Chicago Press, 1985.

Feyerabend, Paul. 'How to Defend Society Against Science'. In *Scientific Revolutions*. Edited by Ian Hacking. Oxford: Oxford University Press, 1981.

————. 'Popper, Kuhn, Lakatos: A Crisis of Modern Intellect'. In *Science and Culture In the Western Tradition: Sources and Interpretations*. Scottsdale, Arizona: Gorsuch Scarisbrick, 1987.

Galilei, Galileo. 'Letter to Madame Christine of Lorraine, Grand Duchess of Tuscany, Concerning the Use of Biblical Quotation in Matters of Science'. In *Men of Physics: Galileo Galilei, His Life and His Works*. Translated by Raymond J. Seeger. Oxford: Pergamon, 1966.

Gibson, Roger F. 'Stroud on Naturalized Epistemology'. *Metaphilosophy*. 20 (January 1989): 1–11.

Goldman, Alvin. 'Epistemics: The Regulative Theory of Cognition'. *Journal of Philosophy* 75, no. 10 (October 1978): 509–523.

Goodman, Nelson. 'On Infirmities of Confirmation-Theory'. *Philosophy and Phenomenological Research*. 8, no. 1 (September 1947): 149–151.

————. 'The Way the World Is'. In *Problems and Projects*. New York: Bobbs-Merrill, 1972.

Habermas. 'A Review of Gadamer's *Truth and Method*'. In *Understanding and Human Inquiry*. Edited by Fred Dallmayr and Thomas McCarthy. Notre Dame: University of Notre Dame Press, 1977.

Hacking, Ian. 'Lakatos's Philosophy of Science'. In *Scientific Revolutions*. Edited by Ian Hacking. Oxford: Oxford University Press, 1981.

Haraway, Donna J. 'In the Beginning Was the Word: The Genesis of Biological Theory'. *Signs: Journal of Women in Culture and Society* 6, no. 3, 469–481.

Harding, Sandra. 'Why Has the Sex/Gender System Become Visible Only Now?' In *Discovering Reality: Feminists Perspectives on Epistemology, Metaphysics, Methodology, and Philosophy of Science*. Edited by Sandra Harding and Merill B. Hintikka. Dordrecht: Reidel, 1983.

Harris, James F. 'Achilles Replies'. *Australasian Journal of Philosophy* 47, no. 3 (December 1969): 322–324.

————. 'Dogmas of "Two Dogmas"'. *The Southern Journal of Philosophy* 11, no. 4 (Winter 1973): 285–289.

————. 'Language, Language Games, and Ostensive Definition'. *Synthese* 69 (October-December 1986): 41–49.

Harris, James, and Kevin Hoover. 'Abduction and the New Riddle of Induction'. *The Monist* 63, no. 3 (July 1980): 329–341.

Hempel, Carl. 'Problems and Changes in the Empiricist Criterion of Meaning'. In *Semantics and the Philosophy of Language*. Edited by Leonard Linsky. Urbana: University of Illinois Press, 1952.

Hesse, M. 'Is There an Independent Observation Language?' In *The Nature and Function of Scientific Theories*. Edited by R. Colodny. Pittsburgh: University of Pittsburgh Press, 1970.

SELECT BIBLIOGRAPHY 217

Hollis, Martin. 'The Limits of Irrationality'. In *Rationality*. Edited by Bryan R. Wilson. Oxford: Basil Blackwell, 1970.

———. 'Reason and Ritual'. In *Rationality*. Edited by Bryan R. Wilson. Oxford: Blackwell, 1970.

Hookway, Christopher. 'Critical Common Sense and Rational Self-Control'. *Nous* 24 (July 1990): 397–411.

———. 'Is Science Really a Pack of Lies?' *Nature* 303 (June 1983): 361–62.

Jackson, Frank. 'Grue'. *Journal of Philosophy* 72, no. 5 (March 13, 1975): 113–131.

James, William. 'The Sentiment of Rationality'. In *Essays on Faith and Morals*. New York: New American Library, 1962.

———. 'Pragmatism's Conception of Truth'. In *Pragmatism*. Indianapolis: Hackett, 1987.

Kim, J. 'What is Naturalized Epistemology?' *Philosophical Perspectives* 2, (1988): 381–405.

Kuhn, Thomas S. 'Reflections on My Critics'. In *Criticism and the Growth of Knowledge*. Edited by Imre Lakatos and Alan Musgrave. Cambridge: Cambridge University Press, 1970.

———. 'Objectivity, Value Judgment, and Theory Choice'. In *The Essential Tension: Selected Studies in Scientific Tradition and Change*. Chicago: University of Chicago Press, 1977.

Laudan, L. 'Progress or Rationality: The Prospects for Normative Naturalism'. *American Philosophical Quarterly* 24 (1987): 19–31.

Longino, Helen E. 'Can There Be a Feminist Science?' *Hypatia* 2, 3 (Fall 1987).

———. 'Beyond "Bad Science"'. *Science, Technology, and Human Values* 8, no. 1 (1983): 7–17.

Lukes, Steven. 'Some Problems about Rationality'. In *Rationality*. Edited by Bryan R. Wilson. Oxford: Basil Blackwell, 1970.

———. 'Relativism in Its Place'. In *Rationality and Relativism*. Edited by Martin Hollis and Steven Lukes. Cambridge: MIT Press, 1982.

Lyotard, Jean-Francois. 'The Postmodern Condition'. In *After Philosophy: End or Transformation*. Edited by Kenneth Baynes, James Bohman, and Thomas McCarthy. Cambridge: MIT Press, 1987.

MacIntyre, Alasdair. 'Is Understanding Religion Compatible with Believing?' In *Rationality*. Edited by Bryan R. Wilson. Oxford: Blackwell, 1970.

Martin, Jane Roland. 'Ideological Critiques and the Philosophy of Science'. *Philosophy of Science* 56 (1989): 1–22.

Neurath, Otto. 'Protocol Sentences'. In *Logical Positivism*. Edited by A.J. Ayer. New York: Free Press, 1959.

Peirce, Charles Sanders. 'Questions Concerning Certain Faculties Claimed for Man'. In *Collected Papers*. Edited by Charles Hartshorne, Paul Weiss, and Arthur Burks. Vol. 5. Cambridge, Massachusetts: Belknap Press of Harvard University Press, 1934.

———. 'Some consequences of Four Incapacities'. In *Collected Papers*. Edited by Charles Hartshorne, Paul Weiss, and Arthur Burks. Vol. 5. Cambridge, Massachusetts: Balknap Press of Harvard University Press, 1934.

Prior, A. N. 'The Runabout Inference-Ticket'. *Analysis* 21 (1960): 38–39.

Putnam, Hilary. 'Why Reason Can't Be Naturalized'. In *After Philosophy: End or Transformation*. Edited by Kenneth Baynes, James Bohman, and Thomas McCarthy. Cambridge: MIT Press, 1987.

Quine, Willard Van Orman. 'Two Dogmas of Empiricism'. In *From a Logical Point of View*. New York: Harper and Row, 1953.

——. 'On What There Is'. In *From a Logical Point of View*. New York: Harper and Row, 1953.

——. 'Identity, Ostension, and Hypostasis'. In *From a Logical Point of View*. New York: Harper and Row, 1953.

——. 'Ontological Relativity'. In *Ontological Relativity and Other Essays*. 2d. ed. New York: Columbia University Press, 1969.

——. 'Grades of Theoreticity'. In *Experience and Theory*. Edited by Lawrence Foster and J. W. Swanson. Amherst, Massachusetts: University of Massachusetts Press, 1970.

——. 'Reply to Stroud'. In *The Foundations of Analytic Philosophy: Midwest Studies in Philosophy*. Vol. 6. *The Foundations of Analytic Philosophy*. Minneapolis: University of Minnesota Press, 1981.

——. 'Reply to Morton White'. In *The Philosophy of W.V. Quine*. Edited by L.E. Hahn and P.A. Schilpp. La Salle: Open Court, 1986.

——. 'Epistemology Naturalized'. In *Naturalizing Epistemology*. Edited by Hilary Kornblith. Cambridge: MIT Press, 1987.

Rorty, Richard. 'Pragmatism, Categories, and Language'. *The Philosophical Review* 70 (April 1961): 197–223.

Roth, Paul A. 'Theories of Nature and the Nature of Theories'. *Mind* (1989): 431–38.

Rose, Hilary. 'Hand, Brain, and Heart: A Feminist Epistemology for the Natural Sciences'. *Signs: Journal of Women in Culture and Society* 9, no. 1 (1983): 73–93.

Russell, Bertrand. 'Facts and Propositions'. In *Contemporary Analytic and Linguistic Philosophies*. Edited by E. D. Klemke. Buffalo, New York: Prometheus, 1983.

Shapere, Dudley. 'The Paradigm Concept'. *Science* 172 (1971).

Siegel, Harvey. 'Justification, Discovery, and the Naturalizing of Epistemology'. *Philosophy of Science* 47, no. 2 (June 1980): 297–321.

——. 'Empirical Psychology, Naturalized Epistemology, and First Philosophy'. *Philosophy of Science* 51, no. 4 (December 1984): 667–676.

Smith, John E. 'Community and Reality'. In *Perspectives on Peirce*. Edited by Richard J. Bernstein. New Haven: Yale University Press, 1965.

Stroud, Barry. 'The Significance of Naturalized Epistemology'. In *Naturalizing Epistemology*. Edited by Hilary Kornblith. Cambridge: MIT Press, 1985.

Winch, Peter. 'Understanding a Primitive Society'. In *Rationality*. Edited by Bryan R. Wilson. Oxford: Blackwell, 1970.

BOOKS

Ackermann, Robert J. *Data, Instruments, and Theory*. Princeton: Princeton University Press, 1985.

Agassi, Joseph, *The Gentle Art of Philosophical Polemics: Selected Reviews and Comments*. La Salle: Open Court, 1988.

Bacon, Fracis. *New Organon*. Edited with an Introduction by Fulton H. Anderson. New York: Bobbs-Merrill, 1960.

Baker, G. P. and P. M. S. Hacker. *Skepticism, Rules, and Language.* Oxford: Blackwell, 1984.

Bernstein, Richard J. *Praxis and Action.* Philadelphia: University of Pennsylvania Press, 1971.

———. *Beyond Objectivism and Relativism.* Philadelphia: University of Pennsylvania Press, 1985.

Bleier, Ruth. *Science and Gender: A Critique of Biology and Its Theories on Women.* New York: Pergamon, 1984.

Boorstin, Daniel J. *The Discoverers.* New York: Random House, 1983.

Bordo, Susan R. *The Flight to Objectivity.* Albany: State University of New York Press, 1987.

Brown, Hanbury. *The Wisdom of Science.* Cambridge: Cambridge University Press, 1986.

Brown, Harold. *Rationality.* New York: Routledge, 1988.

Carnap, Rudolf. *The Logical Syntax of Language.* New York: Harcourt, Brace, 1937.

———. *Introduction to Semantics.* Cambridge: Harvard University Press, 1942.

———. *Formalization of Logic.* Cambridge: Harvard University Press, 1943.

———. *Meaning and Necessity.* Chicago: University of Chicago Press, 1947.

———. *The Philosophy of Rudolf Carnap.* Edited by Paul Arthur Schilpp. La Salle: Open Court, 1963.

———. *The Logical Structure of the World.* Berkeley: University of California Press, 1967.

Casti, John L., *Paradigms Lost: Images of Man in the History of Science.* New York: Morrow, 1989.

Colodny, Robert G., *The Nature and Function of Scientific Theories.* Pittsburg: University of Pittsburg Press, 1970.

Davidson, Donald and Jaakko Hintikka, eds. *Words and Objections: Essays on the Work of W.V. Quine.* Dordrecht: Reidel, 1969.

Descartes, René. *Discourse on Method and Meditations.* Translated with an Introduction by Laurence J. Lafleur. New York: Bobbs-Merrill, 1960.

Feyerabend, Paul. *Against Method.* New York: Verso, 1975.

———. *Farewell to Reason.* New York: Verso, 1987.

Foster, Lawrence and J. W. Swanson. *Experience and Theory.* Amherst, Massachusetts: University of Massachusetts Press, 1970.

Gadamer, Hans-Georg. *Truth and Method.* New York: Seabury Press, 1975.

———. *Philosophical Hermeneutics.* Translated by David Linge. Berkeley: University of California Press, 1976.

Gadamer, Habermas, and others in *Hermeneutik und Ideologiekritik.* Edited by Karl-Otto Apel, et al. Frankfurt: Suhrkamp, 1971.

Galileo Galilei, *Sidereus Nuncius.* Translated by Albert Van Helden. Chicago: University of Chicago Press, 1989.

———. *Dialogue Concerning the Two Chief World Systems—Ptolemaic and Copernican.* Translated by Stillman Drake. Berkeley: University of California Press, 1962.

Garry, Ann and Marilyn Pearsall, eds. *Women, Kowledge, and Reality.* Boston: Unwin Hyman, 1989.

Gay, Peter. *The Enlightenment: An Interpretation.* Vol. 2. *The Science of Freedom.* New York: Knopf, 1969.

Geertz, Clifford. *Local Knowledge: Further Essays in Interpretative Anthropology.* New York: Basic Books, 1983.

Goodman, Nelson. *The Structure of Appearance.* Cambridge: Harvard University Press, 1951.

———. *Fact, Fiction, and Forecast.* 2d ed. New York: Bobbs-Merrill, 1965.

———. *Problems and Projects.* New York: Bobbs-Merrill Co., 1972.

———. *Ways of Worldmaking.* Cambridge: Hackett Publishing Co., 1978.

Grandy, Richard E., ed. *Theories and Observation in Science.* Princeton: Prentice-Hall, 1973.

Grimshaw, Jean. *Philosophy and Feminist Thinking.* Minneapolis: University of Minnesota Press, 1986.

Grunfeld, Joseph. *Method and Language.* Amsterdam: Gruner, 1982.

Habermas, Jürgen. *Knowledge and Human Interests.* Translated by J.J. Shapiro. Boston: Beacon Press, 1971.

Hanson, Norwood Russell. *Patterns of Discovery.* Cambridge: Cambridge University Press, 1961.

Harding, Sandra. *The Science Question in Feminism.* Ithaca: Cornell University Press, 1986.

Hartsock, Nancy M. *Money, Sex, and Power.* New York: Longman, 1983.

Hesse, Mary. *Revolutions and Reconstructions in the Philosophy of Science.* Bloomington: Indiana University Press, 1980.

Hirsch, E.D. Jr. *Validity in Interpretation.* New Haven: Yale University Press, 1967.

———. *The Aims of Interpretation.* Chicago: University of Chicago Press, 1976.

Hollis, Martin and Steven Lukes, eds. *Rationality and Relativism.* Cambridge: MIT Press, 1982.

Horton, Robin, and Ruth Finnegan. *Modes of Thought: Essays on Thinking in Western and Non-Western Societies.* London: Faber and Faber, 1973.

Hoy, David Couzens. *The Critical Circle: Literature, History, and Philosophical Hermeneutics.* Berkeley: University of California Press, 1978.

Hull, David L. *Science as A Process: An Evolutionary Account of the Social and Conceptual Development of Science.* Chicago: University of Chicago Press, 1988.

Hume, David. *An Enquiry Concerning Human Understanding.* Edited with an Introduction by L.A. Selby-Bigge. Oxford: Clarendon Press, 1961.

Keller, Evelyn Fox. *Reflections on Gender and Science.* New Haven: Yale University Press, 1985.

Kornblith, Hilary, ed. *Naturalizing Epistemology.* Cambridge: MIT Press, 1985.

Kripke, Saul A. *Wittgenstein on Rules and Private Language.* Cambridge: Harvard University Press, 1982.

Kuhn, Thomas S. *The Structure of Scientific Revolutions.* 2d ed. Chicago: University of Chicago Press, 1970.

———. *The Copernican Revolution.* Cambridge: Harvard University Press, 1957.

Laudan, Larry. *Progress and Its Problems.* Berkeley: University of California Press, 1977.

———. *Science and Values.* Berkeley: University of California Press, 1984.

Locke, John. *Some Thoughts Concerning Education.* Edited by John W. and Jean S. Yolton. Oxford: Clarendon, 1988.

Lough, John. *The Encyclopédie.* New York: David McKay, 1971.

Margolis, Joseph. *Pragmatism Without Foundations: Reconciling Realism and Relativism.* Oxford: Blackwell, 1986.

Merchant, Carolyn. *The Death of Nature: Women, Ecology, and the Scientific Revolution.* New York: Harper and Row, 1980.

Merton, Robert K. and Jerry Gaston. *The Sociology of Science in Europe.* Carbondale: Southern Illinois University Press, 1977.

Midwest studies in Philosophy. Edited by Peter A. French, Theodore E. Uehling Jr., and Howard K. Wettstein. Vol. 6. *The Foundations of Analytic Philosophy.* Minneapolis: University of Minnesota Press, 1981.

Murphey, Murray G. *The Development of Peirces's Philosophy.* Cambridge: Harvard University Press, 1961.

Murray, Gilbert. *The Five Stages of Greek Religion.* New York: Columbia University Press, 1935.

Nagel, Ernest. *The Structure of Science.* New York: Harcourt, Brace, 1961.

Peirce, Charles Sanders. *Collected Papers.* Edited by Charles Hartshorne, Paul Weiss, and Arthur Burks. 8 Vols. Cambridge: Harvard University Press, 1931–58.

Polanyi, Michael. *Personal Knowledge: Towards a Post-Critical Philosophy.* Chicago: University of Chicago Press, 1958.

Popper, Karl. *The Poverty of Historicism.* New York: Basic Books, 1957.

———. *The Logic of Scientific Discovery.* New York: Basic Books, 1959.

———. *Conjectures and Refutations: The Growth of Scientific Knowledge.* London: Routledge, 1963.

———. *The Open Society and Its Enemies.* Vol. 2. *The High Tide of Prophecy: Hegel, Marx, and the Aftermath.* Princeton: Princeton University Press, 1963.

Putnam, Hilary. *Reason, Truth and History.* Cambridge: Cambridge University Press, 1981.

Quine, Willard Van Orman. *Pursuit of Truth.* Cambridge: Harvard University Press, 1990.

———. *Word and Object.* Cambridge: MIT Press, 1960.

Quine, Willard Van Orman, and J. S. Ullian. *The Web of Belief.* New York: Random House, 1970.

Radnitzky, Gerard and W.W. Bartley III, eds. *Evolutionary Epistemology, Rationality, and the Sociology of Knowledge.* La Salle: Open Court, 1987.

Rajchman, John, and Cornel West, eds. *Post-Analytic Philosophy.* New York: Columbia University Press, 1985.

Rorty, Richard. *Philosophy and the Mirror of Nature.* Princeton: Princeton University Press, 1979.

———. *Consequences of Pragmatism.* Minneapolis: University of Minnesota Press, 1982.

Rossiter, Margaret W. *Women Scientists in America: Struggles and Strategies to 1940.* Baltimore: Johns Hopkins University Press, 1982.

Scheffler, Israel. *Science and Subjectivity.* Indianapolis: Hackett, 1967.

Schilpp, P.A. and L.E. Hahn, eds. *The Philosophy of W. V. Quine.* La Salle: Open Court, 1986.

Siegel, Harvey. *Relativism Refuted: A Critique of Contemporary Epistemological Relativism.* Dordrecht: Reidel, 1987.

Shea, William R., *Galileo's Intellectual Revolution.* New York: Science History Publications, 1972.

Shimony, A. and D. Nails, eds. *Naturalistic Epistemology: A Symposium of Two Decades.* Dordrecht: Reidel, 1987.

Strawson, P.F. *Skepticism and Naturalism: Some Varieties.* New York: Columbia University Press, 1985.

Stroud, Barry. *The Significance of Philosophical Skepticism.* Oxford: Clarendon, 1984.

Tambiah, Stanley Jeyaraja. *Magic, Science, Religion, and the Scope of Rationality.* Cambridge: Cambridge University Press, 1990.

Wallace, *Galileo and His Sources.* Princeton: Princeton University Press, 1984.

Weinsheimer, Joel C. *Gadamer's Hermeneutics: A Reading of Truth and Method.* New Haven: Yale University Press, 1985.

Whitehead, Alfred North. *Process and Reality.* New York: Macmillan, 1929.

Winch, Peter. *The Idea of a Social Science and Its Relation to Philosophy.* London: Routledge, 1958.

Wittgenstein, Ludwig. *Philosophical Investigations.* Translated by G.E.M. Anscombe. 3d ed. New York: Macmillan, 1953.

―――. *Tractatus Logico-Philosophicus.* Translated by D.F. Pears and B.F. McGuinness. London: Routledge, 1961.

INDEX